The Essays Of Samuel Johnson: Selected From The Rambler, 1750-1752; The Adventurer, 1753; And The Idler, 1758-1760

Samuel Johnson

The Essays of Samuel Johnson.
Selected from The Rambler,
1750-1752; The Adventurer, 1753: and The Idler, 1758-1760.

With Biographical Introduction and Notes
By STUART J. REID,
Author of "The Life and Times of Sydney Smith."

LONDON: WALTER SCOTT, LTD.,
PATERNOSTER SQUARE.

Printing Statement:

Due to the very old age and scarcity of this book,
many of the pages may be hard to read due to the
blurring of the original text, possible missing pages,
missing text, dark backgrounds and other issues
beyond our control.

Because this is such an important and rare work, we
believe it is best to reproduce this book regardless of
its original condition.

Thank you for your understanding.

TABLE OF CONTENTS.

THE ADVENTURER.

THE IDLER.

SAMUEL JOHNSON.

1709-1784.

IN the early years of the Eighteenth Century the dim and unpretending book-shop of Michael Johnson, at the corner of the Market-place in Lichfield, was one of the established resorts of the more leisured and learned inhabitants of that quaint and somewhat sleepy old city. In the closing years of the Nineteenth Century the house still stands, and has become a place of pilgrimage, for there—on the 18th September 1709—that "great master of reason," Samuel Johnson, was born. Booksellers in the reign of George the First were not to be found in every town; yet it is charitable to suppose that Lichfield, being the seat of a bishopric, must needs even then have been also a seat of learning. There, accordingly, Michael Johnson fixed his abode and proffered his wares. That he did so with some degree of success is evident from the following sentence from a letter written from Nentham to Lord Gower's chaplain in 1716:—"Johnson, the Lichfield librarian, is now here; he propagates learning all over this diocese, and advanceth knowledge to its just height; all the clergy here are his pupils, and suck all they have from him." Though old Mr. Johnson kept a shop, the shop would not have kept him if he had not acted occasionally on the aggressive. He, therefore, was accustomed, at set times and seasons, to journey to Birmingham, Uttoxeter, and other neighbouring towns, in order that he might tempt local patrons of literature by displaying his choicest volumes for their inspection. Samuel Johnson was thus cradled amongst books, and such a circumstance, no doubt, did much to awaken within him at an early age not only a thirst for knowledge, but also some degree of literary ambition.

His mother seems to have been a peevish woman, of gloomy temperament and slender education. She knew nothing of books, and her chief topic of conversation over the family fireside was the rather embarrassed condition of her husband's affairs. This was a subject which poor Michael Johnson, who was manfully struggling with debts contracted in early life, would gladly have shunned, and hence, after vainly attempting to lift the household talk to other levels, the badgered bookseller sought refuge in silence. "My father and mother," relates Johnson, "had not much happiness from each other. They seldom conversed, for my father could not bear to talk of his affairs; and my mother, being unacquainted with books, cared not to talk of anything else. Had my mother been more literate, they had been better companions. She might have sometimes introduced her unwelcome topic with more success, if she could have diversified her conversation. Of business she had no distinct conception; and therefore her discourse was composed only of complaint, fear, and suspicion." Unfortunately, in one particular at least, husband and wife were but too much alike; years after the little shop at Lichfield had become only a treasured memory, Dr. Johnson was compelled to confess that "neither of them ever tried to calculate the profits of trade or the cost of living." All that is known of Michael Johnson—except his debts—is to his credit. Unlike many booksellers who know only the titles of the books they handle, he was a man of more than average attainments.

The clerical gossips of a cathedral city found his shop a pleasant lounge, and Michael Johnson seems to have been able to hold his own with the best of them. In a small way he aspired to the dignity of a publisher, and stray volumes may even yet be occasionally picked up with his name on the title-page. With the citizens at large he stood well, and after holding several minor appointments, his character and public spirit won emphatic recognition by his election to the office of chief magistrate in 1725. As for Mrs. Johnson, notwithstanding the failings of training and temperament which fell to her share, she was unquestionably a woman of firm religious principle, and the upward bias which she gave to her child's life in twilight whispers in a little room at the top of the house was never afterwards lost. Whatever devotion the good woman displayed towards her boy was repaid a hundredfold by him in after years. Nothing, even in a singularly noble life, was more touching and beautiful than the reverent loyalty with which Johnson cherished his widowed mother.

The conditions under which he began the battle of life were in other respects singularly unfavourable. Scrofula played havoc with his features, and hypochondria cast its shadow over his spirit. Disease had scarred his face, and he had lost the sight of one eye; whilst the melancholy from which he suffered, from youth to old age, was frequently intense enough to cloak his life in gloom. Boswell has described those "convulsive starts and odd gesticulations which tended to excite at once surprise and ridicule;" and Johnson himself states—in a letter written when he was seventy-three—"My health has been, from my twentieth year, such as has seldom afforded me a single day of ease." His curious trick of touching the top of the posts as he walked through the streets, as well as the anxious and awkward strides which he took in order to avoid placing his feet on the cracks in the flags, were habits which doubtless were unconsciously acquired. In later life Dr. Johnson's tall and burly figure conveyed the impression of rude health; yet, in spite of the energy which marked his movements, and the vivacity which characterised his speech, this appearance of physical vigour was deceptive, and only his intimate friends were aware of the extent to which he suffered at times from extreme lassitude.

The children of the middle classes at the beginning of the Eighteenth Century were not coddled in the maudlin fashion which prevails to-day, and Johnson was no exception to the rule. At the age of three he was sent to a dame's school, and it was not long before his natural independence of spirit and vehemence of temper were curiously displayed. The servant who usually took him to and fro one day failed to appear, and the sturdy little fellow, impatient for his dinner, set off alone. His schoolmistress, afraid of some mishap, followed him at a short distance. Suddenly the child turned round and saw her, and indignant at being thought unable to take care of himself, ran back in a temper and struck his would-be protectress again and again. Trivial though the incident is in itself, it is noteworthy as the earliest glimpse of that self-reliance which distinguished his entire career. Before he was eight years old he was sent to Lichfield Grammar School, where he speedily became known as a lad in whom great natural parts were linked to a dilatory and indolent temperament. He possessed a most retentive memory, and was able, as one of his friends said, to "tear the heart out of a book" with wonderful rapidity; this enabled him to glean more at a glance than other boys were able to gather in an hour. The head-master was a stern disciplinarian. "My master," he used to say in after years, "whipt me very well. Without that, I should have done nothing." In spite of his physical inertness, he could not bear to be second to another lad, and under the stimulus of his master's cane and his own ambition he contrived to keep at the head of the school. "They never," he told Boswell, with evident pride, "thought to raise me by comparing me to anyone; they never said, Johnson is as good a scholar as such a one, but such a one is as good a scholar as Johnson; and this was said but of Lowe; and I do not think he was as good a scholar." At the age of fifteen he was sent for a year to a school at Stonebridge in Worcestershire. The master was an able but idle man, and treated Johnson with great severity, yet, he admits, "he taught me a great deal." Years afterwards, in talking over his boyish experiences with Bishop Percy, Dr. Johnson declared that at Lichfield he learnt much in the school, and little from the master; but whilst at Stonebridge, the master taught him much and the school little.

In 1726 he returned to Lichfield, and the next two years were chiefly spent in his father's shop. During this period he read hard, though in a fitful and indiscriminate fashion. Michael Johnson's shelves provided him with an abundance of provender, and if he did not study systematically he duly availed himself of the resources which were placed at his command. His wide acquaintance with books dates from the years which he thus spent browsing amid the literary treasures of the corner shop in Lichfield market-place. Full of ambition, and conscious of his own powers, Samuel Johnson was both restless and proud, and chafed not a little at the drudgery and restraint of his father's business. One day Michael Johnson was too ill to take his accustomed stand behind a stall of books in

Uttoxeter market, and naturally he looked to his son to occupy his place. But the young scholar, moved by false shame, flatly refused to play the shopman in the open air. Half a century later, Dr. Johnson, in the fulness of his fame, did voluntary penance for that impulse of false pride: "To do away with the sin of this disobedience, I this day went in a post-chaise to Uttoxeter, and going into the market at the time of high business, uncovered my head and stood with it bare an hour before the stall which my father had formerly used, exposed to the sneers of the standers-by and the inclemency of the weather; a penance by which I trust I have propitiated heaven for this only instance, I believe, of contumacy to my father." The quality and depth of the great moralist's nature leaps to light in an act of atonement which vividly reveals the reverence and tenderness of a troubled and self-accusing heart.

In October 1728, when in his twentieth year, Johnson went as a Commoner to Pembroke College, Oxford. Dr. Adams, afterwards Master of Pembroke, told the awkward and ungainly scholar that he was the best-equipped student that had ever come to the University. His rooms at Pembroke College were upon the second floor over the gateway. The force of character which had made him supreme amongst his companions at school asserted itself equally at college. He was accustomed to lounge at the gate, the centre of an admiring group; but an empty purse and hypochondria raised a barrier between him and other young men, and he seems to have formed no intimate friendships at the University. Boswell says that during his residence at Oxford, Johnson was "depressed by poverty and irritated by disease," and yet, in the reminiscences of the men who knew him there, he is pictured as reckless and gay. Never were appearances more deceptive, as his own words testify—" Ah, sir, I was mad and violent. It was bitterness which they mistook for frolick. I was miserably poor, and I thought to fight my way by my literature and wit; so I disregarded all power and all authority." So great, indeed, was his poverty, that it could not be hid; his stockings appeared through the holes in his shoes. Yet Johnson felt that there was one thing worse than poverty, and that was patronage. In haughty independence, and with bitter chagrin, he flung contemptuously away the well-meant dole of shoe leather placed by some friendly hand outside his door. Privation he could endure: in that lay no degradation; but at least he would not escape from it by accepting the windfall of a beggar. At the end of three years—in the autumn of 1731—Johnson was driven to bay by the three-headed monster, pounds, shillings, and pence, and abruptly quitted the University. As he had not completed the prescribed term of residence, he was compelled to leave without a degree.

Whilst at Oxford a book had fallen into his hands which left a deep and abiding impression on his mind. It was Law's *Serious Call to a Holy Life.* He relates that he took the volume up, expecting to find it dull and open to ridicule. " But I found Law quite an over-match for me; and this was the first occasion of my thinking in earnest of Religion, after I became capable of rational enquiry." Henceforth it was impossible for him to live any longer at random; he took a Master, and was done with doubt. In Boswell's words—" From this time forward Religion was the predominant object of his thoughts; though, with the just sentiments of a conscientious Christian, he lamented that his practice of its duties fell far short of what it ought to be." His father's affairs were rapidly falling into disorder, and he was no longer able to dole out the pittance on which his son had contrived to support life at the University. " Poor Samuel Johnson "—to quote Boswell again—accordingly " returned to his native city, destitute, and not knowing how he should gain even a decent livelihood." Shortly after he returned home, in the autumn of 1731, his father died. At length he obtained a situation as an usher in a school at Market Bosworth, but he was ill adapted to the monotonous drudgery of this position. In a letter to his old school-fellow, Mr. Hector, of Birmingham, we find him stating that his life was as " unvaried as the note of the cuckoo ; " nor did he know " whether it was more disagreeable for him to teach, or the boys to learn the grammar rules." He appears to have been treated with harshness at Market Bosworth, and that studied insolence which never allowed him to forget his poverty and dependence. Such a life was intolerable to a man of the temperament of Johnson, and at the end of a few months, unable to endure the slights which it brought him, he quitted an uncongenial and irksome position.

Thrown once more upon his own resources, and without any definite plans, he gladly availed himself of an invitation from his friend Hector to visit Birmingham, and thither he accordingly went in the summer of 1732. His sojourn in that town was rendered memorable by two circumstances, one of which was his first attempt at literature and the other his marriage to Mrs. Porter. It chanced that Mr Hector lodged with a bookseller called Warren, who was also proprietor of the *Birmingham Journal.* To this paper Johnson contributed essays, and undertook also to translate and abridge from the French *A Voyage to Abyssinia,* by Father Lobo, a Portuguese Jesuit. He had read the book at Oxford, and it was at his own suggestion that Mr. Warren commissioned him to translate it. He began this literary

task with characteristic ardour, but presently his constitutional indolence asserted itself, and the printer was in
despair. It was only when Mr. Hector informed him that
the poor man and his family were suffering through the delay
that Johnson resumed his work. The book was published in 1735, and he received five guineas for his
labour; a smaller sum, it has been said, than "was
paid to the mechanic who set up the type." Traces
of the vigour and originality which distinguished the
prose of his later years are apparent in the lucid and
forcible preface to a volume which would long ago have
sunk into utter oblivion but for its association with Samuel
Johnson's tentative efforts in literature. Boswell was
probably correct in supposing that his study of Lobo's
Abyssinia suggested, many years later, to Johnson the scene
in which the story of *Rasselas* is laid. Extremely little is
known concerning his life in Birmingham; he was full of
literary plans and projects, but they all fell to the ground;
he attempted to obtain the post of head-master of a school,
but the fact that he could not boast of a degree spoilt his
chances; it was a period of uncertainty and privation—a fit
prelude to the long struggle which awaited him elsewhere.

The rashness of genius is proverbial, and when Johnson's battle for bread at the point of the pen was but
beginning, he complicated matters by marrying, on the 9th
of July 1735, Mrs. Elizabeth Porter, the buxom and mature
widow of a Birmingham mercer. Johnson was not quite
twenty-six when he took this step, and his personal appearance was the reverse of prepossessing; he is described as
being at that time "lean and lank, so that his immense
structure of bones was hideously striking to the eye, and the
scars of the scrofula were deeply visible." Love enters a
woman's heart through hearing; Mrs. Porter was captivated

by her ungainly suitor's conversational powers, and she declared that he was the most sensible man she had ever met in her life—a compliment which the moralist may be said to have won at the expense of the mercer. If the bridegroom was lean and lank, the bride was stout and small, and in point of age there was no comparison between them, for she was twenty years his senior. That Johnson loved his "dear Tetty" with deep and beautiful devotion, and saw in her a thousand excellencies which were hidden from other eyes, we have abundant evidence; and if her tenderness towards him must be largely taken on trust, we at least know that she proved in years that were dark and dreary, in spite of a good deal of foolish affectation, a brave and practical wife. Her first husband died insolvent, but under a settlement she brought her second eight hundred pounds. Straightway the young scholar determined to set up a private academy, and with this end in view he hired a large house within a mile or two of his native city. An announcement duly appeared in the *Gentleman's Magazine* for 1736, which ran as follows :—"At Edial, near Lichfield in Staffordshire, young gentlemen are boarded and taught the Latin and Greek Languages, by Samuel Johnson." Poor fellow ! he quickly found that it was an easier matter to issue an advertisement than to get satisfactory replies. Only three young gentlemen came to board, and to be taught Latin and Greek by Samuel Johnson ; but one of them, David Garrick by name, was worthy of his master.

Presently, the old question of ways and means had again to be faced ; the rent of the "large house" was on a corresponding scale, and the parents of the three pupils were not in a position, even if they had been so minded, to spend a fortune over the education of their sons. In short, the Edial enterprise did not prosper, and it was well for the world that that particular advertisement evoked so little response. Destiny had other work for Samuel Johnson, and young gentlemen were to be drilled elsewhere in the classics by other and more conventional pedagogues. In weariness and chagrin of spirit, the school was abandoned, and with one tragedy in his pocket, Johnson, in 1736, turned his back on the spires of Lichfield, and entered London to begin another. Lord Macaulay points to that precise period as one in which the condition of a man of letters was most miserable and degraded. "It was a dark night between two sunny days. The age of Mæcenases had passed away. The age of general curiosity and intelligence had not arrived." Grub Street, moreover, was no mere figure of speech, for with its poverty and squalor the author by profession was only too well acquainted. When Johnson arrived in London he sought out a bookseller called Wilcox, and told him that he meant to get his livelihood by literature. With a significant glance at his robust frame, Wilcox replied, "You had better buy a porter's knot." Literature and London were, however, to share between them the energy and resources of that wise and valiant heart, and though for galling years of obscurity the rewards of the one were small and the neglect of the other great, with both, long before the end of his life came, the fame of Samuel Johnson was indissolubly linked.

During his residence at Birmingham an impecunious painter had indoctrinated Johnson into the mystery involved in "living in a garret on eighteenpence a week," and circumstances over which he had no control now brought the friendless scholar perilously near to the practical application of the art. London, in the reign of George the Second, was full of literary hacks, some of whom were in the pay of the publishers, whilst others lived from hand to mouth supporting existence in Grub Street on a still more miserable and precarious pittance. Swift, in describing his "Hospital for Incurables," declared that "at least forty thousand incurable scribblers" would require asylum within its walls. According to Smollett, "Authorlings," to quote his own expressive phrase, were the castaways of other professions; and frequently it happened that their only qualification for the vocation of letters was their absolute failure in some less difficult field. The plight to which "distressed poets" were reduced may be gathered from the pictures of Hogarth and the prose of Johnson. The *Life of Richard Savage*, for example, reflects not only the abject poverty of the poet but of his biographer, in those dark and troubled years when whole nights were spent by the pair in tramping round and round St. James' Square because between them they could not raise the few pence necessary to procure the mean shelter of a cellar.

Johnson never described the real nature of the struggle through which he passed between the years 1737 and 1747, though late in life he burst into tears at the remembrance of the privations he had then endured. Yet even when his fortunes were at their lowest ebb he never lost faith in himself, or stooped to those mean artifices by which less scrupulous men pushed their way into notice. Not without justice has Carlyle placed him foremost in his "dust and dimness, with the sick body and the rusty coat," as the representative of the "Hero as Man of Letters"—"The largest soul that was in all England, and provision made for it of 'fourpence-halfpenny a day.'" Cave, the publisher of the *Gentleman's Magazine*, gave him multifarious but scantily paid tasks, and the best years of his life were spent in this obscure drudgery. In 1738 he published anonymously, "London, a Satire." The merit of the poem was instantly recognised, and Pope declared that the author would soon be known. There are passages in "London" which suggest the difficulties with which its author was gallantly contending, and one line at least was manifestly borrowed from his own experience :—

> "Slow rises worth by poverty depressed."

If further commentary be asked on such a text, it certainly is furnished by the six additional years of troubled indigence which awaited Johnson before he finally emerged from obscurity with his *Life of Richard Savage*—a classic biography which reflects the lights and shadows which marked the course of an unhappy child of genius. In Johnson's estimate of the unprincipled poet's career, justice and mercy are admirably blended ; and if the warmth of the friend tempers the severity of the moralist, commiseration of Savage in his suffering and distress is associated with emphatic condemnation of those reckless and vicious habits which—far more than any outward misfortune—were the real cause of the pitiful and tragic collapse of a life which once was full of brilliant promise.

Johnson threw his whole soul into this vivid piece of portraiture ; and yet he contrived to finish it with surprising celerity. "I wrote," he relates, "forty-eight of the printed octavo pages at a sitting; but then I sat up all night." This book brought him fame, and the friendship of Sir Joshua Reynolds; but the fifteen guineas for which he sold the copyright to Cave, though welcome enough, did not do much towards placing him in a sound financial position ! He was still so shabbily dressed that when Cave invited him to a meal at his house he sat behind a screen, as if ashamed to be seen by the other guests. In 1745 he published in pamphlet form his "Miscellaneous

Observations on the Tragedy of Macbeth" together with a prospectus for a new edition of Shakespeare. Nothing then came of the suggestion, but Bishop Warburton, struck with the ability of Johnson's criticisms, spoke in genial terms of the pamphlet—a circumstance which was never forgotten—"He praised me at a time when praise was of value to me." Two years later, in 1747, a great literary project, which he afterwards declared was "not the effect of particular study but had grown up in his mind insensibly," took definite shape by the publication of his "Plan of the Dictionary of the English Language." Dodsley was the first to suggest the idea of the Dictionary, and the "Plan," which was addressed to the Earl of Chesterfield, was not published until Johnson had definitely accepted the offer of a syndicate of booksellers to compile such a work for £1575, a sum which represented eight years of continuous toil; not only on the part of the "great lexicographer," but of the six "harmless drudges" whom he was compelled to employ.

Meanwhile, though he had acquired a certain degree of fame, his fight with poverty was by no means ended; indeed, fifteen years had yet to roll away before a pension of £300—granted to him in 1762, when he was fifty-three years of age—gave him that lettered ease which he was so peculiarly fitted to adorn. The year 1749 witnessed his final attempt to court the muses; the "Vanity of Human Wishes" was then published, and "Irene," a tragedy, which he regarded with great expectations, was placed upon the boards of Drury Lane, through the friendly offices of his former pupil, David Garrick. The "Vanity of Human Wishes," in spite of its ethical suggestiveness and sonorous rhythm, was not so popular as "London;" whilst the tragedy was coldly received, though Garrick did his best to throw vivacity and life into its representation ; the "little fishes" talked like "great whales," and "Irene" herself was but "Dr. Johnson in petticoats" Early in the following year the first number of the *Rambler* appeared, and, in Boswell's words, Johnson came forth as a "majestic teacher of moral and religious wisdom." The first number was published on Tuesday, the 20th of March 1750, and though at first its success was doubtful, its author lived to see ten editions of these collected essays. The *Rambler* was published every Tuesday and Friday until March 1752, and notwithstanding that he was now engrossed with his work on the dictionary, Johnson wrote almost every number ; Cave paid him at the rate of four guineas a-week. Although published without the author's name, Garrick, Samuel Richardson, and others quickly recognised that only one person in London was capable of producing the *Rambler*, a paper which Lady Mary Montagu declared followed the *Spectator* in much the same way as "a pack-horse would do a hunter." Johnson told Sir Joshua Reynolds that he was quite at a loss how to name the paper. "What must be done, sir, *will* be done. I sat down at night upon my bedside, and resolved that I would not go to sleep till I had fixed its title. The *Rambler* seemed the best that occurred, and I took it."

Arthur Murphy, in his essay on the life and genius of Dr. Johnson, published in 1792, hints that the true explanation of the pompous and pedantic terms which occur all too freely in the *Rambler* is to be found in the fact that he was absorbed at the time in the dictionary, and "as he grew familiar with technical and scholastic words, he thought that the bulk of his readers were equally learned, or at least would admire the splendour and dignity of the style." One of the jokes which ran about the town was to the effect that Johnson employed hard words in the *Rambler*

in order to render his forthcoming Dictionary indispensable.
His literary ascendency as a moralist and critic, and the
dictatorship to which it gave rise, dates nevertheless from
the period when his right to speak with authority was
vindicated beyond further challenge, by the appearance of
those wise and profound reflections which arrested the
attention of all thoughtful men in the modest pages of
the *Rambler.*   On the 14th of March 1752 the last number
was published; it was written when the shadow of death
was settling over Johnson's home in Gough Square, Fleet
Street; three days later, his wife died.   To the end of his
life he cherished with fond and reverent affection the
memory of his "dear Tetty."   The anniversary of her death
was spent by him in prayer and self-examination; and the
lapse of years seemed only to reveal in numberless pathetic
ways how tender and enduring was the love he had given her.

The weeks which immediately followed the burial of his
wife in Bromley Churchyard, Kent, were spent by Johnson
in deep and listless dejection.   He was too good a man,
however, to succumb even to such a blow, and his published "Prayers and Meditations" point to the manner in
which he renewed his strength.   The lonely house was
haunted by memories of the happiness he had lost.   He
wandered from room to room, unable to work, for each
recalled too vividly the "touch of a vanished hand, and
the sound of a voice that was still;" at length, climbing to
the top of the stairs, he turned the garret into his study,
because it was the only place in his desolate home in which
he had never seen his wife.   It was a dreary, inconvenient
spot in which to live and labour, but it was less painful to
him to sit there than in any other part of the house.   Dr.
Burney accompanied him one day to his garret in Gough
Square and found "five or six Greek folios, a deal writing-

desk, and a chair and a half. The chair with three legs and one arm Johnson took himself, and gave the other to his guest."

During the darkened months of 1753, Johnson, in Boswell's words, "relieved the drudgery of his Dictionary and the melancholy of his grief" by contributing essays to the *Adventurer*, a publication on the lines of the *Rambler*, which his friend Dr. Hawkesworth had started. Extremely little is known of his life during the next two years beyond the fact that he was toiling over the concluding pages of his great work. In the autumn of 1754 the University of Oxford conferred upon him the degree of Master of Arts, an honour which gratified him exceedingly; in 1765 Dublin bestowed upon him the distinction of Doctor of Laws; and exactly ten years later his own university paid him a similar compliment. Towards the close of his life Dr. Johnson often visited Oxford, and on these occasions, according to Lord Stowell, he "wore his gown almost ostentatiously."

The year 1755 was rendered memorable by the publication of the Dictionary—an event which placed his reputation as a scholar beyond all further challenge. When, after a thousand vexatious delays, the last sheet of the Dictionary had been placed in the hands of the publisher, Johnson demanded of the messenger, "What did he say?" "Sir," was the somewhat reluctant reply, "he said, 'Thank God, I have done with him!'" "I am glad," was the amused lexicographer's retort, "that he thanks God for anything." Seven years before, under the belief that the Earl of Chesterfield meant what he said when he promised to befriend him, Johnson had dedicated to that dilettante patron of learning his "Plan of a Dictionary of the English Language." Chesterfield at that

b

time was Secretary of State, whilst Johnson was poor, and comparatively unknown. Nothing, however, came of the earl's assurances, and the struggling author was treated with contemptuous neglect. But when the Dictionary was at length on the verge of publication, and the public curiosity concerning it was thoroughly aroused, Chesterfield dashed off in the columns of the *World* a couple of laudatory articles on the forthcoming book and its author, which called forth in reply the celebrated " Letter " which demolished not merely the pretensions of that particular " patron," but the hateful system of patronage itself:—
" Seven years, my lord, have now passed, since I waited in your outward rooms, or was repulsed from your door ; during which time I have been pushing on my Work through difficulties, of which it is useless to complain, and have brought it, at last, to the verge of publication, without one act of assistance, one word of encouragement, or one smile of favour. Such treatment I did not expect, for I never had a patron before. . . . Is not a patron, my lord, one who looks with unconcern on a man struggling for life in the water, and, when he has reached ground, encumbers him with help? The notice which you have been pleased to take of my labours, had it been early, had been kind ; but it has been delayed till I am indifferent, and I cannot enjoy it ; till I am solitary, and cannot impart it ; till I am known, and do not want it. I hope it is no very cynical asperity, not to confess obligations where no benefit has been received, or to be unwilling that the public should consider me as owing that to a patron, which Providence has enabled me to do for myself." The " retired and uncourtly scholar," as Johnson describes himself in an earlier part of this scathing epistle, not only by it " gave the world assurance of a man," but made a new departure in

literature, by teaching authors to appeal directly to the public, and to abandon princes and peers to their own devices.

The compilation of the Dictionary brought fame to Johnson, but it did not relieve his financial embarrassments; for the truth was, that a great part of the sum for which he had agreed to compile the work had been advanced to him during the progress of his labours. After the completion of the book, he seems to have rested for a while on his oars; but at length, on the 15th of April 1758, he began the *Idler*—a periodical essay, which possibly received its title from his own condition at the moment, to which it was meant to act as a corrective; for dotted down in his private journal just then are the words, "This year I hope to learn diligence." It was published every Saturday in the columns of the *Universal Chronicle*, and was printed in bold type in a prominent part of the paper, like a modern leading article. The essays were continued until 5th April 1760, and out of the hundred and three which appeared, all except twelve were written by Johnson.

The publication of the Dictionary—a monumental work which displays the range of his powers and the breadth of his scholarship—lifted Johnson to supremacy amongst contemporary men of letters. On the death of Dryden, in 1700, Pope, after an interval of eleven years, had succeeded, by the publication of his *Essay on Criticism*, to the vacant literary dictatorship, a position which he held to his death in 1744. Curiously enough, another period of eleven years elapsed, which ended in Johnson's elevation to power by the appearance of the Dictionary in 1755. Dryden, Pope, and Johnson exercised a lordship in letters which has had no parallel in the present century, though it is possible to trace, even amid the widely changed conditions of modern life, at least a reflection of it in the Victorian Age, in the oracular literary and social judgments on men, movements, and books of Thomas Carlyle. In a letter which Smollett wrote to Wilkes in 1759, Johnson is described as the "great Cham of literature," a term which—like those which were afterwards given him of "Dictator" and "Sultan" of English literature—sufficiently attests the unique place and power to which the once friendless scholar had at length fought his way. That very year Johnson's tender heart was filled with anguish by tidings of the death of his mother at the home of his childhood in the market-place of Lichfield. He had always been a loyal and affectionate son, and out of the poor pittance with which literature had rewarded him, he had given constantly with a reverent and generous hand to his aged mother. Yet he vexed his great heart with imaginary remissness, and was sorely troubled by the thought that perhaps he ought to have done more. To pay the expenses of his mother's funeral, and to wipe off the few modest debts which remained, he sat alone in his garret with his grief and wrote the classic pages of *Rasselas*—his only romance. It was written in the evenings of one week, and it more than procured the sum which its author needed. Always keenly alive to painful associations, Johnson could not bear to look at the book when it appeared, and he never read it in print until many years afterwards, when on a journey he came across a copy by chance.

One of the earliest and best rewards of literary success is the opportunity which it brings of intercourse with kindred minds. The *Rambler* introduced Johnson—just at the time when he most needed solace—to a group of men who quickly became his loyal and devoted friends. Foremost stands Bennet Langton, an amiable young Lincolnshire squire, very tall and equally polite, of polished manners and courtly bearing. Mr. Langton was so much charmed with the wisdom and wit of the *Rambler* that, in an acute fit of hero-worship, he took coach to town to pay homage to its author. Bennet Langton was one of those men who seem to go through life apologising for their own existence. He used to sit "with one leg twisted round the other, as if fearing to occupy more space than was equitable;" and this characteristic led him to be compared to the meditative stork standing on one leg near the shore, in Raphael's cartoon of the Miraculous Draught of Fishes. Johnson playfully declared that Bennet Langton's mind was as exalted as his stature; and, like a good Tory of the old school, he loved his new acquaintance none the less for being a man of ancient family. When thirty years had rolled away, and Johnson's life was closing, Bennet Langton—tender as a woman—was by his side.

A very different man was Topham Beauclerk—versatile, fascinating, accomplished, travelled, sarcastic in speech, light of heart, and of easy morals. It is hard at first sight to understand what two such men as Johnson and Beauclerk could have had in common; but the difficulty at least partially disappears when we remember that Beauclerk was at once a wit, a scholar, and a brilliant talker, who had seen much of the world, and was not blind either to its foibles or his own. These qualities in themselves were, however, not enough to win Johnson's friendship, or to conquer his scruples. He scolded Bennet Langton for associating with so dangerous a companion, but gradually his resentment vanished, and though he still shook his head at certain wild pranks, he became really attached to the genial scrapegrace. Far on in the Georgian era, the House of Stuart, in spite of its sins and short-comings, was regarded with a degree of romantic reverence which seems both ridiculous and misplaced to-day, and Johnson, who shared this sentiment with other old-fashioned Jacobites, treated Topham Beauclerk with marked consideration, because, forsooth, the blood of Charles II. and Nell Gwynne ran in his veins. A fancied resemblance to the "merry monarch" completed the moralist's subjugation. Topham Beauclerk was one of the few men who ventured to maintain a dispute with Dr. Johnson, and apparently he did not always come off second best. Johnson's affection for him was so great that he declared, with a faltering voice, when his friend lay dying, that he would walk to the "extent of the diameter of the earth to save Beauclerk."

Oliver Goldsmith, that gentle-hearted, vain, bright, blundering child of genius, and Edmund Burke, eloquent, stately, impassioned—the greatest thinker, in the judgment of Buckle, who ever devoted himself to English politics, Bacon alone excepted, and a man who took a wide and philosophic survey of every problem he discussed— were amongst the friends who now began to rally around Johnson. It was Burke's affluent and vigorous talk which made Johnson exclaim, "Sir, that fellow calls forth all my powers!" So greatly, indeed, was he impressed with Burke's commanding gifts, that he declared that if he went into a stable and began to talk with the ostlers, they would "venerate him as the wisest man they had ever seen." Sir Joshua Reynolds, the amiable painter, whose graceful brush shares with Boswell's garrulous pen the glory of having presented to all generations an inimitable portrait of the burly and outspoken moralist, whose massive figure still seems to haunt the narrow courts which descend into Fleet Street—a thoroughfare with which his name and fame are forever linked—was another of the intimate and endeared companions of Johnson's later London life.

Last, but not least, comes James Boswell, whom somebody, in a fit of petulance, once called "a Scotch cur." "No, no," replied Goldsmith, who stood by, "he is not a Scotch cur; he is merely a Scotch *bur.* Tom Davies threw him at Johnson in sport, and he has the faculty of *sticking.*" Washington Irving called Boswell the incarnation of toadyism, and it is certain that he flattered Johnson to the top of his bent; but he was neither a coxcomb nor a clown, and there was more to admire in the man than the constancy of his friendship, or his facility in taking notes; and, as Carlyle says, the "fact of his reverence for Johnson will ever remain noteworthy." Macaulay, with his fondness for dramatic contrasts, seeks to heighten the character of Johnson by pouring contempt on his biographer; but even he is compelled to admit that Boswell, who was a very small man, has beaten, in the region of biography, the greatest men who ever tried their hands at that difficult art.

Boswell was twenty-three, and Johnson fifty-five, when they first met in May 1736, in Davies the bookseller's shop. The young Scotch lawyer had a great hankering after personal introductions to eminent men, and not unnaturally he was extremely wishful to make the acquaintance of Johnson. He was drinking tea with the bookseller and his comely wife, when Johnson's shadow fell across the glass door which divided the shop from the parlour in which the little group was seated. Davies, who had but recently retired from the boards, true to his histrionic instincts, "announced his awful approach somewhat in the manner of an actor in the part of Horatio, when he addresses Hamlet on the appearance of his father's ghost—'Look, my lad; he comes.'" Boswell, who knew Johnson's violent prejudice against the Scotch, forgetful of the fact that his own speech would immediately betray him, implored Davies, in a hurried aside, not to mention where he came from. But Davies loved his joke too well to comply, and judged, moreover, like a sensible man, that it was best to take the bull by the horns, so "Mr. Boswell from Scotland" was duly presented. Afraid that such an announcement would close the door to further parley, Boswell gasped out in apologetic tones— "Mr. Johnson, I do indeed come from Scotland—but I cannot help it!" Instantly came the characteristic response, "That, sir, I find is what a very great many of your countrymen cannot help." From that day forward, for twenty years, Boswell followed Johnson about from place to place, watching his daily conduct, treasuring his chance remarks, eliciting his opinions, receiving his rebukes, and crowding the pages of his note-books with exact and picturesque details and racy sayings, which render the biography which he afterwards wrote a most realistic description of the man and his surroundings, as well as a perfect store-house of "wise saws and modern instances."

Of Boswell, indeed, when his theme is Johnson, it is not too much to say that "age cannot wither, nor custom stale, his infinite variety." From childhood to old age, at work or play, in hours of boisterous mirth and in seasons of deep melancholy, at church, at home, in Fleet Street, or at the "Club;" when Burke's arguments called forth all his powers, Goldsmith's debts all his pity, or blind Mrs. Williams's fretfulness all his patience, James Boswell never fails to bring us face to face with the great "Sultan of English Literature," whom he dogged so persistently down the last twenty years of an ever-widening career. If Boswell sometimes irritated Dr. Johnson by his pointless remarks and shallow inquisitiveness, it must at least be owned that he eventually made handsome amends for his tiresome behaviour. Throughout his life, Boswell remained conspicuous for a certain mature puerility; and this, to a man like Johnson, whose character every year which passed more deeply mellowed, must have proved exasperating in the extreme; but, on the other hand, though at heart kindly, tender, and generous even to a fault, the sturdy but somewhat slovenly moralist was himself far from perfect, for he had a temper which flashed fire like a flint; and in conversation he was positive, overbearing, and impatient of contradiction.

Out of a friendship so unequal sprang in due time a biography as honest, sympathetic, and minute as ever was penned; a picture, in short, distinguished beyond all others by that perfect art which conceals itself. Boswell has made us all his debtors, for in his graphic pages Dr. Johnson lives and laughs, and walks and talks before us. Let it be granted once for all that the honest fellow, with his ridiculous family pride, childish vanity, and too palpable hero-worship, said and did many foolish things; yet it would be wholly ungracious to pick a quarrel on that account with the patient listener who rescued Johnson's wise and witty table-talk from oblivion. Boswell has, in truth, immortalised himself by this performance; and it goes almost without the saying—so long as Don Quixote is remembered, Sancho Panza, most faithful of squires, will never be forgotten.

When the Tory party obtained a renewal of power soon after the accession of George III., Johnson, who was a zealous champion of Church and State, was not neglected. The king, who was more favourably disposed to men of literary merit than either George I. or George II., bestowed upon him—entirely unsought—a pension of three hundred

pounds a-year. Johnson hesitated; he was, in fact, afraid
that his acceptance might be regarded as a political bribe,
and he was determined to be the tool of no government,
and more especially of one which he held, in Boswell's
words, to be "founded in usurpation." Lord Bute,
however, removed his scruples by assuring him that it was
conferred upon him, not for what he might yet do, but for
what he had actually done. Satisfied that his independence
was not imperilled, and that no political services were
expected from him, he gratefully accepted this opportune
release from the burden of financial care, and for the next
fifteen years, so far as his pen was concerned, he may
almost be said to have obeyed to the letter the well-known
piece of advice—"rest and be thankful." Time had toned
down the fierce Jacobitism of his youth, and he said jocosely
in his later years, "I cannot now curse the House of
Hanover, but I think that the pleasure of cursing the House
of Hanover, and drinking King James's health, are amply
over-balanced by three hundred pounds a-year." It was
soon after this happy escape from care that Boswell was
introduced to him, under circumstances already described,
and from that time forward, in the language of Macaulay's
famous essay—"Johnson grown old, Johnson in the
fulness of his fame, and in the enjoyment of a competent
fortune, is better known to us than any other man
in history. Everything about him—his coat, his wig,
his figure, his face, his scrofula, his St. Vitus's dance,
his rolling walk, his blinking eye, the outward signs
which too clearly marked his approbation of his dinner,
his insatiable appetite for fish-sauce and veal-pie, his inex-
tinguishable thirst for tea, his trick of touching the posts
as he walked, his mysterious practice of treasuring up
scraps of orange-peel, his morning slumbers, his midnight

disputations, his contortions, his mutterings, his gruntings, his puffings, his vigorous, acute, and ready eloquence, his sarcastic wit, his vehemence, his insolence, his fits of tempestuous rage, his queer inmates, old Mr. Levett and blind Mrs. Williams, the cat Hodge, and the negro Frank—all are as familiar to us as the objects by which we have been surrounded from childhood."

Set free from care, Johnson grew genial, and although his temper was always quick, and he was accustomed to call a spade a spade, and had no patience with sentimental grievances or "foppish lamentations," few men who ever lived were more ready to succour the distressed or uplift the fallen. "He loved the poor," relates Mrs. Piozzi, "as I never yet saw anyone else do, with an earnest desire to make them happy." In the sharpest years of his own poverty, he would thrust pence into the hands of sleeping children whom he passed in his dreary midnight rambles about town, in order that when dawn awakened them from their uneasy slumbers on the cold steps of warehouse or mansion, they at least might be able to buy themselves a morsel of bread. He endured with pitying forbearance the querulous complaints of the maimed and helpless folk who, with no other claim upon him than their dire need, had found an asylum in a house, which they darkened with their discontent. He could tenderly uplift the poor, famished outcast of the streets, and bear her gently on his own shoulders to the shelter of his home. Chesterfield's politeness—it is not too much to say—shrivels into contempt in the presence of Johnson's compassion. He might not be able to bow as gracefully to the rich, but his generous heart had taught him to stoop to the poor. Lord Auchinleck, with a sneer, called Johnson "Ursa Major;"

but Goldsmith, who had tested in his own straits the practical kindliness of his nature, declared that there was "nothing of the bear about him but the skin." Roughness of speech and outbursts of temper, these were the flaws in a noble character, which carried all its blemishes on the surface. Johnson knew his faults, and deeply deplored them; and when he lay dying, they weighed upon a soul which had carried a childlike sensitiveness to right and wrong through the storms, the struggles, the temptations, and the toils of more than three score years and ten. But not less beautiful than just was the tender comment of Edmund Burke—"It is well if, when a man comes to die, he has nothing heavier upon his conscience than having been a little rough in his conversation."

The closing decades of Dr. Johnson's life were marked by public honour, private friendship, congenial leisure, and happy associations. To him "a tavern chair was the throne of human felicity;" and he held that the man who was tired of London was tired of life. By the fireside of the Mitre, affable with and accessible to all, Johnson spent many an hour in animated discussion. At the Literary Club—which he himself founded in 1764, at the Turk's Head, in Gerrard Street, Soho—Reynolds and Burke, Goldsmith and Langton, gathered around him, and drew forth the affluence of his talk. His friendship with Mr. and Mrs. Thrale was another source of gladness to him, though his closing days were darkened by the death of the former, and by the desertion of the latter, and the house at Streatham, which had once been to him a second home, thus closed its gates upon his declining years. The tour which he made in Scotland with Boswell in 1773, and his journey to the Western Islands in 1775, were the chief outward incidents of his old age. Death began to make many inroads on his friendships, though, like a wise man, he sought to keep them in repair.

In 1779 he published the first four volumes of *The Lives of the Poets*, and two years later he finished his literary labours with another six volumes of the *Lives*. During the closing years of his career, according to Boswell, "he seemed to be a kind of public oracle, whom everybody thought they had a right to visit and consult; and, doubtless, they were well rewarded." He rose late, "declaimed all the morning," dined at a tavern, drank tea at a friend's house, "over which he loitered a great while," spent his evenings in company, and read and wrote far on into the night. " He walked the streets at all hours, and said he was never robbed, for the rogues knew that he had little money, nor had he the appearance of having much." Mrs. Piozzi states that "it was never against people of coarse life that his contempt was expressed, while poverty of sentiment in men who considered themselves to be *company for the parlour*, as he called it, was what he would not bear." Death, which he had always feared, came gently to him at last, and he met it with the faith and fortitude of a sincere but humble-minded Christian. His last words had no roughness in them. "God bless you, my dear," came faintly to a young lady, the daughter of an old friend, who kneeled reverently for a final benediction by his bed.

Thus ended in victorious peace, on the 13th of December 1784, the life of Samuel Johnson. He found an appropriate grave in Westminster Abbey, and a statue in the nave of St. Paul's Cathedral was also reared in his honour. If his prejudices were stubborn, his principles were of adamant; if his temper was capricious, his heart was tender; if he failed sometimes to observe those little courtesies of life, the neglect of which in some circles seems to constitute the unpardonable sin, he kept with brave fidelity the weightier matters of the law, and reverenced his conscience as his king.

The poetry of Johnson has been overshadowed by his prose, but its quality and scope ought to shield it from the cheap dismissal which it usually receives. Like all his other work, it is unequal, and its prevailing tone is too didactic; in style and pomp of diction it suggests the school of Pope, but in vigour and veracity of sentiment it reflects the moral majesty of its author's character. The prose of Johnson, though always distinguished by stately imagery, masculine common-sense, philosophic insight, and a touch of subtle humour, was somewhat turgid and grandiloquent in earlier life; this fault had, to a large extent, vanished when the *Rambler* appeared; the *Idler* in turn was brighter and less formal; and the *Lives of the Poets*, written in old age, in spite of the occasional unjustness of the strictures they contain, show, in their blended criticism and biography, the hand of Johnson at its best.

Dr. Johnson himself was greater than anything which he accomplished, and perhaps it is to his familiar sayings that we must turn for the most vivid illustration of those noble and exalted qualities of mind and heart which met in him, and which constitute his abiding claim to the gratitude, reverence, and affection of succeeding generations. So long, indeed, as the world continues to render homage to valiant and generous natures in which virtue and genius blend in noble union, "deep in the common heart," the power of Samuel Johnson will survive.

THE RAMBLER.

THE RAMBLER.

1750-1752.

———◆◆———

[BOSWELL gives the following account of the origin of the *Rambler*:— "In 1750 Johnson came forth in the character for which he was eminently qualified—a majestick teacher of moral and religious wisdom. The vehicle which he chose was that of a periodical paper, which he knew had been, upon former occasions, employed with great success. The *Tatler*, *Spectator*, and *Guardian* were the last of the kind published in England which had stood the test of a long trial; and such an interval had now elapsed since their publication as made him justly think that, to many of his readers, this form of instruction would, in some degree, have the advantage of novelty."—(Hill's Boswell's *Life of Johnson*, vol. i., 201.) Dr. Johnson told Sir Joshua Reynolds that he felt at a loss how to name the new venture :—" I sat down at night upon my bedside, and resolved that I would not go to sleep until I had fixed its title. The *Rambler* seemed the best that occurred, and I took it." The period which had elapsed since Addison and Steele had ceased to charm mankind with their essays was certainly long enough to have gathered a new audience for the first and greatest of their successors. The *Tatler* ended on the 2nd of January 1710-11 ; the first series of the *Spectator* on the 6th of December 1712 ; the *Guardian* on the 1st of October 1713 ; and the second series of the *Spectator* on the 20th of December 1714. The first number of the *Rambler* was published on Tuesday, the 20th of March 1750, and it appeared

I

regularly twice a week, on Tuesdays and Saturdays, until Saturday the 14th of March 1752, when the publication came to an end through the deep sorrow which fell across Johnson's life in the death of his wife. With the exception of five essays, those numbered ten, thirty, forty-four, ninety-seven, and one hundred, all the papers were written by Johnson himself, and often at a white heat. Cave, the publisher, used to say that copy was seldom sent to the press till late in the night before the day of publication, and this, of course, was a much more serious embarrassment to the printer before the age of steam! It will be found that the notes are chiefly snatches from Dr. Johnson's conversation, which serve to cast side-lights on many of the themes discussed in the essays.]

Saturday, March 24, 1749-50.

> "*Stare loco nescit, pereunt vestigia mille*
> *Ante fugam, absentemque ferit gravis ungula campum.*"
> > STATIUS.

> " Th' impatient courser pants in every vein,
>   And pawing seems to beat the distant plain ;
>   Hills, vales, and floods appear already crost,
>   And ere he starts, a thousand steps are lost." POPE.

THAT the mind of man is never satisfied with the objects immediately before it, but is always breaking away from the present moment, and losing itself in schemes of future felicity; and that we forget the proper use of the time now in our power, to provide for the enjoyment of that which, perhaps, may never be granted us, has been frequently remarked; and as this practice is a commodious subject of raillery to the gay, and of declamation to the serious, it has been ridiculed with all the pleasantry of wit, and exaggerated with all the amplifications of rhetorick. Every instance, by which its absurdity might appear most flagrant, has been studiously collected; it has been marked with every epithet of contempt, and all the tropes and figures have been called forth against it.

Censure is willingly indulged, because it always implies some superiority; men please themselves with imagining that they have made a deeper search, or wider survey, than others, and detected faults and follies, which escape vulgar observation. And the pleasure of wantoning in common topicks is so tempting to a writer, that he cannot easily resign it; a train of sentiments generally received enables him to shine without labour, and to conquer without a contest. It is so easy to laugh at the folly of him who lives only in idea, refuses immediate ease for distant pleasures, and, instead of enjoying the blessings of life, lets life glide away in preparations to enjoy them; it affords such opportunities of triumphant exultation, to exemplify the uncertainty of the human state, to rouse mortals from their dream, and inform them of the silent celerity of time, that we may believe authors willing rather to transmit than examine so advantageous a principle, and more inclined to pursue a track so smooth and so flowery, than attentively to consider whether it leads to truth.

This quality of looking forward into futurity, seems the unavoidable condition of a being, whose motions are gradual, and whose life is progressive: as his powers are limited, he must use means for the attainment of his ends, and intend first what he performs last; as by continual advances from his first stage of existence, he is perpetually varying the horizon of his prospects, he must always discover new motives of action, new excitements of fear, and allurements of desire.

The end therefore which at present calls forth our efforts, will be found, when it is once gained, to be only one of the means to some remoter end. The natural flights of the human mind are not from pleasure to pleasure, but from hope to hope.

He that directs his steps to a certain point, must frequently turn his eyes to that place which he strives to reach ; he that undergoes the fatigue of labour must solace his weariness with the contemplation of its reward. In agriculture, one of the most simple and necessary employments, no man turns up the ground but because he thinks of the harvest, that harvest which blights may intercept, which inundations may sweep away, or which death or calamity may hinder him from reaping.

Yet as few maxims are widely received or long retained but for some conformity with truth and nature, it must be confessed, that this caution against keeping our view too intent upon remote advantages is not without its propriety or usefulness, though it have been recited with too much levity, or enforced with too little distinction : for not to speak of that vehemence of desire which presses through right and wrong to its gratification, or that anxious inquietude which is justly chargeable with distrust of heaven, subjects too solemn for my present purpose ; it frequently happens that, by indulging early the raptures of success, we forget the measures necessary to secure it, and suffer the imagination to riot in the fruition of some possible good, till the time of obtaining it has slipped away.

There would, however, be few enterprizes of great labour or hazard undertaken, if we had not the power of magnifying the advantages which we persuade ourselves to expect from them. When the knight of La Mancha gravely recounts to his companion the adventures by which he is to signalize himself in such a manner that he shall be summoned to the support of empires, solicitude to accept the heiress of the crown which he has preserved, have honours and riches to scatter about him, and an island to bestow on his worthy squire, very few readers, amidst their mirth or pity, can deny that they have admitted visions of the same kind; though they have not, perhaps, expected events equally strange, or by means equally inadequate. When we pity him, we reflect on our own disappointments; and when we laugh, our hearts inform us that he is not more ridiculous than ourselves, except that he tells what we have only thought.

The understanding of a man naturally sanguine, may, indeed, be easily vitiated by the luxurious indulgence of hope, however necessary to the production of every thing great or excellent, as some plants are destroyed by too open exposure to that sun which gives life and beauty to the vegetable world.

Perhaps no class of the human species requires more to be cautioned against this anticipation of happiness, than those that aspire to the name of authors. A man of lively fancy no sooner finds a hint moving in his mind, than he makes momentaneous excursions to the press, and to the world, and, with a little encouragement from flattery, pushes forward into future ages, and prognosticates the honours to be paid him, when envy is extinct, and faction forgotten, and those, whom partiality now suffers to obscure him, shall have given way to the triflers of as short duration as themselves.

Those who have proceeded so far as to appeal to the tribunal of succeeding times, are not likely to be cured of their infatuation; but all endeavours ought to be used for the prevention of a disease, for which, when it has attained its height, perhaps no remedy will be found in the gardens of philosophy, however she may boast her physick of the mind, her catharticks of vice, or lenitives of passion.

I shall, therefore, while I am yet but lightly touched with the symptoms of the writer's malady, endeavour to fortify myself against the infection, not without some weak hope that my preservatives may extend their virtues to others, whose employment exposes them to the same danger.

> "*Laudis amore tumes? Sunt certa piacula, quæ te*
> *Ter pure lecto poterunt recreare libello.*"

> "Is fame your passion? Wisdom's powerful charm,
> If thrice read over, shall its force disarm." FRANCIS.

It is the sage advice of Epictetus, that a man should accustom himself often to think of what is most shocking and terrible, that by such reflections he may be preserved from too ardent wishes for seeming good, and from too much dejection in real evil.

There is nothing more dreadful to an author than neglect; compared with which, reproach, hatred, and opposition, are names of happiness; yet this worse, this meanest fate, every one who dares to write has reason to fear.

> "*I nunc, et versus tecum meditare canoros.*"

> "Go now, and meditate thy tuneful lays." ELPHINSTON.

It may not be unfit for him who makes a new entrance into the lettered world, so far to suspect his own powers, as to believe that he possibly may deserve neglect; that nature may not have qualified him much to enlarge or embellish knowledge, nor sent him forth entitled by indisputable superiority to regulate the conduct of the rest of mankind; that, though the world must be granted to be yet in ignorance, he is not destined to dispel the cloud, nor to shine out as one of the luminaries of life. For this suspicion, every catalogue of a library will furnish sufficient reason; as he will find it crowded with names of men who, though now forgotten, were once no less enterprising or confident than himself, equally pleased with their own productions, equally caressed by their patrons, and flattered by their friends.

But though it should happen that an author is capable of excelling, yet his merit may pass without notice, huddled in the variety of things, and thrown into the general miscellany of life. He that endeavours after fame by writing, solicits the regard of a multitude, fluctuating in pleasures or immersed in business, without time for intellectual amusements; he appeals to judges, prepossessed by passions, or corrupted by prejudices, which preclude their approbation of any new performance. Some are too indolent to read anything till its reputation is established; others too envious to promote that fame which gives them pain by its increase. What is new is opposed, because most are unwilling to be taught; and what is known is rejected, because it is not sufficiently considered that men more frequently require to be reminded than informed. The learned are afraid to declare their opinion early, lest they should put their reputation in hazard; the ignorant always imagine themselves giving some proof of delicacy, when they refuse to be pleased; and he that finds his way to reputation through all these obstructions, must acknowledge that he is indebted to other causes besides his industry, his learning, or his wit.

Tuesday, March 27, 1750.

" VIRTUS, *repulsæ nescia sordida,*
Intaminatis fulget honoribus,
Nec sumit aut ponit secures
Arbitrio popularis auræ."   HOR.

" Undisappointed in designs,
With native honours virtue shines ;
Nor takes up pow'r, nor lays it down,
As giddy rabbles smile or frown."   ELPHINSTON.

THE task of an author is, either to teach what is not
known, or to recommend known truths by his manner
of adorning them ; either to let new light in upon the mind,
and open new scenes to the prospect, or to vary the dress
and situation of common objects, so as to give them fresh
grace and more powerful attractions, to spread such flowers
over the regions through which the intellect has already made
its progress, as may tempt it to return, and take a second view
of things hastily passed over, or negligently regarded.

Either of these labours is very difficult, because that they
may not be fruitless, men must not only be persuaded of
their errours, but reconciled to their guide ; they must not
only confess their ignorance, but, what is still less pleasing,
must allow that he from whom they are to learn is more
knowing than themselves.

It might be imagined that such an employment was in
itself sufficiently irksome and hazardous ; that none would
be found so malevolent as wantonly to add weight to the
stone of Sisyphus ; and that few endeavours would be used
to obstruct those advances to reputation, which must be

made at such an expense of time and thought, with so great
hazard in the miscarriage, and with so little advantage from
the success.

Yet there is a certain race of men, that either imagine
it their duty, or make it their amusement, to hinder the
reception of every work of learning or genius, who stand as
centinels in the avenues of fame, and value themselves
upon giving IGNORANCE and ENVY the first notice of a
prey.

To these men who distinguish themselves by the appellation of CRITICKS, it is necessary for a new author to find
some means of recommendation. It is probable, that the
most malignant of these persecutors might be somewhat
softened, and prevailed on, for a short time, to remit their
fury. Having for this purpose considered many expedients,
I find in the records of ancient times, that ARGUS was lulled
by musick, and CERBERUS quieted with a sop; and am,
therefore, inclined to believe that modern criticks, who, if
they have not the eyes, have the watchfulness of ARGUS,
and can bark as loud as CERBERUS, though, perhaps, they
cannot bite with equal force, might be subdued by methods
of the same kind. I have heard how some have been
pacified with claret and a supper, and others laid asleep
with the soft notes of flattery.

Though the nature of my undertaking gives me sufficient
reason to dread the united attacks of this virulent generation, yet I have not hitherto persuaded myself to take any
measures for flight or treaty. For I am in doubt whether
they can act against me by lawful authority, and suspect that
they have presumed upon a forged commission, stiled themselves the ministers of CRITICISM, without any authentick
evidence of delegation, and uttered their own determinations
as the decrees of a higher judicature.

CRITICISM,* from whom they derive their claim to decide the fate of writers, was the eldest daughter of LABOUR and TRUTH : she was, at her birth, committed to the care of JUSTICE, and brought up by her in the palace of WISDOM. Being soon distinguished by the celestials, for her .uncommon qualities, she was appointed the governess of FANCY, and empowered to beat time to the chorus of the MUSES, when they sung before the throne of JUPITER.

When the MUSES condescended to visit this lower world, they came accompanied by CRITICISM, to whom, upon her descent from her native regions, JUSTICE gave a sceptre, to be carried aloft in her right hand, one end of which was tinctured with ambrosia, and inwreathed with a golden foliage of amaranths and bays; the other end was encircled with cypress and poppies, and dipped in the waters of oblivion. In her left hand she bore an unextinguishable torch, manufactured by LABOUR, and lighted by TRUTH, of which it was the particular quality immediately to show everything in its true form, however it might be disguised to common eyes. Whatever ART could complicate, or FOLLY could confound, was, upon the first gleam of the Torch of TRUTH, exhibited in its distinct parts and original simplicity; it darted through the labyrinths of sophistry, and showed at once all the absurdities to which they served for refuge; it pierced through the robes which rhetorick often sold to falsehood, and detected the disproportion of parts which artificial veils had been contrived to cover.

Thus furnished for the execution of her office, CRITICISM came down to survey the performances of those who professed themselves the votaries of the MUSES.

* Note I., Appendix.

Whatever was brought before her, she beheld by the steady
light of the Torch of TRUTH, and when her examination
had convinced her, that the laws of just writing had been
observed, she touched it with the amaranthine end of the
sceptre, and consigned it over to immortality.

But it more frequently happened, that in the works
which required her inspection, there was some imposture
attempted; that false colours were laboriously laid; that
some secret inequality was found between the words and
sentiments, or some dissimilitude of the ideas and the
original objects; that incongruities were linked together,
or that some parts were of no use but to enlarge the
appearance of the whole, without contributing to its
beauty, solidity, or usefulness.

Wherever such discoveries were made, and they were
made · whenever these faults were committed, CRITICISM
refused the touch which conferred the sanction of immortality, and, when the errours were frequent and gross,
reversed the sceptre, and let drops of lethe distil from
the poppies and cypress a fatal mildew, which immediately
begun to waste the work away, till it was at last totally
destroyed.

There were some compositions brought to the test, in
which, when the strongest light was thrown upon them,
their beauties and faults appeared so equally mingled, that
CRITICISM stood with her sceptre poised in her hand, in
doubt whether to shed lethe, or ambrosia, upon them.
These at last increased to so great a number, that she
was weary of attending such doubtful claims, and, for
fear of using improperly the sceptre of JUSTICE, referred
the cause to be considered by TIME.

The proceedings of TIME, though very dilatory, were,
some few caprices excepted, conformable to justice: and

many who thought themselves secure by a short forbearance, have sunk under his scythe, as they were posting down with their volumes in triumph to futurity. It was observable that some were destroyed by little and little, and others crushed for ever by a single blow.

CRITICISM having long kept her eye fixed steadily upon TIME, was at last so well satisfied with his conduct, that she withdrew from the earth with her patroness ASTREA, and left PREJUDICE and FALSE TASTE to ravage at large as the associates of FRAUD and MISCHIEF; contenting herself thenceforth to shed her influence from afar upon some select minds, fitted for its reception by learning and by virtue.

Before her departure she broke her sceptre, of which the shivers, that formed the ambrosial end, were caught up by FLATTERY, and those that had been infected with the waters of lethe were, with equal haste, seized by MALEVOLENCE. The followers of FLATTERY, to whom she distributed her part of the sceptre, neither had nor desired light, but touched indiscriminately whatever POWER or INTEREST happened to exhibit. The companions of MALEVOLENCE were supplied by the FURIES with a torch, which had this quality peculiar to infernal lustre, that its light fell only upon faults.

> " No light, but rather darkness visible,
>   Serv'd only to discover sights of woe."

With these fragments of authority, the slaves of FLATTERY and MALEVOLENCE marched out, at the command of their mistresses, to confer immortality, or condemn to oblivion. But this sceptre had now lost its power; and TIME passes his sentence at leisure, without any regard to their determinations.

Saturday, March 31, 1750.

" *Simul et jucunda et idonea dicere vitæ.*"   HOR.

" And join both profit and delight in one." CREECH.

THE works of fiction, with which the present generation
seems more particularly delighted, are such as exhibit
life in its true state, diversified only by accidents that daily
happen in the world, and influenced by passions and
qualities which are really to be found in conversing with
mankind.

This kind of writing may be termed not improperly the
comedy of romance, and is to be conducted nearly by the
rules of comick poetry. Its province is to bring about
natural events by easy means, and to keep up curiosity
without the help of wonder : it is therefore precluded from
the machines and expedients of the heroick romance, and
can neither employ giants to snatch away a lady from the
nuptial rites, nor knights to bring her back from captivity ;
it can neither bewilder its personages in deserts, nor lodge
them in imaginary castles.

I remember a remark made by Scaliger upon Pontanus,
that all his writings are filled with the same images ; and
that if you take from him his lilies and his roses, his satyrs
and his dryads, he will have nothing left that can be called
poetry. In like manner almost all the fictions of the last
age will vanish, if you deprive them of a hermit and a wood,
a battle and a shipwreck.

Why this wild strain of imagination found reception so

long in polite and learned ages, it is not easy to conceive; but we cannot wonder that while readers could be procured, the authors were willing to continue it; for when a man had by practice gained some fluency of language, he had no further care than to retire to his closet, let loose his invention, and heat his mind with incredibilities; a book was thus produced without fear of criticism, without the toil of study, without knowledge of nature, or acquaintance with life.

The task of our present writers is very different; it requires, together with that learning which is to be gained from books, that experience which can never be attained by solitary diligence, but must arise from general converse and accurate observation of the living world. Their performances have, as Horace expresses it, *plus oneris quantum veniæ minus*, little indulgence, and therefore more difficulty. They are engaged in portraits of which every one knows the original, and can detect any deviation from exactness of resemblance. Other writings are safe, except from the malice of learning, but these are in danger from every common reader: as the slipper ill executed was censured by a shoemaker who happened to stop in his way at the Venus of Apelles.

But the fear of not being approved as just copiers of human manners, is not the most important concern that an author of this sort ought to have before him. These books are written chiefly to the young, the ignorant, and the idle, to whom they serve as lectures of conduct, and introductions into life. They are the entertainment of minds unfurnished with ideas, and therefore easily susceptible of impressions; not fixed by principles, and therefore easily following the current of fancy; not informed by experience, and consequently open to every false suggestion and partial account.

That the highest degree of reverence should be paid to youth, and that nothing indecent should be suffered to approach their eyes or ears, are precepts extorted by sense and virtue from an ancient writer, by no means eminent for chastity of thought. The same kind, though not the same degree of caution, is required in every thing which is laid before them, to secure them from unjust prejudices, perverse opinions, and incongruous combinations of images.

In the romances formerly written, every transaction and sentiment was so remote from all that passes among men, that the reader was in very little danger of making any applications to himself; the virtues and crimes were equally beyond his sphere of activity; and he amused himself with heroes and with traitors, deliverers and persecutors, as with beings of another species, whose actions were regulated upon motives of their own, and who had neither faults nor excellencies in common with himself.

But when an adventurer is levelled with the rest of the world, and acts in such scenes of the universal drama, as may be the lot of any other man; young spectators fix their eyes upon him with closer attention, and hope, by observing his behaviour and success, to regulate their own practices, when they shall be engaged in the like part.

For this reason, these familiar histories may perhaps be made of greater use than the solemnities of professed morality, and convey the knowledge of vice and virtue with more efficacy than axioms and definitions. But if the power of example is so great as to take possession of the memory by a kind of violence, and produce effects almost without the intervention of the will, care ought to be taken, that, when the choice is unrestrained, the best examples only should be exhibited; and that which is likely to operate so strongly, should not be mischievous or uncertain in its effects.

The chief advantage which these fictions have over real life is, that their authors are at liberty, though not to invent, yet to select objects, and to cull from the mass of mankind, those individuals upon which the attention ought most to be employed : as a diamond, though it cannot be made, may be polished by art, and placed in such a situation, as to display that lustre which before was buried among common stones.

It is justly considered as the greatest excellency of art, to imitate nature; but it is necessary to distinguish those parts of nature, which are most proper for imitation : greater care is still required in representing life, which is so often discoloured by passion, or deformed by wickedness. If the world be promiscuously described, I cannot see of what use it can be to read the account : or why it may not be as safe to turn the eye immediately upon mankind as upon a mirror which shows all that presents itself without discrimination.

It is, therefore, not a sufficient vindication of a character, that it is drawn as it appears; for many characters ought never to be drawn : nor of a narrative, that the train of events is agreeable to observation and experience; for that observation which is called knowledge of the world, will be found much more frequently to make men cunning than good. The purpose of these writings is surely not only to show mankind, but to provide that they may be seen hereafter with less hazard; to teach the means of avoiding the snares which are laid by Treachery for Innocence, without infusing any wish for that superiority with which the betrayer flatters his vanity; to give the power of counteracting fraud, without the temptation to practise it; to initiate youth by mock encounters in the art of necessary defence, and to increase prudence without impairing virtue.

Many writers, for the sake of following nature, so mingle good and bad qualities in their principal personages, that they are both equally conspicuous; and as we accompany them through their adventures with delight, and are led by degrees to interest ourselves in their favour, we lose the abhorrence of their faults, because they do not hinder our pleasure, or, perhaps, regard them with some kindness, for being united with so much merit.

There have been men indeed splendidly wicked, whose endowments threw a brightness on their crimes, and whom scarce any villany made perfectly detestable, because they never could be wholly divested of their excellencies; but such have been in all ages the great corrupters of the world, and their resemblance ought no more to be preserved than the art of murdering without pain.

Some have advanced, without due attention to the consequences of this notion, that certain virtues have their correspondent faults, and therefore that to exhibit either apart is to deviate from probability. Thus men are observed by Swift to be "grateful in the same degree as they are resentful." This principle, with others of the same kind, supposes man to act from a brute impulse, and pursue a certain degree of inclination, without any choice of the object; for, otherwise, though it should be allowed that gratitude and resentment arise from the same constitution of the passions, it follows not that they will be equally indulged when reason is consulted; yet, unless that consequence be admitted, this sagacious maxim becomes an empty sound, without any relation to practice or to life.

Nor is it evident, that even the first motions to these effects are always in the same proportion. For pride, which produces quickness of resentment, will obstruct gratitude, by unwillingness to admit that inferiority which obligation implies ; and it is very unlikely that he who cannot think he receives a favour, will acknowledge or repay it.

It is of the utmost importance to mankind, that positions of this tendency should be laid open and confuted ; for while men consider good and evil as springing from the same root, they will spare the one for the sake of the other, and in judging, if not of others, at least of themselves, will be apt to estimate their virtues by their vices. To this fatal errour all those will contribute, who confound the colours of right and wrong, and, instead of helping to settle their boundaries, mix them with so much art, that no common mind is able to disunite them.

In narratives where historical veracity has no place, I cannot discover why there should not be exhibited the most perfect idea of virtue ; of virtue not angelical, nor above probability, for what we cannot credit, we shall never imitate, but the highest and purest that humanity can reach, which, exercised in such trials as the various revolutions of things shall bring upon it, may, by conquering some calamities, and enduring others, teach us what we may hope, and what we can perform. Vice, for vice is necessary to be shown, should always disgust ; nor should the graces of gaiety, or the dignity of courage, be so united with it, as to reconcile it to the mind. Wherever it appears, it should raise hatred by the malignity of its practices, and contempt by the meanness of its stratagems : for while it is supported by either parts or spirit, it will be seldom heartily abhorred. The Roman tyrant was content to be hated, if he was but feared ; and there are thousands of the readers of romances willing to be thought wicked, if they may be allowed to be wits. It is therefore to be steadily inculcated, that virtue is the highest proof of understanding, and the only solid basis of greatness; and that vice is the natural consequence of narrow thoughts; that it begins in mistake, and ends in ignominy.

<hr>

Tuesday, April 24, 1750.

<hr>

" *Non Dindymene, non adytis quatit*
Mentem sacerdotum incola Pythius,
Non Liber æque, non acuta
Sic geminant Corybantes æra,
Tristes ut iræ.——" HOR.

" Yet O ! remember, nor the god of wine,
Nor *Pythian Phœbus* from his inmost shrine,
Nor *Dindymene*, nor her priests possest,
Can with their sounding cymbals shake the breast,
Like furious anger." FRANCIS.

THE maxim which Periander of Corinth, one of the seven sages of Greece, left as a memorial of his knowledge and benevolence, was χόλς κράτει, *Be master of thy anger.* He considered anger as the great disturber of human life, the chief enemy both of publick happiness and private tranquillity, and thought that he could not lay on posterity a stronger obligation to reverence his memory, than by leaving them a salutary caution against this outrageous passion.

To what latitude Periander might extend the word, the brevity of his precept will scarce allow us to conjecture. From anger, in its full import, protracted into malevolence, and exerted in revenge, arise, indeed, many of the evils to which the life of man is exposed. By anger operating upon power are produced the subversion of cities, the desolation of countries, the massacre of nations, and all those dreadful and astonishing calamities which fill the histories of the world, and which could not be read at any distant point of time, when the passions stand neutral, and every motive and principle is left to its natural force, without some doubt of the truth of the relation, did we not see the same causes still tending to the same effects, and only acting with less vigour for want of the same concurrent opportunities.

But this gigantick and enormous species of anger falls not properly under the animadversion of a writer, whose chief end is the regulation of common life, and whose precepts are to recommend themselves by their general use. Nor is this essay intended to expose the tragical or fatal effects even of private malignity. The anger which I propose now for my subject, is such as makes those who indulge it more troublesome than formidable, and ranks them rather with hornets and wasps, than with basilisks and lions. I have, therefore, prefixed a motto, which characterises this passion, not so much by the mischief that it causes, as by the noise that it utters.

There is in the world a certain class of mortals, known, and contentedly known, by the appellation of *passionate men*, who imagine themselves entitled by that distinction to be provoked on every slight occasion, and to vent their rage in vehement and fierce vociferations, in furious menaces and licentious reproaches. Their rage, indeed, for the most part, fumes away in outcries of injury, and protestations of vengeance, and seldom proceeds to actual violence, unless a drawer or linkboy falls in their way ; but they interrupt the quiet of those that happen to be within the reach of their clamours, obstruct the course of conversation, and disturb the enjoyment of society.

Men of this kind are sometimes not without understanding or virtue, and are, therefore, not always treated with the severity which their neglect of the ease of all about them might justly provoke; they have obtained a kind of prescription for their folly, and are considered by their companions as under a predominant influence that leaves them not masters of their conduct or language, as acting without consciousness, and rushing into mischief with a mist before their eyes; they are therefore pitied rather than censured, and their sallies are passed over as the involuntary blows of a man agitated by the spasms of a convulsion.

It is surely not to be observed without indignation that men may be found of minds mean enough to be satisfied with this treatment; wretches who are proud to obtain the privilege of madmen, and can, without shame, and without regret, consider themselves as receiving hourly pardons from their companions, and giving them continual opportunities of exercising their patience, and boasting their clemency.

Pride is undoubtedly the original of anger; but pride, like every other passion, if it once breaks loose from reason, counteracts its own purposes. A passionate man upon the review of his day, will have very few gratifications to offer to his pride, when he has considered how his outrages were caused, why they were borne, and in what they are likely to end at last.

Those sudden bursts of rage generally break out upon small occasions; for life, unhappy as it is, cannot supply great evils as frequently as the man of fire thinks it fit to be enraged; therefore the first reflection upon his violence must show him that he is mean enough to be driven from his post by every petty incident, that he is the mere slave of casualty, and that his reason and virtue are in the power of the wind.

One motive there is of these loud extravagancies, which

a man is careful to conceal from others, and does not always discover to himself. He that finds his knowledge narrow, and his arguments weak, and by consequence his suffrage not much regarded, is sometimes in hope of gaining that attention by his clamours which he cannot otherwise obtain, and is pleased with remembering that at least he made himself heard, that he had the power to interrupt those whom he could not confute, and suspend the decision which he could not guide.

Of this kind is the fury to which many men give way among their servants and domesticks ; they feel their own ignorance, they see their own insignificance ; and therefore they endeavour, by their fury, to fright away contempt from before them, when they know it must follow them behind ; and think themselves eminently masters, when they see one folly tamely complied with, only lest refusal or delay should provoke them to a greater.

These temptations cannot but be owned to have some force. It is so little pleasing to any man to see himself wholly overlooked in the mass of things, that he may be allowed to try a few expedients for procuring some kind of supplemental dignity, and use some endeavour to add weight, by the violence of his temper, to the lightness of his other powers. But this has now been long practised, and found, upon the most exact estimate, not to produce advantages equal to its inconveniencies ; for it appears not that a man can by uproar, tumult, and bluster, alter any one's opinion of his understanding, or gain influence, except over those whom fortune or nature have made his dependents. He may, by a steady perseverance in his ferocity, fright his children, and harass his servants, but the rest of the world will look on and laugh ; and he will have the comfort at last of thinking, that he lives only to raise contempt and hatred, emotions to which wisdom and virtue would be always unwilling to give occasion. He has contrived only to make those fear him, whom every reasonable being is endeavouring to endear by kindness, and must content himself with the pleasure of a triumph obtained by trampling on them who could not resist. He must perceive that the apprehension which his presence causes is not the awe of his virtue, but the dread of his brutality, and that he has given up the felicity of being loved, without gaining the honour of being reverenced.

But this is not the only ill consequence of the frequent indulgence of this blustering passion, which a man, by often calling to his assistance, will teach, in a short time, to intrude before the summons, to rush upon him with resistless violence, and without any previous notice of its approach. He will find himself liable to be inflamed at the first touch of provocation, and unable to retain his resentment, till he has a full conviction of the offence, to proportion his anger to the cause, or to regulate it by prudence or by duty. When a man has once suffered his mind to be thus vitiated, he becomes one of the most hateful and unhappy beings. He can give no security to himself that he shall not, at the next interview, alienate by some sudden transport his dearest friend ; or break out, upon some slight contradiction, into such terms of rudeness as can never be perfectly forgotten. Whoever converses with him, lives with the suspicion and solitude of a man that plays with a tame tiger, always under a necessity of watching the moment in which the capricious savage shall begin to growl.

It is told by Prior,* in a panegyrick on the earl of Dorset, that his servants used to put themselves in his way when he

* Note II., Appendix.

was angry, because he was sure to recompense them for any indignities which he made them suffer. This is the round of a passionate man's life; he contracts debts when he is furious, which his virtue, if he has virtue, obliges him to discharge at the return of reason. He spends his time in outrage and acknowledgment, injury and reparation. Or, if there be any who hardens himself in oppression, and justifies the wrong, because he has done it, his insensibility can make small part of his praise, or his happiness; he only adds deliberate to hasty folly, aggravates petulance by contumacy, and destroys the only plea that he can offer for the tenderness and patience of mankind.

Yet, even this degree of depravity we may be content to pity, because it seldom wants a punishment equal to its guilt. Nothing is more despicable or more miserable than the old age of a passionate man. When the vigour of youth fails him, and his amusements pall with frequent repetition, his occasional rage sinks by decay of strength into peevishness; that peevishness, for want of novelty and variety, becomes habitual; the world falls off from around him, and he is left, as Homer expresses it, φθινίθων φίλον κῆ͜ρ, to devour his own heart in solitude and contempt.

Saturday, May 5, 1750.

" ———*Nil fuit unquam
Sic dispar sibi———*" Hor.

"Sure such a various creature ne'er was known." Francis.

AMONG the many inconsistencies which folly produces, or infirmity suffers, in the human mind, there has often been observed a manifest and striking contrariety between the life of an author and his writings; and Milton, in a letter to a learned stranger, by whom he had been visited, with great reason congratulates himself upon the consciousness of being found equal to his own character, and having preserved in a private and familiar interview, that reputation which his works had procured him.

Those whom the appearance of virtue, or the evidence of genius, have tempted to a nearer knowledge of the writer in whose performances they may be found, have indeed had frequent reason to repent their curiosity; the bubble that sparkled before them has become common water at the touch; the phantom of perfection has vanished when they wished to press it to their bosom. They have lost the pleasure of imagining how far humanity may be exalted, and, perhaps, felt themselves less inclined to toil up the steeps of virtue, when they observe those who seem best able to point the way, loitering below, as either afraid of the labour, or doubtful of the reward.

It has been long the custom of the oriental monarchs to hide themselves in gardens and palaces, to avoid the conversation of mankind, and to be known to their subjects only by their edicts. The same policy is no less necessary to him that writes, than to him that governs; for men would not more patiently submit to be taught, than commanded, by one known to have the same follies and weaknesses with themselves. A sudden intruder into the closet of an author would perhaps feel equal indignation with the officer, who having long solicited admission into the presence of Sardanapalus, saw him not consulting upon laws, inquiring into grievances, or modelling armies, but employed in feminine amusements, and directing the ladies in their work.

It is not difficult to conceive, however, that for many

reasons a man writes much better than he lives. For without entering into refined speculations, it may be shown much easier to design than to perform. A man proposes his schemes of life in a state of abstraction and disengagement, exempt from the enticements of hope, the solicitations of affection, the importunities of appetite, or the depressions of fear, and is in the same state with him that teaches upon land the art of navigation, to whom the sea is always smooth, and the wind always prosperous.

The mathematicians are well acquainted with the difference between pure science, which has to do only with ideas, and the application of its laws to the use of life, in which they are constrained to submit to the imperfection of matter and the influence of accidents. Thus, in moral discussions, it is to be remembered that many impediments obstruct our practice, which very easily give way to theory. The speculatist is only in danger of erroneous reasoning; but the man involved in life, has his own passions, and those of others, to encounter, and is embarrassed with a thousand inconveniencies, which confound him with variety of impulse, and either perplex or obstruct his way. He is forced to act without deliberation, and obliged to chuse before he can examine: he is surprised by sudden alterations of the state of things, and changes his measures according to superficial appearances; he is led by others, either because he is indolent, or because he is timorous; he is sometimes afraid to know what is right, and sometimes finds friends or enemies diligent to deceive him.

We are, therefore, not to wonder that most fail, amidst tumult, and snares, and danger, in the observance of those precepts, which they lay down in solitude, safety, and tranquillity, with a mind unbiassed, and with liberty unobstructed. It is the condition of our present state to see more than we can attain; the exactest vigilance and caution can never maintain a single day of unmingled innocence, much less can the utmost efforts of incorporated mind reach the summits of speculative virtue.

It is, however, necessary for the idea of perfection to be proposed, that we may have some object to which our endeavours are to be directed; and he that is most deficient in the duties of life, makes some atonement for his faults, if he warns others against his own failings, and hinders, by the salubrity of his admonitions, the contagion of his example.

Nothing is more unjust, however common, than to charge with hypocrisy him that expresses zeal for those virtues which he neglects to practise; since he may be sincerely convinced of the advantages of conquering his passions without having yet obtained the victory, as a man may be confident of the advantages of a voyage, or a journey, without having courage or industry to undertake it, and may honestly recommend to others those attempts which he neglects himself.

The interest which the corrupt part of mankind have in hardening themselves against every motive to amendment, has disposed them to give to these contradictions, when they can be produced against the cause of virtue, that weight which they will not allow them in any other case. They see men act in opposition to their interest, without supposing that they do not know it; those who give way to the sudden violence of passion, and forsake the most important pursuits for petty pleasures, are not supposed to have changed their opinions, or to approve their own conduct. In moral or religious questions alone, they determine the sentiments by the actions, and charge every man with endeavouring to impose upon the world, whose writings are not confirmed by his life. They never consider that themselves neglect or practise something every day inconsistently with their own settled judgment, nor discover that the conduct of the advocates for virtue can little increase, or lessen, the obligations of their dictates; argument is to be invalidated only by argument, and is in itself of the same force, whether or not it convinces him by whom it is proposed.

Yet since this prejudice, however unreasonable, is always likely to have some prevalence, it is the duty of every man to take care lest he should hinder the efficacy of his own instructions. When he desires to gain the belief of others, he should show that he believes himself; and when he teaches the fitness of virtue by his reasonings, he should, by his example, prove its possibility : Thus much at least may be required of him, that he shall not act worse than others, because he writes better; nor imagine that, by the merit of his genius, he may claim indulgence beyond mortals of the lower classes, and be excused for want of prudence, or neglect of virtue.

Bacon, in his history of the winds, after having offered something to the imagination as desirable, often proposes lower advantages in its place to the reason as attainable. The same method may be sometimes pursued in moral endeavours, which this philosopher observed in natural inquiries; having first set positive and absolute excellence before us, we may be pardoned though we sink down to humbler virtue, trying, however, to keep our point always in view, and struggling not to lose ground, though we cannot gain it.

It is recorded of Sir Matthew Hale, that he, for a long time, concealed the consecration of himself to the stricter duties of religion, lest, by some flagitious and shameful action, he should bring piety into disgrace. For the same reason it may be prudent for a writer, who apprehends that he shall not inforce his own maxims by his domestick character, to conceal his name, that he may not injure them.

There are, indeed, a great number whose curiosity to gain a more familiar knowledge of successful writers, is not so much prompted by an opinion of their power to improve as to delight, and who expect from them not arguments against vice, or dissertations on temperance or justice, but flights of wit, and sallies of pleasantry, or, at least, acute remarks, nice distinctions, justness of sentiment, and elegance of diction.

This expectation is, indeed, specious and probable, and yet, such is the fate of all human hopes, that it is very often frustrated, and those who raise admiration by their books, disgust by their company. A man of letters for the most part spends, in the privacies of study, that season of life in which the manners are to be softened into ease, and polished into elegance; and, when he has gained knowledge enough to be respected, has neglected the minuter acts by which he might have pleased. When he enters life, if his temper be soft and timorous, he is diffident and bashful, from the knowledge of his defects; or if he was born with spirit and resolution, he is ferocious and arrogant, from the consciousness of his merit: he is either dissipated by the awe of company, and unable to recollect his reading, and arrange his arguments; or he is hot and dogmatical, quick in opposition, and tenacious in defence, disabled by his own violence, and confused by his haste to triumph.

The graces of writing and conversation are of different kinds; and though he who excels in one might have been, with opportunities and application, equally successful in the other, yet as many please by extemporary talk, though utterly unacquainted with the more accurate method, and more laboured beauties, which composition requires; so it is very possible that men, wholly accustomed to works of study, may be without that readiness of conception, and affluence of language, always necessary to colloquial entertainment. They may want address to watch the hints which conversation offers for the display of their particular attainments, or they may be so much unfurnished with matter on common subjects, that discourse not professedly literary glides over them as heterogeneous bodies, without admitting their conceptions to mix in the circulation.

A transition from an author's book to his conversation, is too often like an entrance into a large city, after a distant prospect. Remotely, we see nothing but spires of temples and turrets of palaces, and imagine it the residence of splendour, grandeur, and magnificence; but, when we have passed the gates, we find it perplexed with narrow passages, disgraced with despicable cottages, embarrassed with obstructions, and clouded with smoke.*

Saturday, May 12, 1750.

"———*Multis dicendi copia torrens,*
Et sua mortifera est facundia———"   Juv.

" Some who the depths of eloquence have found,
In that unnavigable stream were drown'd." Dryden.

SIR,

I AM the modest young man whom you favoured with your advice, in a late paper; and, as I am very far from suspecting that you foresaw the numberless inconveniencies

* Note III., Appendix.

which I have, by following it, brought upon myself, I will lay my condition open before you, for you seem bound to extricate me from the perplexities in which your counsel, however innocent in the intention, has contributed to involve me.

You told me, as you thought, to my comfort, that a writer might easily find means of introducing his genius to the world, for the *presses of England were open.** This I have now fatally experienced; the press is, indeed, open.

> " ——*Facilis descensus Averni,*
>   *Noctes atque dies patet atri janua Ditis.*"   Juv.

> " The gates of hell are open night and day;
>   Smooth the descent, and easy is the way."
>   Dryden.

The means of doing hurt to ourselves are always at hand. I immediately sent to a printer, and contracted with him for an impression of several thousands of my pamphlet. While it was at the press, I was seldom absent from the printing-house, and continually urged the workmen to haste, by solicitations, promises, and rewards. From the day all other pleasures were excluded, by the delightful employment of correcting the sheets; and from the night, sleep generally was banished, by anticipation of the happiness which every hour was bringing nearer.

At last the time of publication approached, and my heart beat with the raptures of an author. I was above all little precautions, and in defiance of envy or of criticism, set my name upon the title, without sufficiently considering, that what has once passed the press is irrevocable, and that though the printing-house may properly be compared to the

---

* Note IV., Appendix.

infernal regions, for the facility of its entrance, and the difficulty with which authors return from it; yet there is this difference, that a great genius can never return to his former state, by a happy draught of the waters of oblivion.

I am now, Mr. Rambler, known to be an author, and am condemned, irreversibly condemned, to all the miseries of high reputation. The first morning after publication my friends assembled about me; I presented each, as is usual, with a copy of my book. They looked into the first pages, but were hindered, by their admiration, from reading further. The first pages are, indeed, very elaborate. Some passages they particularly dwelt upon, as more eminently beautiful than the rest; and some delicate strokes and secret elegancies, I pointed out to them which had escaped their observation. I then begged of them to forbear their compliments, and invited them, I could do no less, to dine with me at a tavern. After dinner, the book was resumed; but their praises very often so much overpowered my modesty, that I was forced to put about the glass, and had often no means of repressing the clamours of their admiration, but by thundering to the drawer for another bottle.

Next morning another set of my acquaintance congratulated me upon my performance, with such importunity of praise, that I was again forced to obviate their civilities by a treat. On the third day, I had yet a greater number of applauders to put to silence in the same manner; and, on the fourth, those whom I had entertained the first day came again, having, in the perusal of the remaining part of the book, discovered so many forcible sentences and masterly touches, that it was impossible for me to bear the repetition of their commendations. I therefore persuaded them once more to adjourn to the tavern, and chuse some other subject, on which I might share in their conversation. But it was not in their power to withhold their attention from my performance, which had so entirely taken possession of their minds that no entreaties of mine could change their topic, and I was obliged to stifle, with claret, that praise which neither my modesty could hinder, nor my uneasiness repress.

The whole week was thus spent in a kind of literary revel, and I have now found that nothing is so expensive as great abilities, unless there is joined with them an insatiable eagerness of praise; for to escape from the pain of hearing myself above the greatest names, dead and living, of the learned world, it has already cost me two hogsheads of port, fifteen gallons of arrack, ten dozen of claret, and five and forty bottles of champagne.

I was resolved to stay at home no longer, and therefore rose early and went to the coffee-house; but found that I had now made myself too eminent for happiness, and that I was no longer to enjoy the pleasure of mixing, upon equal terms, with the rest of the world. As soon as I enter the room I see part of the company raging with envy, which they endeavour to conceal, sometimes with the appearance of laughter, and sometimes with that of contempt; but the disguise is such that I can discover the secret rancour of their hearts, and as envy is deservedly its own punishment, I frequently indulge myself in tormenting them with my presence.

But though there may be some slight satisfaction received from the mortification of my enemies, yet my benevolence will not suffer me to take any pleasure in the terrours of my friends. I have been cautious, since the appearance of my work, not to give myself more premeditated airs of superiority than the most rigid humility might allow. It is,

3

indeed, not impossible that I may sometimes have laid down my opinion in a manner that showed a consciousness of my ability to maintain it, or interrupted the conversation, when I saw its tendency, without suffering the speaker to waste his time in explaining his sentiments; and, indeed, I did indulge myself for two days in a custom of drumming with my fingers, when the company began to lose themselves in absurdities, or to encroach upon subjects which I knew them unqualified to discuss. But I generally acted with great appearance of respect, even to those whose stupidity I pitied in my heart. Yet, notwithstanding this exemplary moderation, so universal is the dread of uncommon powers, and such the unwillingness of mankind to be made wiser, that I have now for some days found myself shunned by all my acquaintance. If I knock at a door, no body is at home; if I enter a coffee-house, I have the box to myself. I live in the town like a lion in his desert, or an eagle on his rock, too great for friendship or society, and condemned to solitude by unhappy elevation and dreaded ascendency.

Nor is my character only formidable to others, but burdensome to myself. I naturally love to talk without much thinking; to scatter my merriment at random, and to relax my thoughts with ludicrous remarks and fanciful images; but such is now the importance of my opinion, that I am afraid to offer it, lest, by being established too hastily into a maxim, it should be the occasion of errour to half the nation; and such is the expectation with which I am attended, when I am going to speak, that I frequently pause to reflect whether what I am about to utter is worthy of myself.

This, Sir, is sufficiently miserable; but there are still greater calamities behind. You must have read in Pope and Swift how men of parts have had their closets rifled, and their cabinets broke open, at the instigation of piratical booksellers, for the profit of their works ; and it is apparent that there are many prints now sold in the shops, of men whom you cannot suspect of sitting for that purpose, and whose likenesses must have been certainly stolen when their names made their faces vendible. These considerations at first put me on my guard, and I have, indeed, found sufficient reason for my caution, for I have discovered many people examining my countenance, with a curiosity that showed their intention to draw it ; I immediately left the house, but find the same behaviour in another.

Others may be persecuted, but I am haunted ; I have good reason to believe that eleven painters are now dogging me, for they know that he who can get my face first will make his fortune. I often change my wig, and wear my hat over my eyes, by which I hope somewhat to confound them ; for you know it is not fair to sell my face, without admitting me to share the profit.

I am, however, not so much in pain for my face as for my papers, which I dare neither carry with me nor leave behind. I have, indeed, taken some measures for their preservation, having put them in an iron chest, and fixed a padlock upon my closet. I change my lodgings five times a week, and always remove at the dead of night.

Thus I live, in consequence of having given too great proofs of a predominant genius, in the solitude of a hermit, with the anxiety of a miser, and the caution of an outlaw ; afraid to show my face lest it should be copied ; afraid to speak, lest I should injure my character ; and to write, lest my correspondents should publish my letters ; always uneasy lest my servants should steal my papers for the sake of money, or my friends for that of the publick. This it is to soar above the rest of mankind ; and this representation

I lay before you, that I may be informed how to divest myself of the laurels which are so cumbersome to the wearer, and descend to the enjoyment of that quiet, from which I find a writer of the first class so fatally debarred.

MISELLUS.

Tuesday, May 29, 1750.

" *Terra salutiferas herbas, eademque nocentes,*
   Nutrit ; & urticæ proxima sæpe rosa est."   OVID.

" Our bane and physick the same earth bestows,
   And near the noisome nettle blooms the rose."

EVERY man is prompted by the love of himself to imagine, that he possesses some qualities, superiour, either in kind or in degree, to those which he sees allotted to the rest of the world ; and, whatever apparent disadvantages he may suffer in the comparison with others, he has some invisible distinctions, some latent reserve of excellence, which he throws into the balance, and by which he generally fancies that it is turned in his favour.

The studious and speculative part of mankind always seem to consider their fraternity as placed in a state of opposition to those who are engaged in the tumult of publick business ; and have pleased themselves, from age to age, with celebrating the felicity of their own condition, and with recounting the perplexity of politicks, the dangers of greatness, the anxieties of ambition, and the miseries of riches.

Among the numerous topicks of declamation, that their industry has discovered on this subject, there is none which they press with greater efforts, or on which they have more copiously laid out their reason and their imagination, than the instability of high stations, and the uncertainty with which the profits and honours are possessed, that must be acquired with so much hazard, vigilance, and labour.

This they appear to consider as an irrefragable argument against the choice of the statesman and the warriour ; and swell with confidence of victory, thus furnished by the muses with the arms which never can be blunted, and which no art or strength of their adversaries can elude or resist.

It was well known by experience to the nations which employed elephants in war, that though by the terrour of their bulk, and the violence of their impression, they often threw the enemy into disorder, yet there was always danger in the use of them, very nearly equivalent to the advantage; for if their first charge could be supported, they were easily driven back upon their confederates; they then broke through the troops behind them, and made no less havock in the precipitation of their retreat, than in the fury of their onset.

I know not whether those who have so vehemently urged the inconveniencies and danger of an active life, have not made use of arguments that may be retorted with equal force upon themselves; and whether the happiness of a candidate for literary fame be not subject to the same uncertainty with that of him who governs provinces, commands armies, presides in the senate, or dictates in the cabinet.

That eminence of learning is not to be gained without labour, at least equal to that which any other kind of greatness can require, will be allowed by those who wish to elevate the character of a scholar; since they cannot but know, that every human acquisition is valuable in proportion to the difficulty employed in its attainment. And that those who have gained the esteem and veneration of the world, by their knowledge or their genius, are by no means exempt from the solicitude which any other kind of dignity produces, may be conjectured from the innumerable artifices which they make use of to degrade a superiour, to repress a rival, or obstruct a follower ; artifices so gross and mean, as to prove evidently how much a man may excel in learning, without being either more wise or more virtuous than those whose ignorance he pities or despises.

Nothing therefore remains, by which the student can gratify his desire of appearing to have built his happiness on a more firm basis than his antagonist, except the certainty with which his honours are enjoyed. The garlands gained by the heroes of literature must be gathered from summits equally difficult to climb with those that bear the civick or triumphal wreaths, they must be worn with equal envy, and guarded with equal care from those hands that are always employed in efforts to tear them away ; the only remaining hope is, that their verdure is more lasting, and that they are less likely to fade by time, or less obnoxious to the blast of accident.

Even this hope will receive very little encouragement from the examination of the history of learning, or observation of the fate of scholars in the present age. If we look back into past times, we find innumerable names of authors once in high reputation, read perhaps by the beautiful, quoted by the witty, and commented on by the grave ; but of whom we now know only that they once existed. If we consider the distribution of literary fame in our own time, we shall find it a possession of very uncertain tenure ; sometimes bestowed by a sudden caprice of the publick, and again transferred to a new favourite, for no other reason than that he is new ; sometimes refused to long labour and eminent desert, and sometimes granted to very slight pretensions ; lost sometimes by security and negligence, and sometimes by too diligent endeavours to retain it.

A successful author is equally in danger of the diminution of his fame, whether he continues or ceases to write. The regard of the publick is not to be kept but by tribute, and the remembrance of past service will quickly languish, unless successive performances frequently revive it. Yet in every new attempt there is new hazard, and there are few who do not at some unlucky time, injure their own characters by attempting to enlarge them.

There are many possible causes of that inequality which we may so frequently observe in the performances of the same man, from the influence of which no ability or industry is sufficiently secured, and which have so often sullied the splendour of genius, that the wit, as well as the conqueror, may be properly cautioned not to indulge his pride with too early triumphs, but to defer to the end of life his estimate of happiness.

> " ——*Ultima semper*
> *Expectanda dies homini, dicique beatus*
> *Ante obitum nemo supremaque funera debet.*"

> " But no frail man, however great or high,
> Can be concluded blest before he die." ADDISON.

Among the motives that urge an author to undertakings by which his reputation is impaired, one of the most frequent must be mentioned with tenderness, because it is not to be counted among his follies, but his miseries. It very often happens that the works of learning or of wit are performed at the direction of those by whom they are to be rewarded; the writer has not always the choice of his subject, but is compelled to accept any task which is thrown before him without much consideration of his own convenience, and without time to prepare himself by previous studies.

Miscarriages of this kind are likewise frequently the consequence of that acquaintance with the great, which is generally considered as one of the chief privileges of literature and genius. A man who has once learned to think himself exalted by familiarity with those whom nothing but their birth, or their fortunes, or such stations as are seldom gained by moral excellence, set above him, will not be long without submitting his understanding to their conduct; he will suffer them to prescribe the course of his studies, and employ him for their own purposes either of diversion or interest. His desire of pleasing those whose favour he has weakly made necessary to himself, will not suffer him always to consider how little he is qualified for the work imposed. Either his vanity will tempt him to conceal his deficiencies, or that cowardice, which always encroaches fast upon such as spend their lives in the company of persons higher than themselves, will not leave him resolution to assert the liberty of choice.

But, though we suppose that a man by his fortune can avoid the necessity of dependence, and by his spirit can repel the usurpations of patronage, yet he may easily, by writing long, happen to write ill. There is a general succession of events in which contraries are produced by periodical vicissitudes; labour and care are rewarded with success, success produces confidence, confidence relaxes industry, and negligence ruins that reputation which accuracy had raised.

He that happens not to be lulled by praise into supineness, may be animated by it to undertakings above his strength, or incited to fancy himself alike qualified for every kind of composition, and able to comply with the publick taste through all its variations. By some opinion like this, many men have been engaged, at an advanced age, in attempts which they had not time to complete, and after a few weak efforts, sunk into the grave with vexation to see the rising generation gain ground upon them. From these failures the highest genius is not exempt; that judgment which appears so penetrating, when it is employed upon the works of others, very often fails where interest or passion can exert their power. We are blinded in examining our own labours by innumerable prejudices. Our juvenile compositions please us, because they bring to our mind the remembrance of youth; our later performances we are ready to esteem, because we are unwilling to think that we have made no improvement; what flows easily from the pen charms us, because we read with pleasure that which flatters our opinion of our own powers; what was composed with great struggles of the mind we do not easily reject, because we cannot bear that so much labour should be fruitless. But the reader has none of these prepossessions, and wonders that the author is so unlike himself, without considering that the same soil will, with different culture, afford different products.

Saturday, June 2, 1750.

" ——*Ego nec studium sine divite venâ,*
Nec rude quid prosit video ingenium, alterius sic
Altera poscit opem res, & conjurat amice."   HOR.

"Without a genius learning soars in vain ;
And without learning genius sinks again ;
Their force united crowns the sprightly reign." }

ELPHINSTON.

WIT and LEARNING were the children of Apollo, by
different mothers ; WIT was the offspring of EUPHRO-
SYNE, and resembled her in cheerfulness and vivacity ;
LEARNING was borne of SOPHIA, and retained her seriousness
and caution. As their mothers were rivals, they were bred
up by them from their birth in habitual opposition, and all
means were so incessantly employed to impress upon them
a hatred and contempt of each other, that though Apollo,
who foresaw the ill effects of their discord, endeavoured to
soften them, by dividing his regard equally between them,
yet his impartiality and kindness were without effect; the
maternal animosity was deeply rooted, having been inter-
mingled with their first ideas, and was confirmed every
hour, as fresh opportunities occurred of exerting it. No
sooner were they of age to be received into the apartments
of the other celestials, than WIT began to entertain Venus
at her toilet, by aping the solemnity of LEARNING, and
LEARNING to divert Minerva at her loom, by exposing the
blunders and ignorance of WIT.

Thus they grew up, with malice perpetually increasing, by

the encouragement which each received from those whom
their mothers had persuaded to patronise and support them ;
and longed to be admitted to the table of Jupiter, not so
much for the hope of gaining honour, as of excluding a
rival from all pretensions to regard, and of putting an everlasting stop to the progress of that influence which either
believed the other to have obtained by mean arts and false
appearances.

At last the day came, when they were both, with the usual
solemnities, received into the class of superiour deities, and
allowed to take nectar from the hand of Hebe. But from
that hour CONCORD lost her authority at the table of Jupiter.
The rivals, animated by their new dignity, and incited by
the alternate applauses of the associate powers, harassed
each other by incessant contests, with such a regular vicissitude of victory, that neither was depressed.

It was observable, that, at the beginning of every debate,
the advantage was on the side of WIT; and that, at the first
sallies, the whole assembly sparkled, according to Homer's
expression, with unextinguishable merriment. But LEARN-
ING would reserve her strength till the burst of applause was
over, and the languor with which the violence of joy is
always succeeded, began to promise more calm and patient
attention. She then attempted her defence, and, by comparing one part of her antagonist's objections with another,
commonly made him confute himself ; or, by showing how
small a part of the question he had taken into his view,
proved that his opinion could have no weight. The
audience began gradually to lay aside their prepossessions,
and rose, at last, with great veneration for LEARNING, but
with greater kindness for WIT.

Their conduct was, whenever they desired to recommend
themselves to distinction, entirely opposite. WIT was

daring and adventurous; LEARNING cautious and deliberate. WIT thought nothing reproachful but dulness; LEARNING was afraid of no imputation but that of errour. WIT answered before he understood, lest his quickness of apprehension should be questioned; LEARNING paused, where there was no difficulty, lest any insidious sophism should lie undiscovered. WIT perplexed every debate by rapidity and confusion; LEARNING tired the hearers with endless distinctions, and prolonged the dispute without advantage, by proving that which never was denied. WIT, in hopes of shining, would venture to produce what he had not considered, and often succeeded beyond his own expectation, by following the train of a lucky thought; LEARNING would reject every new notion, for fear of being entangled in consequences which she could not foresee, and was often hindered, by her caution, from pressing her advantages, and subduing her opponent.

Both had prejudices, which in some degree hindered their progress towards perfection, and left them open to attacks. Novelty was the darling of WIT, and antiquity of LEARNING. To WIT, all that was new was specious; to LEARNING, whatever was ancient was venerable. WIT however seldom failed to divert those whom he could not convince, and to convince was not often his ambition; LEARNING always supported her opinion with so many collateral truths, that when the cause was decided against her, her arguments were remembered with admiration.

Nothing was more common, on either side, than to quit their proper characters, and to hope for a complete conquest by the use of the weapons which had been employed against them. WIT would sometimes labour a syllogism, and LEARNING distort her features with a jest; but they always suffered by the experiment, and betrayed themselves to confutation or contempt. The seriousness of WIT was without dignity, and the merriment of LEARNING without vivacity.

Their contests, by long continuance, grew at last important, and the divinities broke into parties. WIT was taken into protection of the laughter-loving Venus, had a retinue allowed him of SMILES and JESTS, and was often permitted to dance among the GRACES. LEARNING still continued the favourite of Minerva, and seldom went out of her palace, without a train of the severer virtues, CHASTITY, TEMPERANCE, FORTITUDE, and LABOUR. WIT, cohabiting with MALICE, had a son named SATYR, who followed him, carrying a quiver filled with poisoned arrows, which, where they once drew blood, could by no skill ever be extracted. These arrows he frequently shot at LEARNING, when she was most earnestly and usefully employed, engaged in abstruse inquiries, or giving instructions to her followers. Minerva therefore deputed CRITICISM to her aid, who generally broke the point of SATYR's arrows, turned them aside, or retorted them on himself.

Jupiter was at last angry that the peace of the heavenly regions should be in perpetual danger of violation, and resolved to dismiss these troublesome antagonists to the lower world. Hither therefore they came, and carried on their ancient quarrel among mortals, nor was either long without zealous votaries. WIT, by his gaiety, captivated the young; and LEARNING, by her authority, influenced the old. Their power quickly appeared by very eminent effects, theatres were built for the reception of WIT; and colleges endowed for the residence of LEARNING. Each party endeavoured to outvie the other in cost and magnificence, and to propagate an opinion, that it was necessary, from the first entrance into life, to enlist in one of the factions; and that none could hope for the regard of either divinity, who had once entered the temple of the rival power.

There were indeed a class of mortals, by whom WIT and LEARNING were equally disregarded : these were the devotees of Plutus, the god of riches ; among these it seldom happened that the gaiety of WIT could raise a smile, or the eloquence of LEARNING procure attention. In revenge of this contempt they agreed to incite their followers against them ; but the forces that were sent on those expeditions frequently betrayed their trust ; and, in contempt of the orders which they had received, flattered the rich in publick, while they scorned them in their hearts ; and when, by this treachery, they obtained the favour of Plutus, affected to look with an air of superiority on those who still remained in the service of WIT and LEARNING.

Disgusted with these desertions, the two rivals, at the same time, petitioned Jupiter for re-admission to their native habitations. Jupiter thundered on the right hand, and they prepared to obey the happy summons. WIT readily spread his wings and soared aloft, but not being able to see far, was bewildered in the pathless immensity of the ethereal spaces. LEARNING, who knew the way, shook her pinions ; but for want of natural vigour could only take short flights : so, after many efforts, they both sunk again to the ground, and learned, from their mutual distress, the necessity of union. They therefore joined their hands, and renewed their flight : LEARNING was borne up by the vigour of WIT, and WIT guided by the perspicacity of LEARNING. They soon reached the dwellings of Jupiter, and were so endeared to each other, that they lived afterwards in perpetual concord. WIT persuaded LEARNING to converse with the GRACES, and LEARNING engaged WIT in the service of the VIRTUES. They were now the favourites of all the powers of heaven, and gladdened every banquet by their presence. They soon after married, at the command of Jupiter, and had a numerous progeny of ARTS and SCIENCES.

Tuesday, June 5, 1750.

" *Tres mihi conviva prope dissentire videntur ;*
  Poscentur vario multum diversa palato."   HOR.

" Three guests I have, dissenting at my feast,
  Requiring each to gratify his taste
  With different food."   FRANCIS.

THAT every man should regulate his actions by his own conscience, without any regard to the opinions of the rest of the world, is one of the first precepts of moral prudence ; justified not only by the suffrage of reason, which declares that none of the gifts of heaven are to lie useless, but by the voice likewise of experience, which will soon inform us that, if we make the praise or blame of others the rule of our conduct, we shall be distracted by a boundless variety of irreconcileable judgments, be held in perpetual suspense between contrary impulses, and consult for ever without determination.

I know not whether, for the same reason, it is not necessary for an author to place some confidence in his own skill, and to satisfy himself in the knowledge that he has not deviated from the established laws of composition, without submitting his works to frequent examinations before he gives them to the publick, or endeavouring to secure success by a solicitous conformity to advice and criticism.

It is, indeed, quickly discoverable, that consultation and compliance can conduce little to the perfection of any literary performance ; for whoever is so doubtful of his own abilities as to encourage the remarks of others, will find himself every day embarrassed with new difficulties, and will harass his mind, in vain, with the hopeless labour of uniting heterogeneous ideas, digesting independent hints, and collecting into one point the several rays of borrowed light, emitted often with contrary directions.

Of all authors, those who retail their labours in periodical sheets would be most unhappy, if they were much to regard the censures or the admonitions of their readers : for, as their works are not sent into the world at once, but by small parts in gradual succession, it is always imagined, by those who think themselves qualified to give instructions, that they may yet redeem their former failings by hearkening to better judges, and supply the deficiencies of their plan, by the help of the criticisms which are so liberally afforded.

I have had occasion to observe, sometimes with vexation, and sometimes with merriment, the different temper with which the same man reads a printed and manuscript performance. When a book is once in the hands of the publick, it is considered as permanent and unalterable ; and the reader, if he be free from personal prejudices, takes it up with no other intention than of pleasing or instructing himself : he accommodates his mind to the author's design ; and, having no interest in refusing the amusement that is offered him, never interrupts his own tranquillity by studied cavils, or destroys his satisfaction in that which is already well, by an anxious inquiry how it might be better ; but is often contented without pleasure, and pleased without perfection.

But if the same man be called to consider the merit of a production yet unpublished, he brings an imagination heated with objections to passages which he has yet never heard; he invokes all the powers of criticism, and stores his memory with Taste and Grace, Purity and Delicacy, Manners and Unities, sounds which, having been once uttered by those that understood them, have been since re-echoed without meaning, and kept up to the disturbance of the world, by a constant repercussion from one coxcomb to another. He considers himself as obliged to show, by some proof of his abilities, that he is not consulted to no purpose, and therefore watches every opening for objection, and looks round for every opportunity to propose some specious alteration. Such opportunities a very small degree of sagacity will enable him to find; for, in every work of imagination, the disposition of parts, the insertion of incidents, and use of decorations, may be varied a thousand ways with equal propriety; and as in things nearly equal, that will always seem best to every man which he himself produces; the critick, whose business is only to propose, without the care of execution, can never want the satisfaction of believing that he has suggested very important improvements, nor the power of enforcing his advice by arguments, which, as they appear convincing to himself, either his kindness or his vanity will press obstinately and importunately, without suspicion that he may possibly judge too hastily in favour of his own advice, or inquiry whether the advantage of the new scheme be proportionate to the labour.

It is observed by the younger Pliny, that an orator ought not so much to select the strongest arguments which his cause admits, as to employ all which his imagination can afford: for, in pleading, those reasons are of most value,

4

which will most affect the judges; and the judges, says he, will be always most touched with that which they had before conceived. Every man who is called to give his opinion of a performance, decides upon the same principle; he first suffers himself to form expectations, and then is angry at his disappointment. He lets his imagination rove at large, and wonders that another, equally unconfined in the boundless ocean of possibility, takes a different course.

But, though the rule of Pliny be judiciously laid down, it is not applicable to the writer's cause, because there always lies an appeal from domestick criticism to a higher judicature, and the publick, which is never corrupted, nor often deceived, is to pass the last sentence upon literary claims.

Of the great force of preconceived opinions I had many proofs, when I first entered upon this weekly labour. My readers having, from the performances of my predecessors, established an idea of unconnected essays, to which they believed all future authors under a necessity of conforming, were impatient of the least deviation from their system, and numerous remonstrances were accordingly made by each, as he found his favourite subject omitted or delayed. Some were angry that the RAMBLER did not, like the SPECTATOR, introduce himself to the acquaintance of the publick, by an account of his own birth and studies, an enumeration of his adventures, and a description of his physiognomy. Others soon began to remark that he was a solemn, serious, dictatorial writer, without sprightliness or gaiety, and called out with vehemence for mirth and humour. Another admonished him to have a special eye upon the various clubs of this great city, and informed him that much of the spectator's vivacity was laid out upon such assemblies. He has been censured for not imitating the politeness of his predecessors, having hitherto neglected to take the ladies under his protection, and give them rules for the just opposition of colours, and the proper dimensions of ruffles and pinners. He has been required by one to fix a particular censure upon those matrons who play at cards with spectacles : and another is very much offended whenever he meets with a speculation in which naked precepts are comprised without the illustration of examples and characters.

I make not the least question that all these monitors intend the promotion of my design, and the instruction of my readers; but they do not know, or do not reflect, that an author has a rule of choice peculiar to himself; and selects those subjects which he is best qualified to treat, by the course of his studies, or the accidents of his life; that some topicks of amusement have been already treated with too much success to invite a competition; and that he who endeavours to gain many readers must try various arts of invitation, essay every avenue of pleasure, and make frequent changes in his methods of approach.

I cannot but consider myself, amidst this tumult of criticism, as a ship in a poetical tempest, impelled at the same time by opposite winds, and dashed by the waves from every quarter, but held upright by the contrariety of the assailants, and secured in some measure, by multiplicity of distress. Had the opinion of my censurers been unanimous, it might perhaps have overset my resolution; but since I find them at variance with each other, I can, without scruple, neglect them, and endeavour to gain the favour of the publick by following the direction of my own reason, and indulging the sallies of my own imagination.

Saturday, June 23, 1750.

" *Illi mors gravis incubat,*
  Qui, notus nimis omnibus,
  Ignotus moritur sibi."   SENECA.

" To him ! alas ! to him, I fear,
The face of death will terrible appear,
Who in his life, flattering his senseless pride,
By being known to all the world beside,
Does not himself, when he is dying, know,
Nor what he is, nor whither he's to go."   .   COWLEY.

I HAVE shown, in a late essay, to what errours men are
hourly betrayed by a mistaken opinion of their own
powers, and a negligent inspection of their own character.
But as I then confined my observations to common
occurrences and familiar scenes, I think it proper to inquire,
how far a nearer acquaintance with ourselves is necessary to
our preservation from crimes as well as follies, and how
much the attentive study of our own minds may contribute
to secure to us the approbation of that Being, to whom we
are accountable for our thoughts and our actions, and
whose favour must finally constitute our total happiness.

If it be reasonable to estimate the difficulty of any
enterprise by frequent miscarriages, it may justly be concluded that it is not easy for a man to know himself, for
wheresoever we turn our view, we shall find almost all with
whom we converse so nearly as to judge of their sentiments,
indulging more favourable conceptions of their own virtue
than they have been able to impress upon others, and
congratulating themselves upon degrees of excellence, which
their fondest admirers cannot allow them to have attained.

Those representations of imaginary virtue are generally considered as arts of hypocrisy, and as snares laid for confidence and praise. But I believe the suspicion often unjust; those who thus propagate their own reputation, only extend the fraud by which they have been themselves deceived; for this failing is incident to numbers, who seem to live without designs, competitions, or pursuits; it appears on occasions which promise no accession of honour or of profit, and to persons from whom very little is to be hoped or feared. It is, indeed, not easy to tell how far we may be blinded by the love of ourselves, when we reflect how much a secondary passion can cloud our judgment, and how few faults a man, in the first raptures of love, can discover in the person or conduct of his mistress.

To lay open all the sources from which errour flows in upon him who contemplates his own character, would require more exact knowledge of the human heart, than, perhaps, the most acute and laborious observers have acquired. And since falsehood may be diversified without end, it is not unlikely that every man admits an imposture in some respect peculiar to himself, as his views have been accidently directed, or his ideas particularly combined.

Some fallacies, however, there are, more frequently insidious, which it may, perhaps, not be useless to detect; because though they are gross, they may be fatal, and because nothing but attention is necessary to defeat them.

One sophism by which men persuade themselves that they have those virtues which they really want, is formed by the substitution of single acts for habits. A miser who once relieved a friend from the danger of a prison, suffers his imagination to dwell for ever upon his own heroic generosity; he yields his heart up to indignation at those who are blind to merit, or insensible to misery, and who can please themselves with the enjoyment of that wealth, which they never permit others to partake. From any censures of the world, or reproaches of his conscience, he has an appeal to action and to knowledge: and though his whole life is a course of rapacity and avarice, he concludes himself to be tender and liberal, because he has once performed an act of liberality and tenderness.

As a glass which magnifies objects by the approach of one end to the eye, lessens them by the application of the other, so vices are extenuated by the inversion of that fallacy, by which virtues are augmented. Those faults which we cannot conceal from our own notice, are considered, however frequent, not as habitual corruptions, or settled practices, but as casual failures, and single lapses. A man who has from year to year set his country to sale, either for the gratification of his ambition or resentment, confesses that the heat of party now and then betrays the severest virtue to measures that cannot be seriously defended. He that spends his days and nights in riot and debauchery, owns that his passions oftentimes overpower his resolutions. But each comforts himself that his faults are not without precedent, for the best and wisest men have given way to the violence of sudden temptations.

There are men who always confound the praise of goodness with the practice, and who believe themselves mild and moderate, charitable and faithful, because they have exerted their eloquence in commendation of mildness, fidelity, and other virtues. This is an errour almost universal among those that converse much with dependents, with such whose fear or interest disposes them to a seeming reverence for any declamation, however enthusiastick, and submission to any boast, however arrogant. Having none to recall their attention to their lives, they rate themselves by the goodness of their opinions, and forget how much more easily men may show their virtue in their talk than in their actions.

The tribe is likewise very numerous of those who regulate their lives, not by the standard of religion, but the measure of other men's virtue; who lull their own remorse with the remembrance of crimes more atrocious than their own, and seem to believe that they are not bad while another can be found worse.

For escaping these and a thousand other deceits, many expedients have been proposed. Some have recommended the frequent consultation of a wise friend, admitted to intimacy, and encouraged to sincerity. But this appears a remedy by no means adapted to general use : for in order to secure the virtue of one, it presupposes more virtue in two than will generally be found. In the first, such a desire of rectitude and amendment, as may incline him to hear his own accusation from the mouth of him whom he esteems, and by whom, therefore, he will always hope that his faults are not discovered ; and in the second, such zeal and honesty, as will make him content for his friend's advantage to lose his kindness.

A long life may be passed without finding a friend in whose understanding and virtue we can equally confide, and whose opinion we can value at once for its justness and sincerity. A weak man, however honest, is not qualified to judge. A man of the world, however penetrating, is not fit to counsel. Friends are often chosen for similitude of manners, and therefore each palliates the other's failings, because they are his own. Friends are tender, and unwilling to give pain, or they are interested, and fearful to offend.

These objections have inclined others to advise, that he who would know himself, should consult his enemies, remember the reproaches that are vented to his face, and listen for the censures that are uttered in private. For his great business is to know his faults, and those malignity will discover, and resentment will reveal. But this precept may be often frustrated; for it seldom happens that rivals or opponents are suffered to come near enough to know our conduct with so much exactness as that conscience should allow and reflect the accusation. The charge of an enemy is often totally false, and commonly so mingled with falsehood, that the mind takes advantage from the failure of one part to discredit the rest, and never suffers any disturbance afterwards from such partial reports.

Yet it seems that enemies have been always found by experience the most faithful monitors; for adversity has ever been considered as the state in which a man most easily becomes acquainted with himself, and this effect it must produce by withdrawing flatterers, whose business it is to hide our weaknesses from us, or by giving loose to malice, and licence to reproach; or at least by cutting off those pleasures which called us away from meditation on our own conduct, and repressing that pride which too easily persuades us that we merit whatever we enjoy.

Part of these benefits it is in every man's power to procure to himself, by assigning proper portions of his life to the examination of the rest, and by putting himself frequently in such a situation, by retirement and abstraction, as may weaken the influence of external objects. By this practice he may obtain the solitude of adversity without its melancholy, its instructions without its censures, and its sensibility without its perturbations.

The necessity of setting the world at a distance from us, when we are to take a survey of ourselves, has sent many from high stations to the severities of a monastic life; and, indeed, every man deeply engaged in business, if all regard to another state be not extinguished, must have the conviction, though, perhaps, not the resolution of Valdesso, who, when he solicited Charles the Fifth to dismiss him, being asked, whether he retired upon disgust, answered that he laid down his commission, for no other reason but because *there ought to be some time for sober reflection between the life of a soldier and his death.*

There are few conditions which do not entangle us with sublunary hopes and fears, from which it is necessary to be at intervals disencumbered, that we may place ourselves in his presence who views effects in their causes, and actions in their motives; that we may, as Chillingworth expresses it, consider things as if there were no other beings in the world but God and ourselves; or, to use language yet more awful, *may commune with our own hearts, and be still.*

Death, says Seneca, falls heavy upon him who is too much known to others, and too little to himself; and Pontanus, a man celebrated among the early restorers of literature, thought the study of our own hearts of so much importance, that he has recommended it from his tomb. *Sum* Joannes Jovianus Pontanus, *quem amaverunt bonæ musæ, suspexerunt viri probi, honestaverunt reges domini; jam scis qui sim, vel qui potius fuerim; ego vero te, hospes, noscere in tenebris nequeo, sed teipsum ut noscas rogo.* "I am Pontanus, beloved by the powers of litera-"ture, admired by men of worth, and dignified by the "monarchs of the world. Thow knowest now who I am, "or more properly who I was. For thee, stranger, I who "am in darkness cannot know thee, but I entreat thee to "know thyself."

I hope every reader of this paper will consider himself

as engaged to the observation of a precept, which the wisdom and virtue of all ages have concurred to enforce; a precept, dictated by philosophers, inculcated by poets, and ratified by saints.

Saturday, August 4, 1750.

> " ————*Nec dicet, cur ego amicum*
> *Offendam in nugis? Hæ nugæ seria ducent*
> *In mala derisum semel.* HOR.

> " Nor say, for trifles why should I displease
> The man I love? For trifles such as these
> To serious michiefs lead the man I love,
> If once the flatterer's ridicule he prove." FRANCIS.

IT has been remarked, that authors are *genus irritabile*, a *generation very easily put out of temper*, and that they seldom fail of giving proofs of their irascibility upon the slightest attack of criticism, or the most gentle or modest offer of advice and information.

Writers being best acquainted with one another, have represented this character as prevailing among men of literature, which a more extensive view of the world would have shown them to be diffused through all human nature, to mingle itself with every species of ambition and desire of praise, and to discover its effects with greater or less restraint, and under disguises more or less artful, in all places and all conditions.

The quarrels of writers, indeed, are more observed, because they necessarily appeal to the decision of the publick. Their enmities are incited by applauses from their parties, and prolonged by treacherous encouragement for general diversion ; and when the contest happens to rise high between men of genius and learning, its memory is continued for the same reason as its vehemence was at first promoted, because it gratifies the malevolence or curiosity of readers, and relieves the vacancies of life with amusement and laughter. The personal disputes, therefore, of rivals in wit are sometimes transmitted to posterity, when the grudges and heart-burnings of men less conspicuous, though carried on with equal bitterness, and productive of greater evils, are exposed to the knowledge of those only whom they nearly affect, and suffered to pass off and be forgotten among common and casual transactions.

The resentment which the discovery of a fault or folly produces, must bear a certain proportion to our pride, and will regularly be more acrimonious as pride is more immediately the principle of action. In whatever therefore we wish or imagine ourselves to excel, we shall always be displeased to have our claims to reputation disputed; and more displeased, if the accomplishment be such as can expect reputation only for its reward. For this reason it is common to find men break out into rage at any insinuation to the disadvantage of their wit, who have borne with great patience reflections on their morals; and of women it has been always known, that no censure wounds so deeply, or rankles so long, as that which charges them with want of beauty.

As men frequently fill their imaginations with trifling pursuits, and please themselves most with things of small importance, I have often known very severe and lasting malevolence excited by unlucky censures, which would have fallen without any effect, had they not happened to wound a part remarkably tender. Gustulus, who valued himself upon the nicety of his palate, disinherited his eldest son for telling him that the wine, which he was then commending, was the same which he had sent away the day before not fit to be drunk. Proculus withdrew his kindness from a nephew, whom he had always considered as the most promising genius of the age, for happening to praise in his presence the graceful horsemanship of Marius. And Fortunio, when he was privy counsellor, procured a clerk to be dismissed from one of the publick offices, in which he was eminent for his skill and assiduity, because he had been heard to say that there was another man in the kingdom on whose skill at billiards he would lay his money against Fortunio's.

Felicia and Floretta had been bred up in one house, and shared all the pleasures and endearments of infancy together. They entered upon life at the same time, and continued their confidence and friendship; consulted each other in every change of their dress, and every admission of a new lover; thought every diversion more entertaining whenever it happened that both were present, and when separated justified the conduct, and celebrated the excellencies, of one another. Such was their intimacy, and such their fidelity; till a birth-night approached, when Floretta took one morning an opportunity, as they were consulting upon new clothes, to advise her friend not to dance at the ball, and informed her that her performance the year before had not answered the expectation which her other accomplishments had raised. Felicia commended her sincerity, and thanked her for the caution; but told her that she danced to please herself, and was very little concerned what the men might take the liberty of saying, but that if her appearance gave her dear Floretta any uneasiness, she would stay away. Floretta had now nothing left but to make new protestations of sincerity and affection, with which Felicia was so well satisfied, that they parted with more than usual fondness. They still continued to visit, with this only difference, that Felicia was more punctual than before, and often declared how high a value she put upon sincerity, how much she thought that goodness to be esteemed which would venture to admonish a friend of an errour, and with what gratitude advice was to be received, even when it might happen to proceed from mistake.

In a few months, Felicia, with great seriousness, told Floretta, that though her beauty was such as gave charms to whatever she did, and her qualifications so extensive, that she could not fail of excellence in any attempt, yet she thought herself obliged by the duties of friendship to inform her, that if ever she betrayed want of judgment, it was by too frequent compliance with solicitations to sing, for that her manner was somewhat ungraceful, and her voice had no great compass. It is true, says Floretta, when I sung three nights ago at lady Sprightly's, I was hoarse with a cold ; but I sing for my own satisfaction, and am not in the least pain whether I am liked. However, my dear Felicia's kindness is not the less, and I shall always think myself happy in so true a friend.

From this time they never saw each other without mutual professions of esteem, and declarations of confidence, but went soon after into the country to visit their relations. When they came back, they were prevailed on, by the importunity of new acquaintance, to take lodgings in different parts of the town, and had frequent occasion, when they met, to bewail the distance at which they were placed, and the uncertainty which each experienced of finding the other at home.

Thus are the fondest and firmest friendships dissolved,

by such openness and sincerity as interrupt our enjoyment of our own approbation, or recall us to the remembrance of those failings which we are more willing to indulge than to correct.

It is by no means necessary to imagine, that he who is offended at advice, was ignorant of the fault, and resents the admonition as a false charge; for perhaps it is most natural to be enraged, when there is the strongest conviction of our own guilt. While we can easily defend our character, we are no more disturbed at an accusation, than we are alarmed by an enemy whom we are sure to conquer; and whose attack, therefore, will bring us honour without danger. But when a man feels the reprehension of a friend seconded by his own heart, he is easily heated into resentment and revenge, either because he hoped that the fault of which he was conscious had escaped the notice of others; or that his friend had looked upon it with tenderness and extenuation, and excused it for the sake of his other virtues; or had considered him as too wise to need advice, or too delicate to be shocked with reproach : or, because we cannot feel without pain those reflections roused which we have been endeavouring to lay asleep; and when pain has produced anger, who would not willingly believe, that it ought to be discharged on others, rather than on himself?

The resentment produced by sincerity, whatever be its immediate cause, is so certain, and generally so keen, that very few have magnanimity sufficient for the practice of a duty, which, above most others, exposes its votaries to hardships and persecutions; yet friendship without it is of very little value, since the great use of so close an intimacy is, that our virtues may be guarded and encouraged, and our vices repressed in their first appearance by timely detection and salutary remonstrances.

It is decreed by Providence, that nothing truly valuable shall be obtained in our present state, but with difficulty and danger. He that hopes for that advantage which is to be gained from unrestrained communication, must sometimes hazard, by unpleasing truths, that friendship which he aspires to merit. The chief rule to be observed in the exercise of this dangerous office, is to preserve it pure from all mixture of interest or vanity; to forbear admonition or reproof, when our consciences tell us that they are incited, not by the hopes of reforming faults, but the desire of showing our discernment, or gratifying our own pride by the mortification of another. It is not indeed certain, that the most refined caution will find a proper time for bringing a man to the knowledge of his own failings, or the most zealous benevolence reconcile him to that judgment, by which they are detected; but he who endeavours only the happiness of him whom he reproves, will always have either the satisfaction of obtaining or deserving kindness; if he succeeds, he benefits his friend; and if he fails, he has at least the consciousness that he suffers for only doing well.

Tuesday, August 28, 1750.

" *Quanquam his solatiis acquiescam, debilitor & frangor eadem illa humanitate quæ me, ut hoc ipsum permitterem, induxit. Non ideo tamen velim durior fieri: nec ignoro alios hujusmodi casus nihil amplius vocare quam damnum; eoque sibi magnos homines & sapientes videri. Qui an magni sapientesque sint, nescio: homines non sunt. Hominis est enim affici dolore, sentire; resistere tamen, & solatia admittere; non solatiis non egere.*" PLIN.

" These proceedings have afforded me some comfort in my distress;
    notwithstanding which, I am still dispirited and unhinged by the
    same motives of humanity that induced me to grant such in-
    dulgences. However, I by no means wish to become less sus-
    ceptible of tenderness. I know these kind of misfortunes would
    be estimated by other persons only as common losses, and from such
    sensations they would conceive themselves great and wise men. I
    shall not determine either their greatness or their wisdom ; but I
    am certain they have no humanity. It is the part of a man to be
    affected with grief; to feel sorrow, at the same time that he is to
    resist it, and to admit of comfort."   EARL OF ORRERY.

OF the passions with which the mind of man is agitated,
    it may be observed, that they naturally hasten
towards their own extinction, by inciting and quickening
the attainment of their objects. Thus fear urges our flight,
and desire animates our progress ; and if there are some
which perhaps may be indulged till they outgrow the good
appropriated to their satisfaction, as it is frequently observed
of avarice and ambition, yet their immediate tendency is to
some means of happiness really existing, and generally
within the prospect. The miser always imagines that there
is a certain sum that will fill his heart to the brim ; and
every ambitious man, like king Pyrrhus, has an acquisition
in his thoughts that is to terminate his labours, after which
he shall pass the rest of his life in ease or gaiety, in repose
or devotion.

Sorrow is perhaps the only affection of the breast that
can be excepted from this general remark, and it therefore
deserves the particular attention of those who have assumed
the arduous province of preserving the balance of the
mental constitution. The other passions are diseases
indeed, but they necessarily direct us to their proper cure.
A man at once feels the pain and knows the medicine to
which he is carried with greater haste as the evil which

requires it is more excruciating, and cures himself by unerring instinct, as the wounded stags of Crete are related by Ælian to have recourse to vulnerary herbs. But for sorrow there is no remedy provided by nature; it is often occasioned by accidents irreparable, and dwells upon objects that have lost or changed their existence; it requires what it cannot hope, that the laws of the universe should be repealed; that the dead should return, or the past should be recalled.

Sorrow is not that regret for negligence or errour which may animate us to future care or activity, or that repentance of crimes for which, however irrevocable, our Creator has promised to accept it as an atonement; the pain which arises from these causes has very salutary effects, and is every hour extenuating itself by the reparation of those miscarriages that produce it. Sorrow is properly that state of the mind in which our desires are fixed upon the past, without looking forward to the future, an incessant wish that something were otherwise than it has been, a tormenting and harassing want of some enjoyment or possession which we have lost, and which no endeavours can possibly regain. Into such anguish many have sunk upon some sudden diminution of their fortune, an unexpected blast of their reputation, or the loss of children or of friends. They have suffered all sensibility of pleasure to be destroyed by a single blow, have given up for ever the hopes of substituting any other object in the room of that which they lament, resigned their lives to gloom and despondency, and worn themselves out in unavailing misery.

Yet so much is this passion the natural consequence of tenderness and endearment, that, however painful and however useless, it is justly reproachful not to feel it on some occasions; and so widely and constantly has it

5

always prevailed, that the laws of some nations, and the customs of others, have limited a time for the external appearances of grief caused by the dissolution of close alliances, and the breach of domestick union.

It seems determined by the general suffrage of mankind, that sorrow is to a certain point laudable, as the offspring of love, or at least pardonable, as the effect of weakness; but that it ought not to be suffered to increase by indulgence, but must give way, after a stated time, to social duties, and the common avocations of life. It is at first unavoidable, and therefore must be allowed, whether with or without our choice; it may afterwards be admitted as a decent and affectionate testimony of kindness and esteem; something will be extorted by nature, and something may be given to the world. But all beyond the bursts of passion, or the forms of solemnity, is not only useless, but culpable; for we have no right to sacrifice to the vain longings of affection, that time which Providence allows us for the task of our station.

Yet it too often happens that sorrow, thus lawfully entering, gains such a firm possession of the mind, that it is not afterwards to be ejected; the mournful ideas, first violently impressed and afterwards willingly received, so much engross the attention, as to predominate in every thought, to darken gaiety, and perplex ratiocination. An habitual sadness seizes upon the soul, and the faculties are chained to a single object, which can never be contemplated but with hopeless uneasiness.

From this state of dejection it is very difficult to rise to cheerfulness and alacrity; and therefore many who have laid down rules of intellectual health, think preservatives easier than remedies, and teach us not to trust ourselves with favourite enjoyments, not to indulge the luxury of fondness, but to keep our minds always suspended in such indifference, that we may change the objects about us without emotion.

An exact compliance with this rule might, perhaps, contribute to tranquillity, but surely it would never produce happiness. He that regards none so much as to be afraid of losing them, must live for ever without the gentle pleasures of sympathy and confidence; he must feel no melting fondness, no warmth of benevolence, nor any of those honest joys which nature annexes to the power of pleasing. And as no man can justly claim more tenderness than he pays, he must forfeit his share in that officious and watchful kindness which love only can dictate, and those lenient endearments by which love only can soften life. He may justly be overlooked and neglected by such as have more warmth in their heart; for who would be the friend of him, whom, with whatever assiduity he may be courted, and with whatever services obliged, his principles will not suffer to make equal returns, and who, when you have exhausted all the instances of goodwill, can only be prevailed on not to be an enemy?

An attempt to preserve life in a state of neutrality and indifference, is unreasonable and vain. If by excluding joy we could shut out grief, the scheme would deserve very serious attention; but since, however we may debar ourselves from happiness, misery will find its way at many inlets, and the assaults of pain will force our regard, though we may withhold it from the invitations of pleasure, we may surely endeavour to raise life above the middle point of apathy at one time, since it will necessarily sink below it at another.

But though it cannot be reasonable not to gain happiness for fear of losing it, yet it must be confessed, that in proportion to the pleasure of possession, will be for some time our sorrow for the loss; it is therefore the province of the moralist to enquire whether such pains may not quickly give way to mitigation. Some have thought that the most certain way to clear the heart from its embarrassment is to drag it by force into scenes of merriment. Others imagine, that such a transition is too violent, and recommend rather to sooth it into tranquillity, by making it acquainted with miseries more dreadful and afflictive, and diverting to the calamities of others the regards which we are inclined to fix too closely upon our own misfortunes.

It may be doubted whether either of those remedies will be sufficiently powerful. The efficacy of mirth it is not always easy to try, and the indulgence of melancholy may be suspected to be one of those medicines, which will destroy, if it happens not to cure.

The safe and general antidote against sorrow is employment. It is commonly observed, that among soldiers and seamen, though there is much kindness, there is little grief; they see their friend fall without any of that lamentation which is indulged in security and idleness, because they have no leisure to spare from the care of themselves; and whoever shall keep his thoughts equally busy, will find himself equally unaffected with irretrievable losses.

Time is observed generally to wear out sorrow, and its effects might doubtless be accelerated by quickening the succession, and enlarging the variety of objects.

> "———*Si tempore longo*
> *Leniri poterit luctus, tu sperne morari,*
> *Qui sapiet sibi tempus erit.*———"　　　GROTIUS.

> " 'Tis long ere time can mitigate your grief;
> To wisdom fly, she quickly brings relief."　F. LEWIS.

Sorrow is a kind of rust of the soul, which every new idea contributes in its passage to scour away. It is the putrefaction of stagnant life, and is remedied by exercise and motion.

Saturday, Sept. 8, 1750.

" *Credebant hoc grande nefas, et morte piandum,*
 Si juvenis vetulo non assurrexerat, atque
 Barbato cuicunque puer, licet ipse videret
 Plura domi fraga, et majores glandis acervos." JUV.

" And had not men the hoary head rever'd,
 And boys paid rev'rence when a man appear'd,
 Both must have died, though richer skins they wore,
 And saw more heaps of acorns in their store." CREECH.

I HAVE always thought it the business of those who turn their speculations upon the living world, to commend the virtues, as well as to expose the faults of their contemporaries, and to confute a false as well as to support a just accusation ; not only because it is peculiarly the business of a monitor to keep his own reputation untainted, lest those who can once charge him with partiality, should indulge themselves afterwards in disbelieving him at pleasure ; but because he may find real crimes sufficient to give full employment to caution or repentance, without distracting the mind by needless scruples and vain solicitudes.

There are certain fixed and stated reproaches that one part of mankind has in all ages thrown upon another, which are regularly transmitted through continued successions, and which he that has once suffered them is certain to use with the same undistinguishing vehemence, when he has changed his station, and gained the prescriptive right of inflicting on others what he had formerly endured himself.

To these hereditary imputations, of which no man sees the justice, till it becomes his interest to see it, very little regard is to be shown ; since it does not appear that they are produced by ratiocination or inquiry, but received implicitly, or caught by a kind of instantaneous contagion, and supported rather by willingness to credit, than ability to prove, them.

It has been always the practice of those who are desirous to believe themselves made venerable by length of time, to censure the new comers into life, for want of respect to grey hairs and sage experience, for heady confidence in their own understandings, for hasty conclusions upon partial views, for disregard of counsels, which their fathers and grandsires are ready to afford them, and a rebellious impatience of that subordination to which youth is condemned by nature, as necessary to its security from evils into which it would be otherwise precipitated, by the rashness of passion, and the blindness of ignorance.

Every old man complains of the growing depravity of the world, of the petulance and insolence of the rising generation. He recounts the decency and regularity of former times, and celebrates the discipline and sobriety of the age in which his youth was passed ; a happy age, which is now no more to be expected, since confusion has broken in upon the world and thrown down all the boundaries of civility and reverence.

It is not sufficiently considered how much he assumes who dares to claim the privilege of complaining ; for as every man has, in his own opinion, a full share of the miseries of life, he is inclined to consider all clamorous uneasiness, as a proof of impatience rather than of affliction,

and to ask, What merit has this man to show, by which he
has acquired a right to repine at the distributions of nature?
Or, why does he imagine that exemptions should be granted
him from the general condition of man? We find ourselves
excited rather to captiousness than pity, and instead of
being in haste to soothe his complaints by sympathy and
tenderness, we inquire, whether the pain be proportionate
to the lamentation ; and whether, supposing the affliction
real, it is not the effect of vice and folly, rather than
calamity.

The querulousness and indignation which is observed so
often to disfigure the last scene of life, naturally leads us to
inquiries like these. For surely it will be thought at the
first view of things, that if age be thus contemned and
ridiculed, insulted and neglected, the crime must at least be
equal on either part. They who have had opportunities
of establishing their authority over minds ductile and
unresisting, they who have been the protectors of helpless-
ness, and the instructors of ignorance, and who yet retain in
their own hands the power of wealth, and the dignity of
command, must defeat their influence by their own
misconduct, and make use of all these advantages with very
little skill, if they cannot secure to themselves an appearance of respect, and ward off open mockery, and declared
contempt.

The general story of mankind will evince, that lawful and
settled authority is very seldom resisted when it is well
employed. Gross corruption, or evident imbecility, is
necessary to the suppression of that reverence with which
the majority of mankind look upon their governors, and on
those whom they see surrounded by splendour, and
fortified by power. For though men are drawn by their
passions into forgetfulnesss of invisible rewards and

punishments, yet they are easily kept obedient to those who have temporal dominion in their hands, till their veneration is dissipated by such wickedness and folly as can neither be defended nor concealed.

It may, therefore, very reasonably be suspected that the old draw upon themselves the greatest part of those insults which they so much lament, and that age is rarely despised but when it is contemptible. If men imagine that excess of debauchery can be made reverend by time, that knowledge is the consequence of long life, however idly or thoughtlessly employed, that priority of birth will supply the want of steadiness or honesty, can it raise much wonder that their hopes are disappointed, and that they see their posterity rather willing to trust their own eyes in their progress into life, than enlist themselves under guides who have lost their way?

There are, indeed, many truths which time necessarily and certainly teaches, and which might, by those who have learned them from experience, be communicated to their successors at a cheaper rate : but dictates, though liberally enough bestowed, are generally without effect, the teacher gains few proselytes by instruction which his own behaviour contradicts ; and young men miss the benefit of counsel, because they are not very ready to believe that those who fall below them in practice, can much excel them in theory. Thus the progress of knowledge is retarded, the world is kept long in the same state, and every new race is to gain the prudence of their predecessors by committing and redressing the same miscarriages.

To secure to the old that influence which they are willing to claim, and which might so much contribute to the improvement of the arts of life, it is absolutely necessary that they give themselves up to the duties of declining years; and contentedly resign to youth its levity, its pleasures, its frolicks, and its fopperies. It is a hopeless endeavour to unite the contrarieties of spring and winter; it is unjust to claim the privileges of age, and retain the playthings of childhood. The young always form magnificent ideas of the wisdom and gravity of men, whom they consider as placed at a distance from them in the ranks of existence, and naturally look on those whom they find trifling with long beards, with contempt and indignation, like that which women feel at the effeminacy of men. If dotards will contend with boys in those performances in which boys must always excel them; if they will dress crippled limbs in embroidery, endeavour at gaiety with faultering voices, and darken assemblies of pleasure with the ghastliness of disease, they may may well expect those who find their diversions obstructed will hoot them away; and that if they descend to competition with youths, they must bear the insolence of successful rivals.

> " *Lusisti satis, edisti satis, atque bibisti :*
> *Tempus abire tibi est.*"

> " You've had your share of mirth, of meat and drink ;
> 'Tis time to quit the scene—'tis time to think."
>   ELPHINSTON.

Another vice of age, by which the rising generation may be alienated from it, is severity and censoriousness, that gives no allowance to the failings of early life, that expects artfulness from childhood, and constancy from youth, that is peremptory in every command, and inexorable to every failure. There are many who live merely to hinder happiness, and whose descendants can only tell of long life, that it produces suspicion, malignity peevishness, and persecution : and yet even these tyrants can talk of the ingratitude of the age, curse their heirs for impatience, and wonder that young men cannot take pleasure in their father's company.

He that would pass the latter part of his life with honour and decency, must, when he is young, consider that he shall one day be old; and remember, when he is old, that he has once been young. In youth, he must lay up knowledge for his support, when his powers of acting shall forsake him ; and in age forbear to animadvert with rigour on faults which experience only can correct.

Saturday, October 6, 1750.

" ——*Improbæ*
Crescunt divitiæ, tamen
Curtæ nescio quid semper abest rei."　　　HOR.

" But, while in heaps his wicked wealth ascends,
He is not of his wish possess'd ;
There's something wanting still to make him blest."
　　　　　FRANCIS.

AS the love of money has been, in all ages, one of the passions that have given great disturbance to the tranquillity of the world, there is no topick more copiously treated by the ancient moralists than the folly of devoting the heart to the accumulation of riches. They who are acquainted with these authors need not be told how riches excite pity, contempt, or reproach, whenever they are mentioned; with what numbers of examples the danger of large possessions is illustrated ; and how all the powers of reason and eloquence have been exhausted in endeavours to eradicate a desire, which seems to have entrenched itself too strongly in the mind to be driven out, and which, perhaps, had not lost its power, even over those who declaimed against it,* but would have broken out in the poet or the sage, if it had been excited by opportunity, and invigorated by the approximation of its proper object.

Their arguments have been, indeed, so unsuccessful, that I know not whether it can be shown, that by all the wit and reason which this favourite cause has called forth, a single convert was ever made; that even one man has refused to be rich, when to be rich was in his power, from the conviction of the greater happiness of a narrow fortune; or disburthened himself of wealth when he had tried its inquietudes, merely to enjoy the peace and leisure and security of a mean and unenvied state.

It is true, indeed, that many have neglected opportunities of raising themselves to honours and to wealth, and rejected the kindest offers of fortune: but however their moderation may be boasted by themselves, or admired by such as only view them at a distance, it will be, perhaps, seldom found that they value riches less, but that they dread labour or danger more than others; they are unable to rouse themselves to action, to strain in the race of competition, or to stand the shock of contest; but though they, therefore, decline the toil of climbing, they nevertheless wish themselves aloft, and would willingly enjoy what they dare not seize.

Others have retired from high stations, and voluntarily condemned themselves to privacy and obscurity. But, even these will not afford many occasions of triumph to the

* Note V., Appendix.

philosopher; for they have commonly either quitted that only which they thought themselves unable to hold, and prevented disgrace by resignation; or they have been induced to try new measures by general inconstancy, which always dreams of happiness in novelty, or by a gloomy disposition, which is disgusted in the same degree with every state, and wishes every scene of life to change as soon as it is beheld. Such men found high and low stations equally unable to satisfy the wishes of a distempered mind, and were unable to shelter themselves in the closest retreat from disappointment, solicitude, and misery.

Yet though these admonitions have been thus neglected by those, who either enjoyed riches, or were able to procure them, it is not rashly to be determined that they are altogether without use; for since far the greatest part of mankind must be confined to conditions comparatively mean, and placed in situations from which they naturally look up with envy to the eminences before them, those writers cannot be thought ill employed that have administered remedies to discontent almost universal, by showing, that what we cannot reach may very well be forborne, that the inequality of distribution, at which we murmur, is for the most part less than it seems, and that the greatness, which we admire at a distance, has much fewer advantages, and much less splendour, when we are suffered to approach it.

It is the business of moralists to detect the frauds of fortune, and to show that she imposes upon the careless eye, by a quick succession of shadows, which will shrink to nothing in the gripe; that she disguises life in extrinsick ornaments, which serve only for show, and are laid aside in the hours of solitude, and of pleasure; and that when greatness aspires either to felicity or to wisdom, it shakes off those distinctions which dazzle the gazer, and awe the supplicant.

It may be remarked, that they whose condition has not afforded them the light or moral of religious instruction, and who collect all their ideas by their own eyes, and digest them by their own understandings, seem to consider those who are placed in ranks of remote superiority, as almost another and higher species of beings. As themselves have known little other misery than the consequences of want, they are with difficulty persuaded that where there is wealth there can be sorrow, or that those who glitter in dignity, and glide along in affluence, can be acquainted with pains and cares like those which lie heavy upon the rest of mankind.

This prejudice is, indeed, confined to the lowest meanness, and the darkest ignorance; but it is so confined only because others have been shown its folly, and its falsehood, because it has been opposed in its progress by history and philosophy, and hindered from spreading its infection by powerful preservatives.

The doctrine of the contempt of wealth, though it has not been able to extinguish avarice or ambition, or suppress that reluctance with which a man passes his days in a state of inferiority, must, at least, have made the lower conditions less grating and wearisome, and has consequently contributed to the general security of life, by hindering that fraud and violence, rapine and circumvention, which must have been produced by an unbounded eagerness of wealth, arising from an unshaken conviction that to be rich is to be happy.

Whoever finds himself incited, by some violent impulse of passion, to pursue riches as the chief end of being, must surely be so much alarmed by the successive admonitions of those whose experience and sagacity have recommended them as the guides of mankind, as to stop and consider whether he is about to engage in an undertaking that will reward his toil, and to examine, before he rushes to wealth, through right and wrong, what it will confer when he has acquired it; and this examination will seldom fail to repress his ardour, and retard his violence.

Wealth is nothing in itself, it is not useful but when it departs from us; its value is found only in that which it can purchase, which, if we suppose it put to its best use by those that possess it, seems not much to deserve the desire or envy of a wise man. It is certain that, with regard to corporal enjoyment, money can neither open new avenues to pleasure, nor block up the passages of anguish. Disease and infirmity still continue to torture and enfeeble, perhaps exasperated by luxury, or promoted by softness. With respect to the mind, it has rarely been observed, that wealth contributes much to quicken the discernment, enlarge the capacity, or elevate the imagination; but may, by hiring flattery, or laying diligence asleep, confirm errour, and harden stupidity.

Wealth cannot confer greatness, for nothing can make that great, which the decree of nature has ordained to be little. The bramble may be placed in a hot-bed, but can never be an oak. Even royalty itself is not able to give that dignity which it happens not to find, but oppresses feeble minds, though it may elevate the strong. The world has been governed in the name of kings, whose existence has scarcely been perceived by any real effects beyond their own palaces.

When therefore the desire of wealth is taking hold of the heart, let us look round and see how it operates upon those whose industry or fortune has obtained it. When we find them oppressed with their own abundance, luxurious without pleasure, idle without ease, impatient and querulous in themselves, and despised or hated by the rest of mankind, we shall soon be convinced, that if the real wants of our condition are satisfied, there remains little to be sought with solicitude, or desired with eagerness.

Saturday, October 13, 1750.

" Quid sit pulchrum, quid turpe, quid utile, quid non,
Plenius et melius Chrysippo et Crantore dicit." Hor.

" Whose works the beautiful and base contain,
Of vice and virtue more instructive rules,
Than all the sober sages of the schools." Francis.

A LL joy or sorrow for the happiness or calamities of others is produced by an act of the imagination, that realizes the event however fictitious, or approximates it however remote, by placing us, for a time, in the condition of him whose fortune we contemplate ; so that we feel, while the deception lasts, whatever motions would be excited by the same good or evil happening to ourselves.

Our passions are therefore more strongly moved, in proportion as we can more readily adopt the pains or pleasure proposed to our minds, by recognising them as once our own, or considering them as naturally incident to our state of life. It is not easy for the most artful writer to give us an interest in happiness or misery, which we think ourselves never likely to feel, and with which we have never yet been made acquainted. Histories of the downfall of kingdoms, and revolutions of empires, are read with great tranquillity; the imperial tragedy pleases common auditors only by its pomp of ornament and grandeur of ideas; and the man whose faculties have been engrossed by business, and whose heart never fluttered but at the rise or fall of the stocks, wonders how the attention can be seized, or the affection agitated, by a tale of love.

Those parallel circumstances and kindred images, to which we readily conform our minds, are, above all other writings, to be found in narratives of the lives of particular persons; and therefore no species of writing seems more worthy of cultivation than biography, since none can be more delightful or more useful, none can more certainly enchain the heart by irresistible interest, or more widely diffuse instruction to every diversity of condition.

The general and rapid narratives of history, which involve a thousand fortunes in the business of a day, and complicate innumerable incidents in one great transaction, afford a few lessons applicable to private life, which derives its comforts and its wretchedness from the right or wrong management of things, which nothing but their frequency makes considerable, *Parva si non fiunt quotidie,* says Pliny, and which can have no place in those relations which never descend below the consultation of senates, the motions of armies, and the schemes of conspirators.

I have often thought that there has rarely passed a life of which a judicious and faithful narrative would not be useful.* For, not only every man has, in the mighty mass of the world, great numbers in the same condition with himself, to whom his mistakes and miscarriages, escapes and expedients, would be of immediate and apparent use; but there is such an uniformity in the state of man,

* Note VI., Appendix.

considered apart from adventitious and separable decorations and disguises, that there is scarce any possibility of good or ill, but is common to human kind. A great part of the time of those who are placed at the greatest distances by fortune, or by temper, must unavoidably pass in the same manner; and though, when the claims of nature are satisfied, caprice, and vanity, and accident, begin to produce discriminations and peculiarities, yet the eye is not very heedful or quick, which cannot discover the same causes still terminating their influence in the same effects, though sometimes accelerated, sometimes retarded, or perplexed by multiplied combinations. We are all prompted by the same motives, all deceived by the same fallacies, all animated by hope, obstructed by danger, entangled by desire, and seduced by pleasure.

It is frequently objected to relations of particular lives, that they are not distinguished by any striking or wonderful vicissitudes. The scholar who passed his life among his books, the merchant who conducted only his own affairs, the priest, whose sphere of action was not extended beyond that of his duty. are considered as no proper objects of publick regard, however they might have excelled in their several stations, whatever might have been their learning, integrity, and piety. But this notion arises from false measures of excellence and dignity, and must be eradicated by considering, that in the esteem of uncorrupted reason, what is of most use is of most value.

It is, indeed, not improper to take honest advantages of prejudice, and to gain attention by a celebrated name; but the business of the biographer is often to pass slightly over those performances and incidents, which produce vulgar greatness, to lead the thoughts into domestick privacies, and display the minute details of daily life, where exterior

6

appendages are cast aside, and men excel each other only by prudence and by virtue. The account of Thuanus is, with great propriety, said by its author to have been written, that it might lay open to posterity the private and familiar character of that man, *cujus ingenium et candorem ex ipsius scriptis sunt olim semper miraturi*, whose candour and genius will to the end of time be by his writings preserved in admiration.

There are many invisible circumstances which, whether we read as inquirers after natural or moral knowledge, whether we intend to enlarge our science, or increase our virtue, are more important than publick occurrences. Thus Sallust, the great master of nature, has not forgot, in his account of Catiline, to remark that *his walk was now quick, and again slow*, as an indication of a mind revolving something with violent commotion. Thus the story of Melancthon affords a striking lecture on the value of time, by informing us, that when he made an appointment, he expected not only the hour, but the minute to be fixed, that the day might not run out in the idleness of suspense: and all the plans and enterprises of De Witt are now of less importance to the world, than that part of his personal character, which represents him as *careful of his health, and negligent of his life*.

But biography has often been allotted to writers who seem very little acquainted with the nature of their task, or very negligent about the performance. They rarely afford any other account than might be collected from publick papers, but imagine themselves writing a life when they exhibit a chronological series of actions or preferments; and so little regard the manners or behaviour of their heroes, that more knowledge may be gained of a man's real character, by a short conversation with one of his servants,

than from a formal and studied narrative, begun with his
pedigree, and ended with his funeral.

If now and then they condescend to inform the world of
particular facts, they are not always so happy as to select the
most important. I know not well what advantage posterity
can receive from the only circumstance by which Tickell
has distinguished Addison from the rest of mankind, *the
irregularity of his pulse:* nor can I think myself overpaid
for the time spent in reading the life of Malherb, by being
enabled to relate after the learned biographer, that Malherb*
had two predominant opinions; one, that the looseness of
a single woman might destroy all her boast of ancient
descent; the other, that the French beggars made use very
improperly and barbarously of the phrase *noble Gentleman*,
because either word included the sense of both.

There are, indeed, some natural reasons why these narratives are often written by such as were not likely to give
much instruction or delight, and why most accounts of
particular persons are barren and useless. If a life be
delayed till interest and envy are at an end, we may hope
for impartiality, but must expect little intelligence; for the
incidents which give excellence to biography are of a volatile
and evanescent kind, such as soon escape the memory,
and are rarely transmitted by tradition. We know how few
can pourtray a living acquaintance, except by his most
prominent and observable particularities, and the grosser
features of his mind; and it may be easily imagined how
much of this little knowledge may be lost in imparting it,
and how soon a succession of copies will lose all resemblance of the original.

If the biographer writes from personal knowledge, and

* Note VII., Appendix.

makes haste to gratify the publick curiosity, there is danger lest his interest, his fear, his gratitude, or his tenderness, overpower his fidelity, and tempt him to conceal, if not to invent. There are many who think it an act of piety to hide the faults or failings of their friends, even when they can no longer suffer by their detection; we therefore see whole ranks of characters adorned with uniform panegyrick, and not to be known from one another, but by extrinsick and casual circumstances. "Let me remember," says Hale, "when I find myself inclined to pity a criminal, that there "is likewise a pity due to the country." If we owe regard to the memory of the dead, there is yet more respect to be paid to knowledge, to virtue, and to truth.

Tuesday, October 23, 1750.

"————*Habebat sæpe ducentos,*
Sæpe decem servos; modo reges atque tetrarchas,
Omnia magna loquens: modo, sit mihi mensa tripes, et
Concha salis furi, et toga, quæ defendere frigus,
Quamvis crassa, queat."
                                                        HOR.

" Now with two hundred slaves he crowds his train;
Now walks with ten. In high and haughty strain
At morn, of kings and governors he prates;
At night,—' A frugal table, O ye fates,
' A little shell the sacred salt to hold,
' And clothes, tho' coarse, to keep me from the cold.' "
                                                        FRANCIS.

IT has been remarked, perhaps, by every writer who has left behind him observations upon life, that no man is pleased with his present state; which proves equally unsatisfactory, says Horace, whether fallen upon by chance, or chosen with deliberation; we are always disgusted with some circumstance or other of our situation, and imagine the condition of others more abundant in blessings, or less exposed to calamities.

This universal discontent has been generally mentioned with great severity of censure, as unreasonable in itself, since of two, equally envious of each other, both cannot have the larger share of happiness, and as tending to darken life with unnecessary gloom, by withdrawing our minds from the contemplation and enjoyment of that happiness which our state affords us, and fixing our attention upon foreign objects, which we only behold to depress ourselves, and increase our misery by injurious comparisons.

When this opinion of the felicity of others predominates in the heart, so as to excite resolutions of obtaining, at whatever price, the condition to which such transcendent privileges are supposed to be annexed; when it bursts into action, and produces fraud, violence, and injustice, it is to be pursued with all the rigour of legal punishments. But while operating only upon the thoughts, it disturbs none but him who has happened to admit it, and, however it may interrupt content, makes no attack on piety or virtue, I cannot think it so far criminal or ridiculous, but that it may deserve some pity, and admit some excuse.

That all are equally happy, or miserable, I suppose none is sufficiently enthusiastical to maintain; because though we cannot judge of the condition of others, yet every man has found frequent vicissitudes in his own state, and must therefore be convinced that life is susceptible of more or less felicity. What then shall forbid us to endeavour the alteration of that which is capable of being improved, and to grasp at augmentations of good, when we know it possible to be increased, and believe that any particular change of situation will increase it?

If he that finds himself uneasy may reasonably make efforts to rid himself from vexation, all mankind have a sufficient plea for some degree of restlessness, and the fault seems to be little more than too much temerity of conclusion, in favour of something not yet experienced, and too much readiness to believe, that the misery which our own passions and appetites produce, is brought upon us by accidental causes, and external efficients.

It is, indeed, frequently discovered by us, that we complained too hastily of peculiar hardships, and imagined ourselves distinguished by embarrassments, in which other classes of men are equally entangled. We often change a lighter for a greater evil, and wish ourselves restored again to the state from which we thought it desirable to be delivered. But this knowledge, though it is easily gained by the trial, is not always attainable any other way; and that errour cannot justly be reproached, which reason could not obviate, nor prudence avoid.

To take a view at once distinct and comprehensive of human life, with all its intricacies of combination, and varieties of connexion, is beyond the power of mortal intelligences. Of the state with which practice has not acquainted us we snatch a glimpse, we discern a point, and regulate the rest by passion, and by fancy. In this inquiry every favourite prejudice, every innate desire, is busy to deceive us. We are unhappy, at least less happy than our nature seems to admit; we necessarily desire the melioration of our lot; what we desire we very reasonably seek, and what we seek we are naturally eager to believe that we have found. Our confidence is often disappointed, but our reason is not convinced, and there is no man who does not hope for something which he has not, though perhaps his wishes lie unactive, because he foresees the difficulty of attainment. As among the numerous students of Hermetick philosophy, not one appears to have desisted from the task of transmutation, from conviction of its impossibility, but from weariness of toil, or impatience of delay, a broken body, or exhausted fortune.

Irresolution and mutability are often the faults of men whose views are wide, and whose imaginations is vigorous and excursive, because they cannot confine their thoughts within their own boundaries of action, but are continually ranging over all the scenes of human existence, and consequently are often apt to conceive that they fall upon new regions of pleasure, and start new possibilities of happiness. Thus they are busied with a perpetual succession of schemes, and pass their lives in alternate elation and sorrow, for want of that calm and immoveable acquiescence in their condition, by which men of slower understandings are fixed for ever to a certain point, or led on in the plain beaten track which their fathers and grandsires have trod before them.

Of two conditions of life equally inviting to the prospect, that will always have the disadvantage which we have already tried; because the evils which we have felt we cannot extenuate: and though we have, perhaps from nature, the power as well of aggravating the calamity which we fear, as of heightening the blessing we expect, yet in those meditations which we indulge by choice, and which are not forced upon the mind by necessity, we have always the art of fixing our regard upon the more pleasing images, and suffer hope to dispose the lights by which we look upon futurity.

The good and ill of different modes of life are sometimes so equally opposed, that perhaps no man ever yet made his choice between them upon a full conviction, and adequate knowledge ; and therefore fluctuation of will is not more wonderful, when they are proposed to the election, than oscillations of a beam charged with equal weights. The mind no sooner imagines itself determined by some prevalent advantage, than some convenience of equal weight is discovered on the other side, and the resolutions which are suggested by the nicest examination, are often repented as soon as they are taken.

Eumenes, a young man of great abilities, inherited a large estate from a father, long eminent in conspicuous employments. His father, harassed with competitions, and perplexed with multiplicity of business, recommended the quiet of a private station with so much force, that Eumenes for some years resisted every motion of ambitious wishes ; but being once provoked by the sight of oppression, which he could not redress, he began to think it the duty of an honest man to enable himself to protect others, and gradually felt a desire of greatness, excited by a thousand projects of advantage to his country. His fortune placed him in the senate, his knowledge and eloquence advanced him at court, and he possessed that authority and influence which he had resolved to exert for the happiness of mankind.

He now became acquainted with greatness, and was in a short time convinced, that in proportion as the power of doing well is enlarged, the temptations to do ill are multiplied and enforced. He felt himself every moment in danger of being either seduced or driven from his honest purposes. Sometimes a friend was to be gratified, and sometimes a rival to be crushed, by means which his

conscience could not approve. Sometimes he was forced
to comply with the prejudices of the publick, and sometimes
with the schemes of the ministry. He was by degrees
wearied with perpetual struggles to unite policy and virtue,
and went back to retirement as the shelter of innocence,
persuaded that he could only hope to benefit mankind by a
blameless example of private virtue. Here he spent some
years in tranquillity and beneficence ; but finding that
corruption increased, and false opinions in government
prevailed, he thought himself again summoned to posts of
publick trust, from which new evidence of his own weakness
again determined him to retire.

Thus men may be made inconstant by virtue and by vice,
by too much or too little thought ; yet inconstancy, however
dignified by its motives, is always to be avoided, because
life allows us but a small time for inquiry and experiment,
and he that steadily endeavours at excellence, in whatever
employment, will more benefit mankind than he that
hesitates in choosing his part till he is called to the performance. The traveller that resolutely follows a rough
and winding path, will sooner reach the end of his journey,
than he that is always changing his direction, and wastes the
hours of day-light in looking for smoother ground, and
shorter passages.

Saturday, October 27, 1750.

" Idem velle, et idem nolle, ea demum firma amicitia est."

SALLUST.

" To live in friendship is to have the same desires and the same
aversions."

WHEN Socrates was building himself a house at
Athens, being asked by one that observed the
littleness of the design, why a man so eminent would not
have an abode more suitable to his dignity? he replied,
that he should think himself sufficiently accommodated, if
he could see that narrow habitation filled with real friends.
Such was the opinion of this great master of human life,
concerning the infrequency of such an union of minds as
might deserve the name of friendship, that among the
multitudes whom vanity or curiosity, civility or veneration,
crowded about him, he did not expect, that very spacious
apartments would be necessary to contain all that should
regard him with sincere kindness, or adhere to him with
steady fidelity.

So many qualities are indeed requisite to the possibility
of friendship, and so many accidents must concur to its rise
and its continuance, that the greatest part of mankind
content themselves without it, and supply its place as they
can, with interest and dependence.

Multitudes are unqualified for a constant and warm
reciprocation of benevolence, as they are incapacitated for

any other elevated excellence, by perpetual attention to their interest, and unresisting subjection to their passions. Long habits may superinduce inability to deny any desire or repress, by superior motives, the importunities of any immediate gratification, and an inveterate selfishness will imagine all advantages diminished in proportion as they are communicated.

But not only this hateful and confirmed corruption, but many varieties of disposition, not inconsistent with common degrees of virtue, may exclude friendship from the heart. Some ardent enough in their benevolence, and defective neither in officiousness nor liberality, are mutable and uncertain, soon attracted by new objects, disgusted without offence, and alienated without enmity. Others are soft and flexible, easily influenced by reports or whispers, ready to catch alarms from every dubious circumstance, and to listen to every suspicion which envy and flattery shall suggest, to follow the opinion of every confident adviser, and move by the impulse of the last breath. Some are impatient of contradiction, more willing to go wrong by their own judgment, than to be indebted for a better or a safer way to the sagacity of another, inclined to consider counsel as insult, and inquiry as want of confidence, and to confer their regard on no other terms than unreserved submission, and implicit compliance. Some are dark and involved, equally careful to conceal good and bad purposes; and pleased with producing effects by invisible means, and showing their design only in its execution. Others are universally communicative, alike open to every eye, and equally profuse of their own secrets and those of others, without the necessary vigilance of caution, or the honest arts of prudent integrity, ready to accuse without malice, and to betray without treachery. Any of these may be useful to the community, and pass through the world with the reputation of good purposes and uncorrupted morals, but they are unfit for close and tender intimacies. He cannot properly be chosen for a friend, whose kindness is exhaled by its own warmth, or frozen by the first blast of slander; he cannot be a useful counsellor who will hear no opinion but his own; he will not much invite confidence whose principal maxim is to suspect; nor can the candour and frankness of that man be much esteemed, who spreads his arms to humankind, and makes every man, without distinction, a denizen of his bosom.

That friendship may be at once fond and lasting, there must not only be equal virtue on each part, but virtue of the same kind; not only the same end must be proposed, but the same means must be approved by both. We are often, by superficial accomplishments and accidental endearments, induced to love those whom we cannot esteem; we are sometimes, by great abilities, and incontestible evidences of virtue, compelled to esteem those whom we cannot love. But friendship, compounded of esteem and love, derives from one its tenderness, and its permanence from the other; and therefore requires not only that its candidates should gain the judgment, but that they should attract the affections; that they should not only be firm in the day of distress, but gay in the hour of jollity; not only useful in exigencies, but pleasing in familiar life; their presence should give cheerfulness as well as courage, and dispel alike the gloom of fear and of melancholy.

To this mutual complacency is generally requisite an uniformity of opinion, at least of those active and conspicuous principles which discriminate parties in government, and sects in religion, and which every day operate more or less on the common business of life. For though great tenderness has, perhaps, been sometimes known to continue between men eminent in contrary factions; yet such friends are to be shown rather as prodigies than examples, and it is no more proper to regulate our conduct by such instances, than to leap a precipice, because some have fallen from it and escaped with life.

It cannot but be extremely difficult to preserve private kindness in the midst of publick opposition, in which will necessarily be involved a thousand incidents extending their influence to conversation and privacy. Men engaged, by moral or religious motives, in contrary parties, will generally look with different eyes upon every man, and decide almost every question upon different principles. When such occasions of dispute happen, to comply is to betray our cause, and to maintain friendship by ceasing to deserve it; to be silent is to lose the happiness and dignity of independence, to live in perpetual constraint, and to desert, if not to betray : and who shall determine which of two friends shall yield, where neither believes himself mistaken, and both confess the importance of the question? What then remains but contradiction and debate? and from those what can be expected, but acrimony and vehemence, the insolence of triumph, the vexation of defeat, and, in time, a weariness of contest, and an extinction of benevolence? Exchange of endearments and intercourse of civility may continue, indeed, as boughs may for a while be verdant, when the root is wounded; but the poison of discord is infused, and though the countenance may preserve its smile, the heart is hardening and contracting.

That man will not be long agreeable whom we see only in times of seriousness and severity; and therefore, to maintain the softness and serenity of benevolence, it is necessary that friends partake each other's pleasures as well as cares, and be led to the same diversions by similitude of taste. This is, however, not to be considered as equally indispensable with conformity of principles, because any man may honestly, according to the precepts of Horace, resign the gratifications of taste to the humour of another, and friendship may well deserve the sacrifice of pleasure, though not of conscience.

It was once confessed to me, by a painter, that no professor of his art ever loved another. This declaration is so far justified by the knowledge of life, as to damp the hopes of warm and constant friendship between men whom their studies have made competitors, and whom every favourer and every censurer are hourly inciting against each other. The utmost expectation that experience can warrant is, that they should forbear open hostilities and secret machinations, and, when the whole fraternity is attacked, be able to unite against a common foe. Some, however, though few, may perhaps be found, in whom emulation has not been able to overpower generosity, who are distinguished from lower beings by nobler motives than the love of fame, and can preserve the sacred flame of friendship from the gusts of pride, and the rubbish of interest.

Friendship is seldom lasting but between equals, or where the superiority on one side is reduced by some equivalent advantage on the other. Benefits which cannot be repaid, and obligations which cannot be discharged, are not commonly found to increase affection; they excite gratitude indeed, and heighten veneration; but commonly take away that easy freedom and familiarity of intercourse, without which, though there may be fidelity, and zeal, and admiration, there cannot be friendship. Thus imperfect are all earthly blessings; the great effect of friendship is beneficence, yet by the first act of uncommon kindness it

is endangered, like plants that bear their fruit and die.*
Yet this consideration ought not to restrain bounty, or
repress compassion ; for duty is to be preferred before convenience, and he that loses part of the pleasures of friendship by his generosity, gains in its place the gratulation of
his conscience.

Tuesday, November 6, 1750.

" Αἱ δ' ἐλπίδες βόσκσσι φυγάδας, ὡς λόγος,
 Καλῶς βλέωσιν ὄμμασι, μέλλσι δέ."   Eurip.

" Exiles, the proverb says, subsist on hope,
 Delusive hope still points to distant good,
 To good that mocks approach."

THERE is no temper so generally indulged as hope ;
other passions operate by starts on particular
occasions, or in certain parts of life; but hope begins
with the first power of comparing our actual with our
possible state, and attends us through every stage and
period, always urging us forward to new acquisitions, and
holding out some distant blessing to our view, promising us
either relief from pain, or increase of happiness.

Hope is necessary in every condition. The miseries of
poverty, of sickness, of captivity, would, without this
comfort, be insupportable; nor does it appear that the
happiest lot of terrestrial existence can set us above the
want of this general blessing; or that life, when the gifts of
nature and of fortune are accumulated upon it, would not

* Note VIII., Appendix.

still be wretched, were it not elevated and delighted by the expectation of some new possession, of some enjoyment yet behind, by which the wish shall be at last satisfied, and the heart filled up to its utmost extent.

Hope is, indeed, very fallacious, and promises what it seldom gives; but its promises are more valuable than the gifts of fortune, and it seldom frustrates us without assuring us of recompensing the delay by a greater bounty.

I was musing on this strange inclination which every man feels to deceive himself, and considering the advantages and dangers proceeding from this gay prospect of futurity, when, falling asleep, on a sudden I found myself placed in a garden, of which my sight could descry no limits. Every scene about me was gay and gladsome, light with sunshine, and fragrant with perfumes; the ground was painted with all the variety of spring, and all the choir of nature was singing in the groves. When I had recovered from the first raptures, with which the confusion of pleasure had for a time entranced me, I began to take a particular and deliberate view of this delightful region. I then perceived that I had yet higher gratifications to expect, and that, at a small distance from me, there were brighter flowers, clearer fountains, and more lofty groves, where the birds, which I yet heard but faintly, were exerting all the power of melody. The trees about me were beautiful with verdure, and fragrant with blossoms; but I was tempted to leave them by the sight of ripe fruits, which seemed to hang only to be plucked. I therefore walked hastily forwards, but found, as I proceeded, that the colours of the field faded at my approach, the fruit fell before I reached it, the birds flew still singing before me, and though I pressed onward with great celerity, I was still in sight of pleasures of which

I could not yet gain the possession, and which seemed to mock my diligence, and to retire as I advanced.

Though I was confounded with so many alternations of joy and grief, I yet persisted to go forward, in hopes that these fugitive delights would in time be overtaken. At length I saw an innumerable multitude of every age and sex, who seemed all to partake of some general felicity; for every cheek was flushed with confidence, and every eye sparkled with eagerness: yet each appeared to have some particular and secret pleasure, and very few were willing to communicate their intentions, or extend their concern beyond themselves. Most of them seemed, by the rapidity of their motion, too busy to gratify the curiosity of a stranger, and therefore I was content for a while to gaze upon them, without interrupting them with troublesome inquiries. At last I observed one man worn with time, and unable to struggle in the crowd; and therefore, supposing him more at leisure, I began to accost him: but he turned from me with anger, and told me he must not be disturbed, for the great hour of projection was now come when Mercury should lose his wings, and slavery should no longer dig the mine for gold.

I left him, and attempted another, whose softness of mien, and easy movement, gave me reason to hope for a more agreeable reception; but he told me, with a low bow, that nothing would make him more happy than an opportunity of serving me, which he could not now want, for a place which he had been twenty years soliciting would be soon vacant. From him I had recourse to the next, who was departing in haste to take possession of the estate of an uncle, who by the course of nature could not live long. He that followed was preparing to dive for treasure in a new-invented bell; and another was on the point of discovering the longitude.

Being thus rejected wheresoever I applied myself for information, I began to imagine it best to desist from inquiry, and try what my own observation would discover: but seeing a young man, gay and thoughtless, I resolved upon one more experiment, and was informed that I was in the garden of HOPE, the daughter of DESIRE, and that all those whom I saw thus tumultuously bustling round me were incited by the promises of HOPE, and hastening to seize the gifts which she held in her hand.

I turned my sight upward, and saw a goddess in the bloom of youth sitting on a throne: around her lay all the gifts of fortune, and all the blessings of life were spread abroad to view; she had a perpetual gaiety of aspect, and every one imagined that her smile, which was impartial and general, was directed to himself, and triumphed in his own superiority to others, who had conceived the same confidence from the same mistake.

I then mounted an eminence, from which I had a more extensive view of the whole place, and could with less perplexity consider the different conduct of the crowds that filled it. From this station I observed, that the entrance into the garden of HOPE was by two gates, one of which was kept by REASON, and the other by FANCY. REASON was surly and scrupulous, and seldom turned the key without many interrogatories, and long hesitation; but FANCY was a kind and gentle portress, she held her gate wide open, and welcomed all equally to the district under her superintendency: so that the passage was crowded by all those who either fear the examination of REASON, or had been rejected by her.

From the gate of REASON there was a way to the throne of HOPE, by a craggy, slippery, and winding path, called the *Streight of Difficulty*, which those who entered with the permission of the guard endeavoured to climb. But though they surveyed the way very carefully before they began to rise, and marked out the several stages of their progress, they commonly found unexpected obstacles, and were obliged frequently to stop on the sudden, where they imagined the way plain and even. A thousand intricacies embarrassed them, a thousand slips threw them back, and a thousand pitfalls impeded their advance. So formidable were the dangers, and so frequent the miscarriages, that many returned from the first attempt, and many fainted in the midst of the way, and only a very small number were led up to the summit of HOPE, by the hand of FORTITUDE. Of these few the greater part, when they had obtained the gift which HOPE had promised them, regretted the labour which it cost, and felt in their success the regret of disappointment; the rest retired with their prize, and were led by WISDOM to the bowers of CONTENT.

Turning then towards the gate of FANCY, I could find no way to the seat of HOPE; but though she sat full in view, and held out her gifts with an air of invitation, which filled every heart with rapture, the mountain was, on that side, inaccessibly steep, but so channelled and shaded, that none perceived the impossibility of ascending it, but each imagined himself to have discovered a way to which the rest were strangers. Many expedients were indeed tried by this industrious tribe, of whom some were making themselves wings, which others were contriving to actuate by the perpetual motion. But with all their labour, and all their artifices, they never rose above the ground, or quickly fell back, nor ever approached the throne of HOPE, but continued still to gaze at a distance, and laughed at the slow progress of those whom they saw toiling in the *Streight of Difficulty.*

Part of the favourites of FANCY, when they had entered the garden, without making, like the rest, an attempt to climb the mountain, turned immediately to the vale of IDLENESS, a calm and undisturbed retirement, from whence they could always have HOPE in prospect, and to which they pleased themselves with believing that she intended speedily to descend. These were indeed scorned by all the rest; but they seemed very little affected by contempt, advice, or reproof, but were resolved to expect at ease the favour of the goddess.

Among this gay race I was wandering, and found them ready to answer all my questions, and willing to communicate their mirth; but turning round, I saw two dreadful monsters entering the vale, one of whom I knew to be AGE, and the other WANT. Sport and revelling were now at an end, and an universal shriek of affright and distress burst out and awaked me.

Saturday, November 10, 1750.

" *Vivendum rectè, cum propter plurima, tunc his*
 Præcipue causis, ut linguas mancipiorum
 Contemnas ; nam lingua mali pars pessima servi." JUV.

" Let us live well : were it alone for this
 The baneful tongues of servants to despise :
 Slander, that worst of poisons, ever finds
 An easy entrance to ignoble minds." HERVEY.

THE younger Pliny has very justly observed, that of actions that deserve our attention, the most splendid are not always the greatest. Fame, and wonder, and applause, are not excited but by external and adventitious circumstances, often distinct and separate from virtue and heroism. Eminence of station, greatness of effect, and all the favours of fortune, must concur to place excellence in publick view; but fortitude, diligence, and patience, divested of their show, glide unobserved through the crowd of life, and suffer and act, though with the same vigour, and constancy, yet without pity and without praise.

This remark may be extended to all parts of life. Nothing is to be estimated by its effect upon common eyes and common ears. A thousand miseries make silent and invisible inroads on mankind, and the heart feels innumerable throbs, which never break into complaint. Perhaps, likewise, our pleasures are for the most part equally secret, and most are borne up by some private satisfaction, some internal consciousness, some latent hope, some peculiar prospect, which they never communicate, but reserve for solitary hours and clandestine meditations.

The main of life is, indeed, composed of small incidents and petty occurrences; of wishes for objects not remote, and grief for disappointments of no fatal consequence; of insect vexations which sting us and fly away, impertinences which buzz a while about us, and are heard no more; of meteorous pleasures which dance before us and are dissipated; of compliments which glide off the soul like other musick, and are forgotten by him that gave and him that received them.

Such is the general heap out of which every man is to cull his own condition: for, as the chemists tell us, that all bodies are resolvable into the same elements, and that the boundless variety of things arises from the different proportions of very few ingredients; so a few pains and a few pleasures are all the materials of human life, and of these the proportions are partly allotted by Providence, and partly left to the arrangement of reason and of choice.

As these are well or ill disposed, man is for the most part happy or miserable. For very few are involved in great events, or have their thread of life entwisted with the chain of causes on which armies or nations are suspended; and even those who seem wholly busied in publick affairs, and elevated above low cares, or trivial pleasures, pass the chief part of their time in familiar and domestick scenes; from these they came into publick life, to these they are every hour recalled by passions not to be suppressed; in these they have the reward of their toils, and to these at last they retire.

The great end of prudence is to give cheerfulness to those hours which splendour cannot gild, and acclamation cannot exhilarate; those soft intervals of unbended amusement, in which a man shrinks to his natural dimensions, and throws aside the ornaments or disguises, which he feels in privacy to be useless incumbrances, and to lose all effect when they become familiar. To be happy at home is the ultimate result of all ambition, the end to which every enterprise and labour tends, and of which every desire prompts the prosecution.

It is, indeed, at home that every man must be known by those who would make a just estimate either of his virtue or felicity; for smiles and embroidery are alike occasional, and the mind is often dressed for show in painted honour and fictitious benevolence.

Every man must have found some whose lives, in every house but their own, were a continual series of hypocrisy, and who concealed under fair appearances bad qualities, which, whenever they thought themselves out of the reach of censure, broke out from their restraint, like winds imprisoned in their caverns, and whom every one had reason to love, but they whose love a wise man is chiefly solicitous to procure. And there are others who, without any show of general goodness, and without the attractions by which popularity is conciliated, are received among their own families as bestowers of happiness, and reverenced as instructors, guardians, and benefactors.

The most authentick witnesses of any man's character are those who know him in his own family, and see him without any restraint or rule of conduct, but such as he voluntarily prescribes to himself. If a man carries virtue with him into his private apartments, and takes no advantage of unlimited power or probable secrecy; if we trace him through the round of his time, and find that his character, with those allowances which mortal frailty must always want, is uniform and regular, we have all the evidence of his sincerity, that one man can have with regard to another : and, indeed, as hypocrisy cannot be its own reward, we may, without hesitation, determine that his heart is pure.

The highest panegyrick, therefore, that private virtue can receive, is the praise of servants. For, however vanity or insolence may look down with contempt on the suffrage of men undignified by wealth, and unenlightened by education, it very seldom happens that they commend or blame without justice. Vice and virtue are easily distinguished. Oppression, according to Harrington's aphorism, will be felt by those who cannot see it : and, perhaps, it falls out very often that, in moral questions, the philosophers in the gown, and in the livery, differ not so much in their sentiments, as in their language, and have equal power of discerning right, though they cannot point it out to others with equal address.

There are very few faults to be committed in solitude, or

without some agents, partners, confederates, or witnesses; and, therefore, the servant must commonly know the secrets of a master, who has any secrets to entrust; and failings, merely personal, are so frequently exposed by that security which pride and folly generally produce, and so inquisitively watched by that desire of reducing the inequalities of condition, which the lower orders of the world will always feel, that the testimony of a menial domestick can seldom be considered as defective for want of knowledge. And though its impartiality may be sometimes suspected, it is at least as credible as that of equals, where rivalry instigates censure, or friendship dictates palliations.

The danger of betraying our weakness to our servants, and the impossibility of concealing it from them, may be justly considered as one motive to a regular and irreproachable life. For no condition is more hateful or despicable, than his who has put himself in the power of his servant; in the power of him whom, perhaps, he has first corrupted by making him subservient to his vices, and whose fidelity he therefore cannot enforce by any precepts of honesty or reason. It is seldom known that authority thus acquired, is possessed without insolence, or that the master is not forced to confess, by his tameness or forbearance, that he has enslaved himself by some foolish confidence. And his crime is equally punished, whatever part he takes of the choice to which he is reduced; and he is from that fatal hour, in which he sacrificed his dignity to his passions, in perpetual dread of insolence or defamation; of a controller at home, or an accuser abroad. He is condemned to purchase, by continual bribes, that secrecy which bribes never secured, and which, after a long course of submission, promises, and anxieties, he will find violated in a fit of rage, or in a frolick of drunkenness.

To dread no eye, and to suspect no tongue, is the great prerogative of innocence; an exemption granted only to invariable virtue. But guilt has always its horrours and solicitudes; and, to make it yet more shameful and detestable, it is doomed often to stand in awe of those, to whom nothing could give influence or weight, but their power of betraying.

Saturday, November 24, 1750.

" *Omnis* Aristippum *decuit status, et color, et res,*
Tentantem majora, fere presentibus æquum." Hor.

" Yet *Aristippus* ev'ry dress became,
In ev'ry various change of life the same ;
And though he aim'd at things of higher kind,
Yet to the present held an equal mind."   Francis.

TO THE RAMBLER.

Sir,

THOSE who exalt themselves into the chair of instruction, without inquiring whether any will submit to their authority, have not sufficiently considered how much of human life passes in little incidents, cursory conversation, slight business, and casual amusements ; and therefore they have endeavoured only to inculcate the more awful virtues, without condescending to regard those petty qualities, which grow important only by their frequency, and which, though they produce no single acts of heroism, nor astonish us by great events, yet are every moment exerting their influence upon us, and make the draught of life sweet or bitter by imperceptible instillations. They operate unseen and unregarded, as change of air makes us sick or healthy, though we breathe it without attention, and only know the particles that impregnate it by their salutary or malignant effects.

You have shown yourself not ignorant of the value of those subaltern endowments, yet have hitherto neglected to recommend good-humour to the world, though a little reflection will show you that it is the *balm of being*, the quality to which all that adorns or elevates mankind must owe its power of pleasing. Without good-humour, learning and bravery can only confer that superiority which swells the heart of the lion in the desert, where he roars without reply, and ravages without resistance. Without good-humour, virtue may awe by its dignity, and amaze by its brightness ; but must always be viewed at a distance, and will scarcely gain a friend or attract an imitator.

Good-humour may be defined a habit of being pleased ;* a constant and perennial softness of manner, easiness of approach, and suavity of disposition ; like that which every man perceives in himself, when the first transports of new felicity have subsided, and his thoughts are only kept in motion by a slow succession of soft impulses. Good-humour is a state between gaiety and unconcern; the act or emanation of a mind at leisure to regard the gratification of another.

It is imagined by many, that whenever they aspire to please, they are required to be merry, and to show the gladness of their souls by flights of pleasantry, and bursts of laughter. But though these men may be for a time heard with applause and admiration, they seldom delight us long. We enjoy them a little, and then retire to easiness and

* Note IX., Appendix.

good-humour, as the eye gazes a while on eminences glittering with the sun, but soon turns aching away to verdure and to flowers.

Gaiety is to good-humour as animal perfumes to vegetable fragrance ; the one overpowers weak spirits, and the other recreates and revives them. Gaiety seldom fails to give some pain ; the hearers either strain their faculties to accompany its towerings, or are left behind in envy and despair. Good-humour boasts no faculties which every one does not believe in his own power, and pleases principally by not offending.

It is well known that the most certain way to give any man pleasure is to persuade him that you receive pleasure from him, to encourage him to freedom and confidence, and to avoid any such appearance of superiority as may overbear and depress him. We see many that by this art only spend their days in the midst of caresses, invitations, and civilities ; and without any extraordinary qualities or attainments, are the universal favourites of both sexes, and certainly find a friend in every place. The darlings of the world will, indeed, be generally found such as excite neither jealousy nor fear, and are not considered as candidates for any eminent degree of reputation, but content themselves with common accomplishments, and endeavour rather to solicit kindness than to raise esteem ; therefore, in assemblies and places of resort, it seldom fails to happen, that though at the entrance of some particular person, every face brightens with gladness, and every hand is extended in salutation, yet if you pursue him beyond the first exchange of civilities, you will find him of very small importance, and only welcome to the company, as one by whom all conceive themselves admired, and with whom any one is at liberty to amuse himself when he can find no other auditor or companion ; as one with whom all are at ease, who will hear a jest without criticism, and a narrative without contradiction, who laughs with every wit, and yields to every disputer.

There are many whose vanity always inclines them to associate with those from whom they have no reason to fear mortification ; and there are times in which the wise and the knowing are willing to receive praise without the labour of deserving it, in which the most elevated mind is willing to descend, and the most active to be at rest. All therefore are at some hour or another fond of companions whom they can entertain upon easy terms, and who will relieve them from solitude, without condemning them to vigilance and caution. We are most inclined to love when we have nothing to fear, and he that encourages us to please ourselves, will not be long without preference in our affection to those whose learning holds us at the distance of pupils, or whose wit calls all attention from us, and leaves us without importance and without regard.

It is remarked by Prince Henry, when he sees Falstaff lying on the ground, that *he could have better spared a better man.* He was well acquainted with the vices and follies of him whom he lamented ; but while his conviction compelled him to do justice to superior qualities, his tenderness still broke out at the remembrance of Falstaff, of the cheerful companion, the loud buffoon, with whom he had passed his time in all the luxury of idleness, who had gladded him with unenvied merriment, and whom he could at once enjoy and despise.

You may perhaps think this account of those who are distinguished for their good-humour, not very consistent with the praises which I have bestowed upon it. But surely nothing can more evidently show the value of this quality, than that it recommends those who are destitute of all other excellencies, and procures regard to the trifling, friendship to the worthless, and affection to the dull.

Good-humour is indeed generally degraded by the characters in which it is found; for, being considered as a cheap and vulgar quality, we find it often neglected by those that, having excellencies of higher reputation and brighter splendour, perhaps imagine that they have some right to gratify themselves at the expense of others, and are to demand compliance rather than to practise it. It is by some unfortunate mistake that almost all those who have any claim to esteem or love, press their pretensions with too little consideration of others. This mistake, my own interest, as well as my zeal for general happiness, makes me desirous to rectify; for I have a friend, who, because he knows his own fidelity and usefulness, is never willing to sink into a companion: I have a wife whose beauty first subdued me, and whose wit confirmed her conquest, but whose beauty now serves no other purpose than to entitle her to tyranny, and whose wit is only used to justify perverseness.

Surely nothing can be more unreasonable than to lose the will to please, when we are conscious of the power, or show more cruelty than to choose any kind of influence before that of kindness. He that regards the welfare of others, should make his virtue approachable, that it may be loved and copied; and he that considers the wants which every man feels, or will feel, of external assistance, must rather wish to be surrounded by those that love him, than by those that admire his excellencies, or solicit his favours; for admiration ceases with novelty, and interest gains its end and retires. A man whose great qualities want the ornament of superficial attractions, is like a naked mountain with mines of gold, which will be frequented only till the treasure is exhausted.   I am, &c.

PHILOMIDES.

Tuesday, December 11, 1750.

" *Os dignum æterno nitidum quod fulgeat auro,*
Si mallet laudare Deum, cui sordida monstra
Prætulit, et liquidam temeravit crimine vocem."

PRUDENT.

" A golden statue such a wit might claim,
Had God and virtue rais'd the noble flame ;
But ah ! how lewd a subject has he sung !
What vile obscenity profanes his tongue ! "

F. LEWIS.

AMONG those whose hopes of distinction, or riches, arise from an opinion of their intellectual attainments, it has been, from age to age, an established custom to complain of the ingratitude of mankind to their instructors, and the discouragement which men of genius and study suffer from avarice and ignorance, from the prevalence of false taste, and the encroachment of barbarity.

Men are most powerfully affected by those evils which themselves feel, or which appear before their own eyes ; and as there has never been a time of such general felicity, but that many have failed to obtain the rewards to which they had, in their own judgment, a just claim, some offended writer has always declaimed, in the rage of disappointment, against his age or nation ; nor is there one who has not fallen upon times more unfavourable to learning than any former century, or who does not wish, that he had been reserved in the insensibility of non-existence to some happier hour, when literary merit shall no longer be despised, and the gifts and caresses of mankind shall recompense the toils of study, and add lustre to the charms of wit.

Many of these clamours are undoubtedly to be considered only as the bursts of pride never to be satisfied, as the prattle of affectation mimicking distresses unfelt, or as the common-places of vanity solicitous for splendour of sentences, and acuteness of remark. Yet it cannot be denied that frequent discontent must proceed from frequent hardships; and though it is evident, that not more than one age or people can deserve the censure of being more averse from learning than any other, yet at all times knowledge must have encountered impediments, and wit been mortified with contempt, or harassed with persecution.

It is not necessary, however, to join immediately in the outcry, or to condemn mankind as pleased with ignorance, or always envious of superior abilities. The miseries of the learned have been related by themselves; and since they have not been found exempt from that partiality with which men look upon their own actions and sufferings, we may conclude that they have not forgotten to deck their cause with the brightest ornaments and strongest colours. The logician collected all his subtilities when they were to be employed in his own defence; and the master of rhetorick exerted against his adversary all the arts by which hatred is embittered, and indignation inflamed.

To believe no man in his own cause, is the standing and perpetual rule of distributive justice. Since therefore, in the controversy between the learned and their enemies, we have only the pleas of one party, of the party more able to delude our understandings, and engage our passions, we must determine our opinion by facts uncontested, and evidences on each side allowed to be genuine.

By this procedure, I know not whether the students will find their cause promoted, or their compassion which they expect much increased. Let their conduct be impartially surveyed ; let them be allowed no longer to direct attention at their pleasure, by expatiating on their own deserts ; let neither the dignity of knowledge overawe the judgment, nor the graces of elegance seduce it. It will then, perhaps, be found that they were not able to produce claims to kinder treatment, but provoked the calamities which they suffered, and seldom wanted friends, but when they wanted virtue.

That few men, celebrated for theoretick wisdom, live with conformity to their precepts, must be readily confessed ; and we cannot wonder that the indignation of mankind rises with great vehemence against those, who neglect the duties which they appear to know with so strong conviction the necessity of performing. Yet since no man has power of acting equal to that of thinking, I know not whether the speculatist may not sometimes incur censures too severe, and by those who form ideas of his life from their knowledge of his books, be considered as worse than others, only because he was expected to be better.

He, by whose writings the heart is rectified, the appetites counteracted, and the passions repressed, may be considered as not unprofitable to the great republick of humanity, even though his behaviour should not always exemplify his rules. His instructions may diffuse their influence to regions, in which it will not be inquired, whether the author be *albus an ater*, good or bad ; to times, when all his faults and all his follies shall be lost in forgetfulness, among things of no concern or importance to the world ; and he may kindle in thousands and ten thousands that flame which burnt but dimly in himself, through the fumes of passion, or the damps of cowardice. The vicious moralist may be considered as a taper, by which we are lighted through the labyrinth of complicated passions, he extends his radiance further than his heat, and guides all that are within view, but burns only those who make too near approaches.

Yet since good or harm must be received for the most part from those to whom we are familiarly known, he whose vices overpower his virtues, in the compass to which his vices can extend, has no reason to complain that he meets not with affection or veneration, when those with whom he passes his life are more corrupted by his practice than enlightened by his ideas. Admiration begins where acquaintance ceases ; and his favourers are distant, but his enemies at hand.

Yet many have dared to boast of neglected merit, and to challenge their age for cruelty and folly, of whom it cannot be alleged that they have endeavoured to increase the wisdom or virtue of their readers. They have been at once profligate in their lives, and licentious in their compositions ; have not only forsaken the paths of virtue, but attempted to lure others after them. They have smoothed the road of perdition, covered with flowers the thorns of guilt, and taught temptation sweeter notes, softer blandishments, and stronger allurements.

It has been apparently the settled purpose of some writers, whose powers and acquisitions place them high in the rank of literature, to set fashion on the side of wickedness; to recommend debauchery and lewdness, by associating them with qualities most likely to dazzle the discernment, and attract the affections ; and to show innocence and goodness with such attendant weaknesses as necessarily expose them to contempt and derision.

Such naturally found intimates among the corrupt, the

thoughtless, and the intemperate ; passed their lives amidst
the levities of sportive idleness, or the warm professions
of drunken friendship; and fed their hopes with the
promises of wretches, whom their precepts had taught
to scoff at truth. But when fools had laughed away their
sprightliness, and the languors of excess could no longer
be relieved, they saw their protectors hourly drop away,
and wondered and stormed to find themselves abandoned.
Whether their companions persisted in wickedness, or
returned to virtue, they were left equally without assistance ;
for debauchery is selfish and negligent, and from virtue
the virtuous only can expect regard.

It is said by Florus of Catiline, who died in the midst
of slaughtered enemies, that *his death had been illustrious,
had it been suffered for his country.* Of the wits who have
languished away life under the pressures of poverty, or
in the restlessness of suspense, caressed and rejected,
flattered and despised, as they were of more or less use
to those who stiled themselves their patrons, it might be
observed, that their miseries would enforce compassion,
had they been brought upon them by honesty and
religion.

The wickedness of a loose or profane author is more
atrocious than that of the giddy libertine, or drunken
ravisher, not only because it extends its effects wider, as
a pestilence that taints the air is more destructive than
poison infused in a draught, but because it is committed
with cool deliberation. By the instantaneous violence of
desire, a good man may sometimes be surprised before
reflection can come to his rescue ; when the appetites
have strengthened their influence by habit, they are not
easily resisted or suppressed; but for the frigid villany
of studious lewdness, for the calm malignity of laboured

impiety, what apology can be invented? What punishment can be adequate to the crime of him who retires to solitudes for the refinement of debauchery; who tortures his fancy, and ransacks his memory, only that he may leave the world less virtuous than he found it; that he may intercept the hopes of the rising generation; and spread snares for the soul with more dexterity?

What were their motives, or what their excuses, is below the dignity of reason to examine. If having extinguished in themselves the distinction of right and wrong, they were insensible of the mischief which they promoted, they deserved to be hunted down by the general compact, as no longer partaking of social nature; if influenced by the corruption of patrons, or readers, they sacrificed their own convictions to vanity or interest, they were to be abhorred with more acrimony than he that murders for pay; since they committed greater crimes without greater temptations.

Of him, to whom much is given, much shall be required. Those, whom God has favoured with superior faculties, and made eminent for quickness of intuition, and accuracy of distinctions, will certainly be regarded as culpable in his eye, for defects and deviations which, in souls less enlightened, may be guiltless. But, surely, none can think without horror on that man's condition, who has been more wicked in proportion as he had more means of excelling in virtue, and used the light imparted from heaven only to embellish folly, and shed lustre upon crimes.

Tuesday, January 15, 1751.

" *Invidus, iracundus, iners, vinosus, amator,*
   Nemo adeo ferus est, ut non mitescere possit,
   Si modo culturæ patientem commodet aurem."   HOR.

" The slave to envy, anger, wine, or love,
   The wretch of sloth, its excellence shall prove ;
   Fierceness itself shall hear its rage away,
   When list'ning calmly to th' instructive lay."

FRANCIS.

THAT few things are so liberally bestowed, or squandered
   with so little effect, as good advice, has been generally
observed ; and many sage positions have been advanced
concerning the reasons of this complaint, and the means of
removing it.   It is indeed an important and noble inquiry,
for little would be wanting to the happiness of life, if every
man could conform to the right as soon as he was shown
it.

This perverse neglect of the most salutary precepts, and
stubborn resistance of the most pathetick persuasion, is
usually imputed to him by whom the counsel is received,
and we often hear it mentioned as a sign of hopeless
depravity, that though good advice was given, it has
wrought no reformation.

Others, who imagine themselves to have quicker sagacity
and deeper penetration, have found out that the inefficacy
of advice is usually the fault of the counsellor, and rules
have been laid down, by which this important duty may be
successfully performed : We are directed by what tokens to
discover the favourable moment at which the heart is

disposed for the operation of truth and reason, with what
address to administer, and with what vehicles to disguise
the catharticks of the soul.

But, notwithstanding this specious expedient, we find the
world yet in the same state : advice is still given, but still
received with disgust ; nor has it appeared that the
bitterness of the medicine has been yet abated, or its power
increased, by any methods of preparing it.

If we consider the manner in which those who assume
the office of directing the conduct of others execute their
undertaking, it will not be very wonderful that their labours,
however zealous or affectionate, are frequently useless. For
what is the advice that is commonly given? A few general
maxims, enforced with vehemence and inculcated with
importunity, but failing for want of particular reference and
immediate application.

It is not often that any man can have so much knowledge
of another, as is necessary to make instruction useful. We
are sometimes not ourselves conscious of the original
motives of our actions, and when we know them, our first
care is to hide them from the sight of others, and often
from those most diligently, whose superiority either of
power or understanding may entitle them to inspect our lives;
it is therefore very probable that he who endeavours the
cure of our intellectual maladies, mistakes their cause ; and
that his prescriptions avail nothing, because he knows not
which of the passions or desires is vitiated.

Advice, as it always gives a temporary appearance of
superiority, can never be very grateful, even when it is most
necessary or most judicious. But for the same reason every
one is eager to instruct his neighbours. To be wise or to
be virtuous, is to buy dignity and importance at a high price ;
but when nothing is necessary to elevation but detection of

the follies or the faults of others, no man is so insensible to the voice of fame as to linger on the ground.

"——*Tentanda via est, qua me quoque possim*
  Tollere humo, victorque virûm volitare per ora."   VIRG.

" New ways I must attempt, my grovelling name
  To raise aloft, and wing my flight to fame."   DRYDEN.

Vanity is so frequently the apparent motive of advice, that we, for the most part, summon our powers to oppose it without any very accurate inquiry whether it is right. It is sufficient that another is growing great in his own eyes, at our expense, and assumes authority over us without our permission; for many would contentedly suffer the consequences of their own mistakes, rather than the insolence of him who triumphs as their deliverer.

It is, indeed, seldom found that any advantages are enjoyed with that moderation which the uncertainty of all human good so powerfully enforces; and therefore the adviser may justly suspect, that he has inflamed the opposition which he laments by arrogance and superciliousness. He may suspect, but needs not hastily to condemn himself, for he can rarely be certain that the softest language or most humble diffidence would have escaped resentment; since scarcely any degree of circumspection can prevent or obviate the rage with which the slothful, the impotent, and the unsuccessful, vent their discontent upon those that excel them. Modesty itself, if it is praised, will be envied; and there are minds so impatient of inferiority, that their gratitude is a species of revenge, and they return benefits, not because recompence is a pleasure, but because obligation is a pain.

The number of those whom the love of themselves has thus far corrupted, is perhaps not great; but there are few so free from vanity, as not to dictate to those who will hear their instructions with a visible sense of their own benefi- cence; and few to whom it is not unpleasing to receive documents, however tenderly and cautiously delivered, or who are not willing to raise themselves from pupilage, by disputing the propositions of their teacher.

It was the maxim, I think, of Alphonsus of Arragon,* that *dead counsellors are safest.* The grave puts an end to flattery and artifice, and the information that we receive from books is pure from interest, fear, or ambition. Dead counsellors are likewise most instructive; because they are heard with patience and with reverence. We are not unwilling to believe that man wiser than ourselves, from whose abilities we may receive advantage, without any danger of rivalry or opposition, and who affords us the light of his experience, without hurting our eyes by flashes of insolence.

By the consultation of books, whether of dead or living authors, many temptations to petulance and opposition, which occur in oral conferences, are avoided. An author cannot obtrude his services unasked, nor can be often suspected of any malignant intention to insult his readers with his knowledge or his wit. Yet so prevalent is the habit of comparing ourselves with others, while they remain within the reach of our passions, that books are seldom read with complete impartiality, but by those from whom the writer is placed at such a distance that his life or death is indifferent.

We see that volumes may be perused, and perused with attention, to little effect; and that maxims of prudence, or principles of virtue, may be treasured in the memory without influencing the conduct. Of the numbers that pass their

* Note X., Appendix.

lives among books, very few read to be made wiser or better, apply any general reproof of vice to themselves, or try their own manners by axioms of justice. They purpose either to consume those hours for which they can find no other amusement, to gain or preserve that respect which learning has always obtained; or to gratify their curiosity with knowledge, which, like treasures buried and forgotten, is of no use to others or themselves.

"The preacher (says a French author) may spend an hour "in explaining and enforcing a precept of religion, without "feeling any impression from his own performance, because "he may have no further design than to fill up his hour." A student may easily exhaust his life in comparing divines and moralists, without any practical regard to morality or religion; he may be learning not to live, but to reason; he may regard only the elegance of style, justness of argument, and accuracy of method; and may enable himself to criticise with judgment, and dispute with subtilty, while the chief use of his volumes is unthought of, his mind is unaffected, and his life is unreformed.

But though truth and virtue are thus frequently defeated by pride, obstinacy, or folly, we are not allowed to desert them; for whoever can furnish arms which they hitherto have not employed, may enable them to gain some hearts which would have resisted any other method of attack. Every man of genius has some arts of fixing the attention peculiar to himself, by which, honestly exerted, he may benefit mankind; for the arguments for purity of life fail of their due influence, not because they have been considered and confuted, but because they have been passed over without consideration. To the position of Tully, that if Virtue could be seen, she must be loved, may be added, that if Truth could be heard, she must be obeyed.

Tuesday, January 22, 1751.

" *Dulce est desipere in loco.*"   Hor.

" Wisdom at proper times is well forgot."

LOCKE, whom there is no reason to suspect of being a
favourer of idleness or libertinism, has advanced, that
whoever hopes to employ any part of his time with efficacy
and vigour, must allow some of it to pass in trifles. It is
beyond the powers of humanity to spend a whole life in
profound study and intense meditation, and the most
rigorous exacters of industry and seriousness have appointed
hours for relaxation and amusement.

It is certain, that, with or without our consent, many of
the few moments allotted us will slide imperceptibly away,
and that the mind will break, from confinement to its stated
task, into sudden excursions. Severe and connected
attention is preserved but for a short time ; and when a
man shuts himself up in his closet, and bends his thoughts
to the discussion of any abstruse question, he will find his
faculties continually stealing away to more pleasing entertainments. He often perceives himself transported, he
knows not how, to distant tracts of thought, and returns to
his first object as from a dream, without knowing when
he forsook it, or how long he has been abstracted from it.

It has been observed that the most studious are not
always the most learned. There is, indeed, no great difficulty in discovering that this difference of proficiency may
arise from the difference of intellectual powers, of the choice

of books, or the convenience of information. But I believe it likewise frequently happens that the most recluse are not the most vigorous prosecutors of study. Many impose upon the world, and many upon themselves, by an appearance of severe and exemplary diligence, when they, in reality, give themselves up to the luxury of fancy, please their minds with regulating the past, or planning out the future ; place themselves at will in varied situations of happiness, and slumber away their days in voluntary visions. In the journey of life some are left behind, because they are naturally feeble and slow ; some because they miss the way, and many because they leave it by choice, and, instead of pressing onward with a steady pace, delight themselves with momentary deviations, turn aside to pluck every flower, and repose in every shade.

There is nothing more fatal to a man whose business is to think, than to have learned the art of regaling his mind with those airy gratifications. Other vices or follies are restrained by fear, reformed by admonition, or rejected by the conviction which the comparison of our conduct with that of others may in time produce. But this invisible riot of the mind, this secret prodigality of being, is secure from detection, and fearless of reproach. The dreamer retires to his apartments, shuts out the cares and interruptions of mankind, and abandons himself to his own fancy; new worlds rise up before him, one image is followed by another, and a long succession of delights dances round him. He is at last called back to life by nature, or by custom, and enters peevish into society, because he cannot model it to his own will. He returns from his idle excursions with the asperity, though not with the knowledge of a student, and hastens again to the same felicity with the eagerness of a man bent upon the advancement of some favourite science.

* Rousseauistic type of reverie.

The infatuation strengthens by degrees, and, like the poison / of opiates, weakens his powers, without any external symptom | of malignity.

It happens, indeed, that these hypocrites of learning are in time detected, and convinced by disgrace and disappointment of the difference between the labour of thought, and the sport of musing. But this discovery is often not made till it is too late to recover the time that has been fooled away. A thousand accidents may, indeed, awaken drones to a more early sense of their danger and their shame. But they who are convinced of the necessity of breaking from this habitual drowsiness, too often relapse in spite of their resolution ; for these ideal seducers are always near, and neither any particularity of time nor place is necessary to their influence ; they invade the soul without warning, and have often charmed down resistance before their approach is perceived or suspected.

This captivity, however, it is necessary for every man to break, who has any desire to be wise or useful, to pass his life with the esteem of others, or to look back with satisfaction from his old age upon his earlier years. In order to regain liberty, he must find the means of flying from himself; he must, in opposition to the Stoick precept, teach his desires to fix upon external things ; he must adopt the joys and the pains of others, and excite in his mind the want of social pleasures and amicable communication.

It is, perhaps, not impossible to promote the cure of this mental malady, by close application to some new study, which may pour in fresh ideas, and keep curiosity in perpetual motion. But study requires solitude, and solitude is a state dangerous to those who are too much accustomed to sink into themselves. Active employment or publick pleasure is generally a necessary part of this intellectual regimen, without which, though some remission may be obtained, a complete cure will scarcely be effected.

This is a formidable and obstinate disease of the intellect, of which, when it has once become radicated by time, the remedy is one of the hardest tasks of reason and of virtue. Its slightest attacks, therefore, should be watchfully opposed; and he that finds the frigid and narcotick infection beginning to seize him, should turn his whole attention against it, and check it at the first discovery by proper counteraction.

The great resolution to be formed, when happiness and virtue are thus formidably invaded, is, that no part of life be spent in a state of neutrality or indifference; but that some pleasure be found for every moment that is not devoted to labour; and that, whenever the necessary business of life grows irksome or disgusting, an immediate transition be made to diversion and gaiety.

After the exercises which the health of the body requires, and which have themselves a natural tendency to actuate and invigorate the mind, the most eligible amusement of a rational being seems to be that interchange of thoughts which is practised in free and easy conversation; where suspicion is banished by experience, and emulation by benevolence; where every man speaks with no other restraint than unwillingness to offend, and hears with no other disposition than desire to be pleased.

There must be a time in which every man trifles; and the only choice that nature offers us, is, to trifle in company or alone. To join profit with pleasure, has been an old precept among men who have had very different conceptions of profit. All have agreed that our amusements should not terminate wholly in the present moment, but contribute more or less to future advantage. He that

[✱ Add ᴋ abrʒ ✱ 1.]

amuses himself among well chosen companions, can scarcely fail to receive, from the most careless and obstreperous merriment which virtue can allow, some useful hints ; nor can converse on the most familiar topicks, without some casual information. The loose sparkles of thoughtless wit may give new light to the mind, and the gay contention for paradoxical positions rectify the opinions.

This is the time in which those friendships that give happiness or consolation, relief or security, are generally formed. A wise and good man is never so amiable as in his unbended and familiar intervals. Heroick generosity, or philosophical discoveries, may compel veneration and respect, but love always implies some kind of natural or voluntary equality, and is only to be excited by that levity and cheerfulness which disencumber all minds from awe and solitude, invite the modest to freedom, and exalt the timorous to confidence. This easy gaiety is certain to please, whatever be the character of him that exerts it ; if our superiors descend from their elevation, we love them for lessening the distance at which we are placed below them ; and inferiors, from whom we can receive no lasting advantage, will always keep our affections while their sprightliness and mirth contribute to our pleasure.

Every man finds himself differently affected by the sight of fortresses of war, and palaces of pleasure ; we look on the height and strength of the bulwarks with a kind of gloomy satisfaction, for we cannot think of defence without admitting images of danger ; but we range delighted and jocund through the gay apartments of the palace, because nothing is impressed by them on the mind but joy and festivity. Such is the difference between great and amiable characters ; with protectors we are safe, with companions we are happy.

[* Boswell.]

Saturday, March 9, 1751.

" *Ipsa quoque assiduo labuntur tempora motu*
 Non secus ac flumen : neque enim consistere flumen,
 Nec levis hora potest ; sed ut unda impellitur undâ,
 Urgeturque prior veniente, urgetque priorem,
 Tempora sic fugiunt pariter, pariterque sequuntur."

OVID.

" With constant motion as the moments glide,
 Behold in running life the rolling tide !
 For none can stem by art, or stop by pow'r,
 The flowing ocean, or the fleeting hour :
 But wave by wave pursu'd arrives on shore,
 And each impell'd behind impels before :
 So time on time revolving we descry ;
 So minutes follow, and so minutes fly."

ELPHINSTON.

" LIFE," says Seneca, "is a voyage, in the progress "of which we are perpetually changing our scenes : "we first leave childhood behind us, then youth, then "the years of ripened manhood, then the better and more "pleasing part of old age." The perusal of this passage having incited in me a train of reflections on the state of man, the incessant fluctuation of his wishes, the gradual change of his disposition to all external objects, and the thoughtlessness with which he floats along the stream of time, I sunk into a slumber amidst my meditations, and, on a sudden, found my ears filled with the tumult of labour, the shouts of alacrity, the shrieks of alarm, the whistle of winds, and the dash of waters.

My astonishment for a time repressed my curiosity; but soon recovering myself so far as to inquire whither we were going, and what was the cause of such clamour and confusion, I was told that we were launching out into the *ocean of life ;* that we had already passed the streights of infancy, in which multitudes had perished, some by the weakness and fragility of their vessels, and more by the folly, perverseness, or negligence, of those who undertook to steer them; and that we were now on the main sea, abandoned to the winds and billows, without any other means of security than the care of the pilot, whom it was always in our power to choose among great numbers that offered their direction and assistance.

I then looked round with anxious eagerness; and first turning my eyes behind me, saw a stream flowing through flowery islands, which every one that sailed along seemed to behold with pleasure; but no sooner touched, than the current, which, though not noisy or turbulent, was yet irresistible, bore him away. Beyond these islands all was darkness, nor could any of the passengers describe the shore at which he first embarked.

Before me, and on each side, was an expanse of waters violently agitated, and covered with so thick a mist, that the most perspicacious eye could see but a little way. It appeared to be full of rocks and whirlpools, for many sunk unexpectedly while they were courting the gale with full sails, and insulting those whom they had left behind. So numerous, indeed, were the dangers, and so thick the darkness, that no caution could confer security. Yet there were many, who, by false intelligence, betrayed their followers into whirlpools, or by violence pushed those whom they found in their way against the rocks.

The current was invariable and insurmountable ; but

though it was impossible to sail against it, or to return to the place that was once passed, yet it was not so violent as to allow no opportunities for dexterity or courage, since, though none could retreat back from danger, yet they might often avoid it by oblique direction.

It was, however, not very common to steer with much care or prudence; for by some universal infatuation, every man appeared to think himself safe, though he saw his consorts every moment sinking around him; and no sooner had the waves closed over them, than their fate and their misconduct were forgotten; the voyage was pursued with the same jocund confidence; every man congratulated himself upon the soundness of his vessel, and believed himself able to stem the whirlpool in which his friend was swallowed, or glide over the rocks on which he was dashed: nor was it often observed that the sight of a wreck made any man change his course: if he turned aside for a moment, he soon forgot the rudder, and left himself again to the disposal of chance.

This negligence did not proceed from indifference, or from weariness of their present condition; for not one of those who thus rushed upon destruction, failed, when he was sinking, to call loudly upon his associates for that help which could not now be given him; and many spent their last moments in cautioning others against the folly by which they were intercepted in the midst of their course. Their benevolence was sometimes praised, but their admonitions were unregarded.

The vessels in which we had embarked being confessedly unequal to the turbulence of the stream of life, were visibly impaired in the course of the voyage; so that every passenger was certain, that how long soever he might, by favourable accidents, or by incessant vigilance, be preserved, he must sink at last.

This necessity of perishing might have been expected to sadden the gay, and intimidate the daring, at least to keep the melancholy and timorous in perpetual torments, and hinder them from any enjoyments of the varieties and gratifications which nature offered them as the solace of their labours : yet, in effect, none seemed less to expect destruction than those to whom it was most dreadful; they all had the art of concealing their danger from themselves ; and those who knew their inability to bear the sight of the terrours that embarrassed their way, took care never to look forward, but found some amusement for the present moment, and generally entertained themselves by playing with HOPE, who was the constant associate of the voyage of life.

Yet all that HOPE ventured to promise, even to those whom she favoured most, was, not that they should escape, but that they should sink last ; and with this promise every one was satisfied, though he laughed at the rest for seeming to believe it. HOPE, indeed, apparently mocked the credulity of her companions; for, in proportion as their vessels grew leaky, she redoubled her assurance of safety ; and none were more busy in making provisions for a long voyage, than they whom all but themselves saw likely to perish soon by irreparable decay.

In the midst of the current of life was the *gulph of* INTEMPERANCE, a dreadful whirlpool, interspersed with rocks, of which the pointed crags were concealed under water, and the tops covered with herbage, on which EASE spread couches of repose, and with shades, where PLEASURE warbled the song of invitation. Within sight of these rocks all who sailed on the ocean of life must necessarily pass.

9

REASON, indeed, was always at hand to steer the passengers through a narrow outlet by which they might escape ; but very few could, by her entreaties or remonstrances, be induced to put the rudder into her hand, without stipulating that she should approach so near unto the rocks of PLEASURE, that they might solace themselves with a short enjoyment of that delicious region, after which they always determined to pursue their course without any other deviation.

REASON was too often prevailed upon so far by these promises, as to venture her charge within the eddy of the gulph of INTEMPERANCE, where, indeed, the circumvolution was weak, but yet interrupted the course of the vessel, and drew it, by insensible rotations, towards the centre. She then repented her temerity, and with all her force endeavoured to retreat ; but the draught of the gulph was generally too strong to be overcome ; and the passenger, having danced in circles with a pleasing and giddy velocity, was at last overwhelmed and lost. Those few whom REASON was able to extricate, generally suffered so many shocks upon the points which shot out from the rocks of PLEASURE, that they were unable to continue their course with the same strength and facility as before, but floated along timorously and feebly, endangered by every breeze, and shattered by every ruffle of the water, till they sunk, by slow degrees, after long struggles, and innumerable expedients, always repining at their own folly, and warning others against the first approach of the gulph of INTEMPERANCE.

There were artists who professed to repair the breaches and stop the leaks of the vessels which had been shattered on the rocks of PLEASURE. Many appeared to have great confidence in their skill, and some, indeed, were preserved by it from sinking, who had received only a single blow; but I remarked that few vessels lasted long which had been much repaired, nor was it found that the artists themselves continued afloat longer than those who had least of their assistance.

The only advantage which, in the voyage of life, the cautious had above the negligent, was, that they sunk later, and more suddenly; for they passed forward till they had sometimes seen all those in whose company they had issued from the streights of infancy, perish in the way, and at last were overset by a cross breeze, without the toil of resistance, or the anguish of expectation. But such as had often fallen against the rocks of PLEASURE, commonly subsided by sensible degrees, contended long with the encroaching waters, and harassed themselves by labours that scarce HOPE herself could flatter with success.

As I was looking upon the various fate of the multitude about me, I was suddenly alarmed with an admonition from some unknown Power, "Gaze not idly upon others when "thou thyself art sinking. Whence is this thoughtless "tranquillity, when thou and they are equally endangered?" I looked, and seeing the gulph of INTEMPERANCE before me, started and awaked.

Saturday, March 30, 1751.

"——*Sapere aude,*
Incipe.   Vivendi rectè qui prorogat horam,
Rusticus expectat dum defluat amnis. at ille
Labitur, & labetur in omne volubilis ævum."   HOR.

" Begin, be bold, and venture to be wise;
He who defers his work from day to day,
Does on a river's bank expecting stay,
Till the whole stream, which stopp'd him, should be gone,
That runs, and as it runs, for ever will run on."   COWLEY.

A N ancient poet, unreasonably discontented at the present
state of things, which his system of opinions obliged
him to represent in its worst form, has observed of the earth,
" that its greater part is covered by the uninhabitable ocean;
" that of the rest some is encumbered with naked mountains,
" and some lost under barren sands; some scorched with
" unintermitted heat, and some petrified with perpetual
" frost; so that only a few regions remain for the production
" of fruits, and the pasture of cattle, and the accommodation
" of man."

The same observation may be transferred to the time
allotted us in our present state. When we have deducted
all that is absorbed in sleep, all that is inevitably appropriated to the demands of nature, or irresistibly engrossed
by the tyranny of custom; all that passes in regulating the
superficial decorations of life, or is given up in the recipro-
cations of civility to the disposal of others; all that is torn
from us by the violence of disease, or stolen imperceptibly
away by lassitude and languor; we shall find that part of our

duration very small of which we can truly call ourselves masters, or which we can spend wholly at our own choice. Many of our hours are lost in a rotation of petty cares, in a constant recurrence of the same employments; many of our provisions for ease or happiness are always exhausted by the present day; and a great part of our existence serves no other purpose, than that of enabling us to enjoy the rest.

Of the few moments which are left in our disposal, it may reasonably be expected, that we should be so frugal, as to let none of them slip from us without some equivalent: and perhaps it might be found, that as the earth, however straitened by rocks and waters, is capable of producing more than all its inhabitants are able to consume, our lives, though much contracted by incidental distraction, would yet afford us a large space vacant to the exercise of reason and virtue; that we want not time, but diligence, for great performances; and that we squander much of our allowance, even while we think it sparing and insufficient.

This natural and necessary comminution of our lives, perhaps, often makes us insensible of the negligence with which we suffer them to slide away. We never consider ourselves as possessed at once of time sufficient for any great design, and therefore indulge ourselves in fortuitous amusements. We think it unnecessary to take an account of a few supernumerary moments, which, however employed, could have produced little advantage, and which were exposed to a thousand chances of disturbance and interruption.

It is observable that, either by nature or by habit, our faculties are fitted to images of a certain extent, to which we adjust great things by division, and little things by accumulation. Of extensive surfaces we can only take a survey, as the parts succeed one another; and atoms we cannot

perceive till they are united into masses.   Thus we break
the vast periods of time into centuries and years ; and
thus, if we would know the amount of moments, we must
agglomerate them into days and weeks.

The proverbial oracles of our parsimonious ancestors have
informed us, that the fatal waste of fortune is by small
expenses, by the profusion of sums too little singly to alarm
our caution, and which we never suffer ourselves to consider together.   Of the same kind is the prodigality of life ;
he that hopes to look back hereafter with satisfaction upon
past years, must learn to know the present value of single
minutes, and endeavour to let no particle of time fall useless
to the ground.

It is usual for those who are advised to the attainment of
any new qualification, to look upon themselves as required
to change the general course of their conduct, to dismiss
business, and exclude pleasure, and to devote their days
and nights to a particular attention.   But all common
degrees of excellence are attainable at a lower price ; he
that should steadily and resolutely assign to any science
or language those interstitial vacancies which intervene in
the most crowded variety of diversion or employment, would
find every day new irradiations of knowledge, and discover
how much more is to be hoped from frequency and
perseverance, than from violent efforts and sudden desires ;
efforts which are soon remitted when they encounter
difficulty, and desires, which, if they are indulged too often,
will shake off the authority of reason, and range capriciously
from one object to another.

The disposition to defer every important design to a time
of leisure, and a state of settled uniformity, proceeds
generally from a false estimate of the human powers.   If we
except those gigantick and stupendous intelligences who are

said to grasp a system by intuition, and bound forward from one series of conclusions to another, without regular steps through intermediate propositions, the most successful students make their advances in knowledge by short flights, between each of which the mind may lie at rest. For every single act of progression a short time is sufficient ; and it is only necessary, that whenever that time is afforded, it be well employed.

Few minds will be long confined to severe and laborious meditation ; and when a successful attack on knowledge has been made, the student recreates himself with the contemplation of his conquest, and forbears another incursion, till the new-acquired truth has become familiar, and his curiosity calls upon him for fresh gratifications. Whether the time of intermission is spent in company, or in solitude, in necessary business, or in voluntary levities, the understanding is equally abstracted from the object of inquiry ; but perhaps, if it be detained by occupations less pleasing, it returns again to study with greater alacrity, than when it is glutted with ideal pleasures, and surfeited with intemperance of application. He that will not suffer himself to be discouraged by fancied impossibilities, may sometimes find his abilities invigorated by the necessity of exerting them in short intervals, as the force of a current is increased by the contraction of its channel.

From some cause like this it has probably proceeded, that among those who have contributed to the advancement of learning, many have risen to eminence in opposition to all the obstacles which external circumstances could place in their way, amidst the tumult of business, the distresses of poverty, or the dissipations of a wandering and unsettled state. A great part of the life of Erasmus was one con-tinual peregrination ; ill supplied with the gifts of fortune, and led from city to city, and from kingdom to kingdom, by the hopes of patrons and preferment, hopes which always flattered and always deceived him ; he yet found means, by unshaken constancy, and a vigilant improvement of those hours, which, in the midst of the most restless activity, will remain unengaged, to write more than another in the same condition would have hoped to read.   Compelled by want to attendance and solicitation, and so much versed in common life, that he has transmitted to us the most perfect delineation of the manners of his age, he joined to his knowledge of the world, such application to books, that he will stand for ever in the first rank of literary heroes.   How this proficiency was obtained he sufficiently discovers, by informing us, that the *Praise of Folly*, one of his most celebrated performances, was composed by him on the road to Italy ; *ne totum illud tempus quo equo fuit insidendum, illiteratis fabulis terreretur,* lest the hours which he was obliged to spend on horseback should be tattled away without regard to literature.

An Italian philosopher expressed in his motto, that *time was his estate;* an estate indeed, which will produce nothing without cultivation, but will always abundantly repay the labours of industry, and satisfy the most extensive desires, if no part of it be suffered to lie waste by negligence, to be overrun with noxious plants, or laid out for show rather than for use.

Tuesday, April 30, 1751.

"Ὄσσαν ἐπ' Οὐλύμπῳ μέμασαν θέμεν αὐτὰζ ἐπ' Ὄσσῃ,
Πήλιον εἰνοσιφυλλον, ἴν ἀρανὸς ἀμβατὸς εἴη." HOM.

"The gods they challenge, and affect the skies :
Heav'd on Olympus tott'ring Ossa stood ;
On Ossa, Pelion nods with all his wood." POPE.

TO THE RAMBLER.

SIR,

NOTHING has more retarded the advancement of learning than the disposition of vulgar minds to ridicule and vilify what they cannot comprehend. All industry must be excited by hope ; and as the student often proposes no other reward to himself than praise, he is easily discouraged by contempt and insult. He who brings with him into a clamorous multitude the timidity of recluse speculation, and has never hardened his front in publick life, or accustomed his passions to the vicissitudes and accidents, the triumphs and defeats of mixed conversation, will blush at the stare of petulant incredulity, and suffer himself to be driven by a burst of laughter, from the fortresses of demonstration. The mechanist will be afraid to assert before hardy contradiction, the possibility of tearing down bulwarks with a silkworm's thread ; and the astronomer of relating the rapidity of light, the distance of the fixed stars, and the height of the lunar mountains.

If I could by any efforts have shaken off this cowardice, I had not sheltered myself under a borrowed name, nor applied to you for the means of communicating to the

publick the theory of a garret; a subject which, except
some slight and transient strictures, has been hitherto
neglected by those who were best qualified to adorn it,
either for want of leisure to prosecute the various researches
in which a nice discussion must engage them, or because it
requires such diversity of knowledge, and such extent of
curiosity, as is scarcely to be found in any single intellect;
or perhaps others foresaw the tumults which would be
raised against them, and confined their knowledge to their
own breasts, and abandoned prejudice and folly to the
direction of chance.

That the professors of literature generally reside in the
highest stories, has been immemorially observed.* The
wisdom of the ancients was well acquainted with the
intellectual advantages of an elevated situation: why else
were the Muses stationed on Olympus, or Parnassus, by
those who could with equal right have raised them bowers
in the vale of Tempe, or erected their altars among the
flexures of Meander? Why was Jove himself nursed upon
a mountain? or why did the goddesses, when the prize of
beauty was contested, try the cause upon the top of Ida?
Such were the fictions by which the great masters of the
earlier ages endeavoured to inculcate to posterity the
importance of a garret, which, though they had been long
obscured by the negligence and ignorance of succeeding
times, were well enforced by the celebrated symbol of
Pythagoras, ἀνεμῶν ὠνεόντων τὴν ἠχω προσκύνει; "when the
"wind blows, worship its echo." This could not but be
understood by his disciples as an inviolable injunction to
live in a garret, which I have found frequently visited by the
echo and the wind. Nor was the tradition wholly obliterated

* Note XI., Appendix.

in the age of Augustus, for Tibullus evidently congratulates himself upon his garret, not without some allusion to the Pythagorean precept :

> " *Quàm juvat immites ventos audire cubantem——*
> *Aut, gelidas hybernus aquas cùm fuderit auster,*
> *Securum somnos, imbre juvante, sequi !* "

> " How sweet in sleep to pass the careless hours,
> Lull'd by the beating winds and dashing show'rs !

And it is impossible not to discover the fondness of Lucretius, an earlier writer, for a garret, in his description of the lofty towers of serene learning, and of the pleasure with which a wise man looks down upon the confused and erratick state of the world moving below him :

> " *Sed nil dulcius est, bene quàm munita tenere*
> *Editâ doctrinâ sapientum templa serena;*
> *Despicere unde queas alios, passimque videre*
> *Errare, atque viam palanteis quærere vitæ.*"

> "———'Tis sweet thy lab'ring steps to guide
> To virtue's heights, with wisdom well supply'd,
> And all the magazines of learning fortify'd :
> From thence to look below on human kind,
> Bewilder'd in the maze of life, and blind." DRYDEN.

The institution has, indeed, continued to our own time; the garret is still the usual receptacle of the philosopher and poet; but this, like many ancient customs, is perpetuated only by an accidental imitation, without knowledge of the original reason for which it was established :

> " *Causa latet : res est notissima.*"

> " The cause is secret, but th' effect is known." ADDISON.

Conjectures have, indeed, been advanced concerning these habitations of literature, but without much satisfaction to the judicious inquirer. Some have imagined, that the garret is generally chosen by the wits as most easily rented; and concluded that no man rejoices in his aërial abode, but on the days of payment. Others suspect, that a garret is chiefly convenient, as it is remoter than any other part of the house from the outer door, which is often observed to be infested by visitants, who talk incessantly of beer, or linen, or a coat, and repeat the same sounds every morning, and sometimes again in the afternoon, without any variation, except that they grow daily more importunate and clamorous, and raise their voices in time from mournful murmurs to raging vociferations. This eternal monotony is always detestable to a man whose chief pleasure is to enlarge his knowledge, and vary his ideas. Others talk of freedom from noise, and abstraction from common business or amusements; and some, yet more visionary, tell us, that the faculties are enlarged by open prospects, and that the fancy is more at liberty, when the eye ranges without confinement.

These conveniencies may perhaps all be found in a well-chosen garret; but surely they cannot be supposed sufficiently important to have operated unvariably upon different climates, distant ages, and separate nations. Of an universal practice, there must still be presumed an universal cause, which, however recondite and abstruse, may be perhaps reserved to make me illustrious by its discovery, and you by its promulgation.

It is universally known that the faculties of the mind are invigorated or weakened by the state of the body, and that the body is in a great measure regulated by the various compressions of the ambient element. The effects of the air in the production or cure of corporeal maladies have been acknowledged from the time of Hippocrates; but no man has yet sufficiently considered how far it may influence the operations of the genius, though every day affords instances of local understanding, of wits and reasoners, whose faculties are adapted to some single spot, and who, when they are removed to any other place, sink at once into silence and stupidity. I have discovered, by a long series of observations, that invention and elocution suffer great impediments from dense and impure vapours, and that the tenuity of a defecated air at a proper distance from the surface of the earth, accelerates the fancy, and sets at liberty those intellectual powers which were before shackled by too strong attraction, and unable to expand themselves under the pressure of a gross atmosphere. I have found dulness to quicken into sentiment in a thin ether, as water, though not very hot, boils in a receiver partly exhausted; and heads, in appearance empty, have teemed with notions upon rising ground, as the flaccid sides of a football would have swelled out into stiffness and extension.

For this reason I never think myself qualified to judge decisively of any man's faculties, whom I have only known in one degree of elevation; but take some opportunity of attending him from the cellar to the garret, and try upon him all the various degrees of rarefaction and condensation, tension and laxity. If he is neither vivacious aloft, nor serious below, I then consider him as hopeless; but as it seldom happens, that I do not find the temper to which the texture of his brain is fitted, I acccommodate him in time with a tube of mercury, first marking the points most favourable to his intellects, according to rules which I have long studied, and which I may, perhaps, reveal to mankind in a complete treatise of barometrical pneumatology.

Another cause of the gaiety and sprightliness of the dwellers in garrets is probably the increase of that vertiginous motion, with which we are carried round by the diurnal revolution of the earth. The power of agitation upon the spirits is well known ; every man has felt his heart lightened in a rapid vehicle, or on a galloping horse ; and nothing is plainer, than that he who towers to the fifth storey, is whirled through more space by every circum-rotation, than another that grovels upon the ground-floor. The nations between the tropicks are known to be fiery, inconstant, inventive, and fanciful ; because, living at the utmost length of the earth's diameter, they are carried about with more swiftness that those whom nature has placed nearer to the poles ; and therefore, as it becomes a wise man to struggle with the inconveniencies of his country, when-ever celerity and acuteness are requisite, we must actuate our languor by taking a few turns round the centre in a garret.

If you imagine that I ascribe to air and motion effects which they cannot produce, I desire you to consult your own memory, and consider whether you have never known a man acquire reputation in his garret, which, when fortune or a patron had placed him upon the first floor, he was unable to maintain ; and who never recovered his former vigour of understanding, till he was restored to his original situation. That a garret will make every man a wit, I am very far from supposing ; I know there are some who would continue blockheads even on the summit of the Andes, or on the peak of Teneriffe. But let not any man be considered as unimproveable till this potent remedy has been tried ; for perhaps he was formed to be great only in a garret, as the joiner of Aretæus was rational in no other place but his own shop.

I think a frequent removal to various distances from the centre, so necessary to a just estimate of intellectual abilities, and consequently of so great use in education, that if I hoped that the publick could be persuaded to so extensive an experiment, I would propose, that there should be a cavern dug, and a tower erected, like those which Bacon describes in Solomon's house, for the expansion and concentration of understanding, according to the exigence of different employments, or constitutions. Perhaps some that fume away in meditations upon time and space in the tower, might compose tables of interest at a certain depth ; and he that upon level ground stagnates in silence, or creeps in narrative, might, at the height of half a mile, ferment into merriment, sparkle with repartee, and froth with declamation.

Addison observes, that we may find the heat of Virgil's climate in some lines of his Georgick : so, when I read a composition, I immediately determine the height of the author's habitation.   As an elaborate performance is commonly said to smell of the lamp, my commendation for a noble thought, a sprightly sally, or a bold figure, is to pronounce it fresh from the garret ; an expression which would break from me upon the perusal of most of your papers, did I not believe, that you sometimes quit the garret, and ascend into the cock-loft.*

Hypertatus.

* Note XII., Appendix.

Tuesday, June 4, 1751.

" *Cœpisti melius quàm desinis: ultima primis*
   Cedunt: dissimiles hic vir, et ille puer."   OVID.

" Succeeding years thy early fame destroy ;
  Thou, who began'st a man, wilt end a boy."

POLITIAN, a name eminent among the restorers of
polite literature, when he published a collection of
epigrams, prefixed to many of them the year of his age at
which they were composed.   He might design by this
information, either to boast the early maturity of his genius,
or to conciliate indulgence to the puerility of his performances.   But, whatever was his intent, it is remarked by
Scaliger, that he very little promoted his own reputation,
because he fell below the promise which his first productions
had given, and in the latter part of his life seldom equalled
the sallies of his youth.

It is not uncommon for those who, at their first entrance
into the world, were distinguished for attainments or
abilities, to disappoint the hopes which they had raised, and
to end in neglect and obscurity that life which they began
in celebrity and honour.   To the long catalogue of the
inconveniencies of old age, which moral and satirical writers
have so copiously displayed, may be often added the loss of
fame.

The advance of the human mind towards any object of
laudable pursuit, may be compared to the progress of a
body driven by a blow.   It moves for a time with great
velocity and vigour, but the force of the first impulse is

perpetually decreasing, and, though it should encounter no obstacle capable of quelling it by a sudden stop, the resistance of the medium through which it passes, and the latent inequalities of the smoothest surface, will in a short time, by continued retardation, wholly overpower it. Some hindrances will be found in every road of life, but he that fixes his eyes upon any thing at a distance, necessarily loses sight of all that fills up the intermediate space, and therefore sets forward with alacrity and confidence, nor suspects a thousand obstacles by which he afterwards finds his passage embarrassed and obstructed. Some are indeed stopt at once in their career by a sudden shock of calamity, or diverted to a different direction by the cross impulse of some violent passion; but far the greater part languish by slow degrees, deviate at first into slight obliquities, and themselves scarcely perceive at what time their ardour forsook them, or when they lost sight of their original design.

Weariness and negligence are perpetually prevailing by silent encroachments, assisted by different causes, and not observed till they cannot, without great difficulty, be opposed. Labour necessarily requires pauses of ease and relaxation, and the deliciousness of ease commonly makes us unwilling to return to labour. We, perhaps, prevail upon ourselves to renew our attempts, but eagerly listen to every argument for frequent interpositions of amusement; for, when indolence has once entered upon the mind, it can scarcely be dispossessed but by such efforts as very few are willing to exert.

It is the fate of industry to be equally endangered by miscarriage and success, by confidence and despondency. He that engages in a great undertaking, with a false opinion of its facility, or too high conceptions of his own strength, is easily discouraged by the first hindrance of his advances, because he had promised himself an equal and perpetual progression without impediment or disturbance; when unexpected interruptions break in upon him, he is in the state of a man surprised by a tempest, where he purposed only to bask in the calm, or sport in the shallows.

It is not only common to find the difficulty of an enterprize greater, but the profit less, than hope had pictured it. Youth enters the world with very happy prejudices in her own favour. She imagines herself not only certain of accomplishing every adventure, but of obtaining those rewards which the accomplishment may deserve. She is not easily persuaded to believe that the force of merit can be resisted by obstinacy and avarice, or its lustre darkened by envy and malignity. She has not yet learned that the most evident claims to praise or preferment may be rejected by malice against conviction, or by indolence without examination; that they may be sometimes defeated by artifices, and sometimes overborne by clamour; that, in the mingled numbers of mankind, many need no other provocation to enmity than that they find themselves excelled; that others have ceased their curiosity, and consider every man who fills the mouth of report with a new name, as an intruder upon their retreat, and disturber of their repose; that some are engaged in complications of interest which they imagine endangered by every innovation; that many yield themselves up implicitly to every report which hatred disseminates or folly scatters; and that whoever aspires to the notice of the publick, has in almost every man an enemy and a rival; and must struggle with the opposition of the daring, and elude the stratagems of the timorous, must quicken the frigid and soften the obdurate, must reclaim perverseness and inform stupidity.

It is no wonder that when the prospect of reward has

vanished, the zeal of enterprise should cease; for who would persevere to cultivate the soil which he has, after long labour, discovered to be barren? He who hath pleased himself with anticipated praises, and expected that he should meet in every place with patronage or friendship, will soon remit his vigour, when he finds that, from those who desire to be considered as his admirers, nothing can be hoped but cold civility, and that many refuse to own his excellence, lest they should be too justly expected to reward it.

A man, thus cut off from the prospect of that port to which his address and fortitude had been employed to steer him, often abandons himself to chance and to the wind, and glides careless and idle down the current of life, without resolution to make another effort, till he is swallowed up by the gulph of mortality.

Others are betrayed to the same desertion of themselves by a contrary fallacy. It was said of Hannibal, that he wanted nothing to the completion of his martial virtues, but that when he had gained a victory he should know how to use it. The folly of desisting too soon from successful labours, and the haste of enjoying advantages before they are secured, are often fatal to men of impetous desire, to men whose consciousness of uncommon powers fills them with presumption, and who, having borne opposition down before them, and left emulation panting behind, are early persuaded to imagine that they have reached the heights of perfection, and that now, being no longer in danger from competitors, they may pass the rest of their days in the enjoyment of their acquisitions, in contemplation of their own superiority, and in attention to their own praises, and look unconcerned from their eminence upon the toils and contentions of meaner beings.

It is not sufficiently considered in the hour of exultation, that all human excellence is comparative ; that no man performs much but in proportion to what others accomplish, or to the time and opportunities which have been allowed him ; and that he who stops at any point of excellence is every day sinking in estimation, because his improvement grows continually more incommensurate to his life. Yet, as no man willingly quits opinions favourable to himself, they who have been once justly celebrated, imagine that they still have the same pretensions to regard, and seldom perceive the diminution of their character while there is time to recover it. Nothing then remains but murmurs and remorse ; for if the spendthrift's poverty be embittered by the reflection that he once was rich, how must the idler's obscurity be clouded by the remembering that he once had lustre !

These errors all arise from an original mistake of the true motives of action. He that never extends his view beyond the praises or rewards of men, will be dejected by neglect and envy, or infatuated by honours and applause. But the consideration that life is only deposited in his hands to be employed in obedience to a Master who will regard his endeavours, not his success, would have preserved him from trivial elations and discouragements, and enabled him to proceed with constancy and cheerfulness, neither enervated by commendation, nor intimidated by censure.

Tuesday, July 9, 1751.

" Dum vitant stulti vitia, in contraria currunt." HOR.

" —— Whilst fools one vice condemn,
They run into the opposite extreme." CREECH.

THAT wonder is the effect of ignorance, has been often
observed. The awful stillness of attention, with which
the mind is overspread at the first view of an unexpected
effect, ceases when we have leisure to disentangle complications and investigate causes. Wonder is a pause of
reason, a sudden cessation of the mental progress, which
lasts only while the understanding is fixed upon some single
idea, and is at an end when it recovers force enough to
divide the object into its parts, or mark the intermediate
gradations from the first agent to the last consequence.

It may be remarked with equal truth, that ignorance is
often the effect of wonder. It is common for those who
have never accustomed themselves to the labour of inquiry,
nor invigorated their confidence by conquests over difficulty,
to sleep in the gloomy quiescence of astonishment, without
any effort to animate inquiry, or dispel obscurity. What
they cannot immediately conceive, they consider as too high
to be reached, or too extensive to be comprehended ; they
therefore content themselves with the gaze of folly, forbear
to attempt what they have no hopes of performing, and
resign the pleasure of rational contemplation to more
pertinacious study or more active faculties.

Among the productions of mechanick art, many are of a
form so different from that of their first materials, and many
consist of parts so numerous and so nicely adapted to each

other, that it is not possible to view them without amazement. But when we enter the shops of artificers, observe the various tools by which every operation is facilitated, and trace the progress of a manufacture through the different hands, that, in succession to each other, contribute to its perfection, we soon discover that every single man has an easy task, and that the extremes, however remote, of natural rudeness and artificial elegance, are joined by a regular concatenation of effects, of which every one is introduced by that which precedes it, and equally introduces that which is to follow.

The same is the state of intellectual and manual performances. Long calculations or complex diagrams affright the timorous and unexperienced from a second view; but if we have skill sufficient to analyze them into simple principles, it will be discovered that our fear was groundless. *Divide and conquer*, is a principle equally just in science as in policy. Complication is a species of confederacy which, while it continues united, bids defiance to the most active and vigorous intellect; but of which every member is separately weak, and which may therefore be quickly subdued, if it can once be broken.

The chief art of learning, as Locke has observed, is to attempt but little at a time. The widest excursions of the mind are made by short flights frequently repeated; the most lofty fabrics of science are formed by the continued accumulation of single propositions.

It often happens, whatever be the cause, that impatience of labour, or dread of miscarriage, seizes those who are most distinguished for quickness of apprehension; and that they who might with greatest reason promise themselves victory, are least willing to hazard the encounter. This diffidence,*

* Note XIII., Appendix.

where the attention is not laid asleep by laziness, or dissipated by pleasures, can arise only from confused and general views, such as negligence snatches in haste, or from the disappointment of the first hopes formed by arrogance without reflection. To expect that the intricacies of science will be pierced by a careless glance, or the eminences of fame ascended without labour, is to expect a particular privilege, a power denied to the rest of mankind; but to suppose that the maze is inscrutable to diligence, or the heights inaccessible to perseverance, is to submit tamely to the tyranny of fancy, and enchain the mind in voluntary shackles.

It is the proper ambition of the heroes in literature to enlarge the boundaries of knowledge by discovering and conquering new regions of the intellectual world. To the success of such undertakings, perhaps, some degree of fortuitous happiness is necessary, which no man can promise or procure to himself; and therefore doubt and irresolution may be forgiven in him that ventures into the unexplored abysses of truth, and attempts to find his way through the fluctuations of uncertainty, and the conflicts of contradiction. But when nothing more is required, than to pursue a path already beaten, and to trample obstacles which others have demolished, why should any man so much distrust his own intellect as to imagine himself unequal to the attempt?

It were to be wished that they who devote their lives to study would at once believe nothing too great for their attainment, and consider nothing as too little for their regard; that they would extend their notice alike to science and to life, and unite some knowledge of the present world to their acquaintance with past ages and remote events.

Nothing has so much exposed men of learning to

contempt and ridicule, as their ignorance of things which are known to all but themselves. Those who have been taught to consider the institutions of the schools, as giving the last perfection to human abilities, are surprised to see men wrinkled with study, yet wanting to be instructed in the minute circumstances of propriety, or the necessary forms of daily transaction; and quickly shake off their reverence for modes of education, which they find to produce no ability above the rest of mankind.

Books, says Bacon, *can never teach the use of books.* The student must learn by commerce with mankind to reduce his speculations to practice, and accommodate his knowledge to the purposes of life.

It is too common for those who have been bred to scholastick professions, and passed much of their time in academies where nothing but learning confers honours, to disregard every other qualification, and to imagine that they shall find mankind ready to pay homage to their knowledge, and to crowd about them for instruction. They therefore step out from their cells into the open world with all the confidence of authority and dignity of importance; they look round about them at once with ignorance and scorn on a race of beings to whom they are equally unknown and equally contemptible, but whose manners they must imitate, and with whose opinions they must comply, if they desire to pass their time happily among them.

To lessen that disdain with which scholars are inclined to look on the common business of the world, and the unwillingness with which they condescend to learn what is not to be found in any system of philosophy, it may be necessary to consider that, though admiration is excited by abstruse researches and remote discoveries, yet pleasure is not given, nor affection conciliated, but by softer accomplishments, and qualities more easily communicable to those about us. He that can only converse upon questions, about which only a small part of mankind has knowledge sufficient to make them curious, must lose his days in unsocial silence, and live in the crowd of life without a companion. He that can only be useful on great occasions, may die without exerting his abilities, and stand a helpless spectator of a thousand vexations which fret away happiness, and which nothing is required to remove but a little dexterity of conduct and readiness of expedients.

No degree of knowledge attainable by man is able to set him above the want of hourly assistance, or to extinguish the desire of fond endearments, and tender officiousness; and therefore, no one should think it unnecessary to learn those arts by which friendship may be gained. Kindness is preserved by a constant reciprocation of benefits or interchange of pleasures; but such benefits only can be bestowed, as others are capable to receive, and such pleasures only imparted, as others are qualified to enjoy.

By this descent from the pinnacles of art no honour will be lost; for the condescensions of learning are always overpaid by gratitude. An elevated genius employed in little things, appears, to use the simile of Longinus, like the sun in his evening declination, he remits his splendour but retains his magnitude, and pleases more though he dazzles less.

Tuesday, July 30, 1751.

" ——*Moveat cornicula risum*
  Furtivis nudata coloribus."——   Hor.

"Lest when the birds their various colours claim,
 Stripp'd of his stolen pride, the crow forlorn
 Should stand the laughter of the publick scorn." Francis.

AMONG the innumerable practices by which interest or
  envy have taught those who live upon literary fame
to disturb each other at their airy banquets, one of the most
common is the charge of plagiarism. When the excellence
of a new composition can no longer be contested, and
malice is compelled to give way to the unanimity of
applause, there is yet this one expedient to be tried, by
which the author may be degraded, though his work be
reverenced ; and the excellence which we cannot obscure,
may be set at such a distance as not to overpower our
fainter lustre.

This accusation is dangerous, because, even when it is
false, it may be sometimes urged with probability. Bruyere
declares that we are come into the world too late to produce any thing new, that nature and life are preoccupied,
and that description and sentiment have been long
exhausted. It is indeed certain, that whoever attempts any
common topick, will find unexpected coincidences of his
thoughts with those of other writers ; nor can the nicest
judgment always distinguish accidental similitude from artful imitation. There is likewise a common stock of images,

a settled mode of arrangement, and a beaten track of transition, which all authors suppose themselves at liberty to use, and which produce the resemblance generally observable among contemporaries. So that in books which best deserve the name of originals, there is little new beyond the disposition of materials already provided; the same ideas and combinations of ideas have been long in the possession of other hands; and, by restoring to every man his own, as the Romans must have returned to their cots from the possession of the world, so the most inventive and fertile genius would reduce his folios to a few pages. Yet the author who imitates his predecessors only by furnishing himself with thoughts and elegancies out of the same general magazine of literature, can with little more propriety be reproached as a plagiary, than the architect can be censured as a mean copier of Angelo or Wren, because he digs his marble from the same quarry, squares his stones by the same art, and unites them in columns of the same orders.

Many subjects fall under the consideration of an author, which, being limited by nature, can admit only of slight and accidental diversities. All definitions of the same thing must be nearly the same; and descriptions, which are definitions of a more lax and fanciful kind, must always have in some degree that resemblance to each other which they all have to their object. Different poets describing the spring or the sea would mention the zephyrs and the flowers, the billows and the rocks; reflecting on human life, they would, without any communication of opinions, lament the deceitfulness of hope, the fugacity of pleasure, the fragility of beauty, and the frequency of calamity; and for palliatives of these incurable miseries, they would concur in recommending kindness, temperance, caution, and fortitude.

When therefore there are found in Virgil and Horace two similar passages :

> " *Hæ tibi erunt artes——*
> *Parcere subjectis, et debellare superbos.*"——   VIRG.

> " To tame the proud, the fetter'd slave to free :
> These are imperial arts, and worthy thee." DRYDEN.

> " *Imperet bellante prior, jacentem*
> *Lenis in hostem.*"   HOR.

> " Let Cæsar spread his conquests far,
> Less pleas'd to triumph than to spare."

it is surely not necessary to suppose with a late critick, that one is copied from the other, since neither Virgil nor Horace can be supposed ignorant of the common duties of humanity, and the virtue of moderation in success.

Cicero and Ovid have on very different occasions remarked how little of the honour of a victory belongs to the general, when his soldiers and his fortune have made their deductions ; yet why should Ovid be suspected to have owed to Tully an observation which perhaps occurs to every man that sees or hears of military glories ?

Tully observes of Achilles, that had not Homer written, his valour had been without praise.

> " *Nisi Ilias illa extitisset, idem tumulus qui corpus ejus contexerat,*
> *nomen ejus obruisset.*"

> " Unless the Iliad had been published, his name had been lost in the tomb that covered his body."

Horace tells us with more energy that there were brave

men before the wars of Troy, but they were lost in oblivion for want of a poet:

> " *Vixere fortes ante Agamemnona*
> *Multi ; sed omnes illachrymabiles*
> *Urgentur, ignotique longâ*
> *Nocte, carent quia vate sacro.*"

> " Before great Agamemnon reign'd,
>   Reign'd kings as great as he, and brave,
> Whose huge ambition's now contain'd
>   In the small compass of a grave :
> In endless night they sleep, unwept, unknown:
> No bard had they to make all time their own."

FRANCIS.

Tully enquires, in the same oration, why, but for fame, we disturb a short life with so many fatigues?

> " *Quid est quod in hoc tam exiguo vitæ curriculo et tam brevi, tantis*
> *nos in laboribus exerceamus ?* "

> " Why in so small a circuit of life should we employ ourselves in so many fatigues? "

Horace enquires in the same manner,

> " *Quid brevi fortes jaculamur ævo*
> *Multa ?* "

> " Why do we aim, with eager strife,
>   At things beyond the mark of life?" FRANCIS.

when our life is of so short duration, why we form such numerous designs? But Horace, as well as Tully, might discover that records are needful to preserve the memory of actions, and that no records were so durable as poems ;

either of them might find out that life is short, and that we consume it in unnecessary labour.

There are other flowers of fiction so widely scattered and so easily cropped, that it is scarcely just to tax the use of them as an act by which any particular writer is despoiled of his garland ; for they may be said to have been planted by the ancients in the open road of poetry for the accommodation of their successors, and to be the right of every one that has art to pluck them without injuring their colours or their fragrance.   The passage of Orpheus to hell, with the recovery and second loss of Eurydice, have been described after Boetius by Pope, in such a manner as might justly leave him suspected of imitation, were not the images such as they might both have derived from more ancient writers.

> " *Quæ sontes agitant metu*
>   *Ultrices scelerum deæ*
>   *Jam mæstæ lacrymis madent,*
>   *Non Ixionium caput*
>   *Velox præcipitat rota.*"

> " The pow'rs of vengeance, while they hear,
>   Touch'd with compassion, drop a tear ;
>   Ixion's rapid wheel is bound,
>   Fix'd in attention to the sound."   F. LEWIS.

> " Thy stone, O Sysiphus, stands still,
>   Ixion rests upon his wheel,
>   And the pale spectres dance !
>   The furies sink upon their iron beds."

> " *Tandem, vicimur, arbiter*
>   *Umbrarum, miserans, ait——*
>   *Donemus, comitem viro,*
>   *Emtam carmine, conjugem.*"

" Subdu'd at length, Hell's pitying monarch cry'd,
    The song rewarding, let us yield the bride."

                                        F. LEWIS.

    " He sung, and hell consented
        To hear that poet's prayer ;
    Stern Proserpine relented,
        And gave him back the fair."

    " *Heu, noctis prope terminos*
    Orpheus Eurydicen suam
    Vidit, perdidit, occidit."

" Nor yet the golden verge of day begun,
    When Orpheus, her unhappy lord,
    Eurydice to life restor'd,
At once beheld, and lost, and was undone."

                                        F. LEWIS.

" But soon, too soon, the lover turns his eyes ;
    Again she falls, again she dies, she dies !"

No writer can be fully convicted of imitation, except there
is a concurrence of more resemblance than can be imagined
to have happened by chance ; as where the same ideas are
conjoined without any natural series or necessary coherence,
or where not only the thought but the words are copied.
Thus it can scarcely be doubted, that in the first of the
following passages Pope remembered Ovid, and that in the
second he copied Crashaw :

    " *Sæpe pater dixit, studium quid inutile tentas ?*
    Mæonides nullas ipse reliquit opes——
    Sponte suâ carmen numeros veniebat ad aptos,
    Et quod conabar scribere, versus erat."   OVID.

"Quit, quit this barren trade, my father cry'd ;
    Ev'n Homer left no riches when he dy'd——
    In verse spontaneous flow'd my native strain,
    Forc'd by no sweat or labour of the brain."   F. LEWIS.

"I left no calling for this idle trade ;
    No duty broke, no father disobey'd ;
    While yet a child, ere yet a fool to fame,
    I lisp'd in numbers, for the numbers came."   POPE.

"——This plain floor,
    Believe me, reader, can say more
    Than many a braver marble can,
    Here lies a truly honest man."   CRASHAW.

"This modest stone, what few vain marbles can,
    May truly say, Here lies an honest man."   POPE.

Conceits, or thoughts not immediately impressed by
sensible objects, or necessarily arising from the coalition or
comparison of common sentiments, may be with great
justice suspected whenever they are found a second time.
Thus Waller probably owed to Grotius an elegant compliment :

"Here lies the learned Savil's heir,
    So early wise, and lasting fair,
    That none, except her years they told,
    Thought her a child, or thought her old."   WALLER.

"*Unica lux sæcli, genitoris gloria, nemo*
    Quem puerum, nemo credidit esse senem."   GROTIUS.

"The age's miracle, his father's joy !
    Nor old you wou'd pronounce him, nor a boy."   F. LEWIS.

And Prior was indebted for a pretty illustration to
Alleyne's poetical history of Henry the Seventh.

"For nought but light itself, itself can shew,
    And only kings can write, what kings can do."   ALLEYNE.

> " Your musick's power, your musick must disclose,
> For what light is, 'tis only light that shews." PRIOR.

And with yet more certainty may the same writer be censured for endeavouring the clandestine appropriation of a thought which he borrowed, surely without thinking himself disgraced, from an epigram of Plato :

> " Τῇ Παφίῃ τὸ κάτοπτρον· ἐπεὶ τοίη μὲν ὁρᾶσθαι
> Οὐκ ἐθέλω, οἵη δ' ἦν πάρος, θ' δύναμαι."

> " Venus, take my votive glass,
> Since I am not what I was ;
> What from this day I shall be,
> Venus, let me never see."

As not every instance of similitude can be considered as a proof of imitation, so not every imitation ought to be stigamatized as plagiarism. The adoption of a noble sentiment, or the insertion of a borrowed ornament, may sometimes display so much judgment as will almost compensate for invention : and an inferior genius may, without any imputation of servility, pursue the path of the ancients, provided he declines to tread in their footsteps.

Tuesday, September 10, 1751.

" ——*Steriles transmisimus annos,*
  Hæc ævi mihi prima dies, hæc limina vitæ."
                                        STAT.

" ——Our barren years are past;
  Be this of life the first, of sloth the last."
                                    ELPHINSTON.

NO weakness of the human mind has more frequently incurred animadversion, than the negligence with which men overlook their own faults, however flagrant, and the easiness with which they pardon them, however frequently repeated.

It seems generally believed, that, as the eye cannot see itself, the mind has no faculties by which it can contemplate its own state, and that therefore we have not means of becoming acquainted with our real characters; an opinion which, like innumerable other postulates, an inquirer finds himself inclined to admit upon very little evidence, because it affords a ready solution of many difficulties. It will explain why the greatest abilities frequently fail to promote the happiness of those who possess them; why those who can distinguish with the utmost nicety the boundaries of vice and virtue, suffer them to be confounded in their own conduct; why the active and vigilant resign their affairs implicitly to the management of others; and why the cautious and fearful make hourly approaches towards ruin, without one sigh of solicitude or struggle for escape.

When a position teems thus with commodious consequences, who can without regret confess it to be false?
Yet it is certain that declaimers have indulged a disposition
to describe the dominion of the passions as extended
beyond the limits that nature assigned. Self-love is often
rather arrogant than blind : it does not hide our faults from
ourselves, but persuades us that they escape the notice of
others, and disposes us to resent censures lest we should
confess them to be just. We are secretly conscious of
defects and vices which we hope to conceal from the publick
eye, and please ourselves with innumerable impostures, by
which, in reality, nobody is deceived.

In proof of the dimness of our internal sight, or the
general inability of man to determine rightly concerning his
own character, it is common to urge the success of the most
absurd and incredible flattery, and the resentment always
raised by advice, however soft, benevolent, and reasonable.
But flattery, if its operation be nearly examined, will be
found to owe its acceptance, not to our ignorance but
knowledge of our failures, and to delight us rather as it
consoles our wants than displays our possessions. He that
shall solicit the favour of his patron by praising him for
qualities which he can find in himself, will be defeated by the
more daring panegyrist who enriches him with adscititious
excellence. Just praise is only a debt, but flattery is a
present. The acknowledgment of those virtues on which
conscience congratulates us, is a tribute that we can at any
time exact with confidence ; but the celebration of those
which we only feign, or desire without any vigorous
endeavours to attain them, is received as a confession of
sovereignty over regions never conquered, as a favourable
decision of disputable claims, and is more welcome as it is
more gratuitous.

Advice is offensive, not because it lays us open to unexpected regret, or convicts us of any fault which had escaped our notice, but because it shows us that we are known to others as well as to ourselves; and the officious monitor is persecuted with hatred, not because his accusation is false, but because he assumes that superiority which we are not willing to grant him, and has dared to detect what we desired to conceal.

For this reason advice is commonly ineffectual. If those who follow the call of their desires, without inquiry whither they are going, had deviated ignorantly from the paths of wisdom, and were rushing upon dangers unforeseen, they would readily listen to information that recalls them from their errors, and catch the first alarm by which destruction or infamy is denounced. Few that wander in the wrong way mistake it for the right; they only find it more smooth and flowery, and indulge their own choice rather than approve it: therefore few are persuaded to quit it by admonition or reproof, since it impresses no new conviction, nor confers any powers of action or resistance. He that is gravely informed how soon profusion will annihilate his fortune, hears with little advantage what he knew before, and catches at the next occasion of expense, because advice has no force to suppress his vanity. He that is told how certainly intemperance will hurry him to the grave, runs with his usual speed to a new course of luxury, because his reason is not invigorated, nor his appetite weakened.

The mischief of flattery is, not that it persuades any man that he is what he is not, but that it suppresses the influence of honest ambition, by raising an opinion that honour may be gained without the toil of merit; and the benefit of advice arises commonly, not from any new light imparted to the mind, but from the discovery which it affords of the publick suffrages. He that could withstand conscience is frighted at infamy, and shame prevails when reason was defeated.

As we all know our own faults, and know them commonly with many aggravations which human perspicacity cannot discover, there is, perhaps, no man, however hardened by impudence or dissipated by levity, sheltered by hypocrisy or blasted by disgrace, who does not intend some time to review his conduct, and to regulate the remainder of his life by the laws of virtue. New temptations indeed attack him, new invitations are offered by pleasure and interest, and the hour of reformation is always delayed ; every delay gives vice another opportunity of fortifying itself by habit ; and the change of manners, though sincerely intended and rationally planned, is referred to the time when some craving passion shall be fully gratified, or some powerful allurement cease its importunity.

Thus procrastination is accumulated on procrastination, and one impediment succeeds another, till age shatters our resolution, or death intercepts the project of amendment. Such is often the end of salutary purposes, after they have long delighted the imagination, and appeased that disquiet which every mind feels from known misconduct, when the attention is not diverted by business or by pleasure.

Nothing surely can be more unworthy of a reasonable nature, than to continue in a state so opposite to real happiness, as that all the peace of solitude, and felicity of meditation, must arise from resolutions of forsaking it. Yet the world will often afford examples of men, who pass months and years in a continual war with their own convictions, and are daily dragged by habit, or betrayed by passion, into practices which they closed and opened their eyes with purposes to avoid ; purposes which, though settled on conviction, the first impulse of momentary desire totally overthrows.

The influence of custom is indeed such, that to conquer it will require the utmost efforts of fortitude and virtue ; nor can I think any men more worthy of veneration and renown, than those who have burst the shackles of habitual vice. This victory, however, has different degrees of glory as of difficulty ; it is more heroick as the objects of guilty gratification are more familiar, and the recurrence of solicitation more frequent. He that, from experience of the folly of ambition, resigns his offices, may set himself free at once from temptation to squander his life in courts, because he cannot regain his former station. He who is enslaved by an amorous passion, may quit his tyrant in disgust, and absence will, without the help of reason, overcome by degrees the desire of returning. But those appetites to which every place affords their proper object, and which require no preparatory measures or gradual advances, are more tenaciously adhesive ; the wish is so near the enjoyment, that compliance often precedes consideration ; and, before the powers of reason can be summoned, the time for employing them is past.

Indolence is therefore one of the vices from which those whom it once infects are seldom reformed. Every other species of luxury operates upon some appetite that is quickly satiated, and requires some concurrence of art or accident which every place will not supply ; but the desire of ease acts equally at all hours, and the longer it is indulged is the more increased. To do nothing is in every man's power ; we can never want an opportunity of omitting duties. The lapse to indolence is soft and imperceptible, because it is only a mere cessation of activity ; but the return to diligence is difficult, because it implies a change from rest to motion, from privation to reality.

> " *Facilis descensus averni:*
> *Noctes atque dies patet atri janua ditis ;*
> *Sed revocare gradum, superasque evadere ad auras,*
> *Hoc opus, hic labor est.*"
>
> VIRG.

> " The gates of Hell are open night and day;
> Smooth the descent, and easy is the way;
> But to return, and view the cheerful skies,
> In this the task and mighty labour lies."
>
> DRYDEN.

Of this vice, as of all others, every man who indulges it is conscious : we all know our own state, if we could be induced to consider it ; and it might perhaps be useful to the conquest of all these ensnarers of the mind, if, at certain stated days, life was reviewed. Many things necessary are omitted, because we vainly imagine that they may be always performed ; and what cannot be done without pain will for ever be delayed, if the time of doing it be left unsettled. No corruption is great but by long negligence, which can scarcely prevail in a mind regularly and frequently awakened by periodical remorse. He that thus breaks his life into parts, will find in himself a desire to distinguish every stage of his existence by some improvement, and delight himself with the approach of the day of recollection, as of the time which is to begin a new series of virtue and felicity.

Tuesday, October 1, 1751.

"Οἰή γαρ φύλλων γενέη, τόιηδε καὶ ἀνδρων." HOM.

"Frail as the leaves that quiver on the sprays,
Like them man flourishes, like them decays."

MR. RAMBLER.

SIR,

YOU have formerly observed that curiosity often terminates in barren knowledge, and that the mind is prompted to study and inquiry rather by the uneasiness of ignorance than the hope of profit. Nothing can be of less importance to any present interest, than the fortune of those who have been long lost in the grave, and from whom nothing now can be hoped or feared. Yet, to rouse the zeal of a true antiquary, little more is necessary than to mention a name which mankind have conspired to forget; he will make his way to remote scenes of action through obscurity and contradiction, as Tully sought amidst bushes and brambles the tomb of Archimedes.

It is not easy to discover how it concerns him that gathers the produce, or receives the rent of an estate, to know through what families the land has passed, who is registered in the Conqueror's survey as its possessor, how often it has been forfeited by treason, or how often sold by prodigality. The power or wealth of the present inhab itants of a country cannot be much increased by an inquiry after the names of those barbarians, who destroyed one another, twenty centuries ago, in contests for the shelter of woods or convenience of pasturage. Yet we see that no man can be at rest in the enjoyment of a new purchase, till he has learned the history of his grounds from the ancient inhabitants of the parish, and that no nation omits to record the actions of their ancestors, however bloody, savage, and rapacious.

The same disposition, as different opportunities call it forth, discovers itself in great or little things. I have always thought it unworthy of a wise man to slumber in total inactivity, only because he happens to have no employment equal to his ambition or genius: it is therefore my custom to apply my attention to the objects before me; and as I cannot think any place wholly unworthy of notice that affords a habitation to a man of letters, I have collected the history and antiquities of the several garrets in which I have resided.

"Quantulacunque estis, vos ego magna voco."

" How small to others, but how great to me!"

Many of these narratives my industry has been able to extend to a considerable length; but the woman with whom I now lodge has lived only eighteen months in the house, and can give no account of its ancient revolutions; the plaisterer having, at her entrance, obliterated, by his white-wash, all the smoky memorials which former tenants had left upon the ceiling, and perhaps drawn the veil of oblivion over politicians, philosophers, and poets.

When I first cheapened my lodgings, the landlady told me, that she hoped I was not an author, for the lodgers on the first floor had stipulated that the upper rooms should not be occupied by a noisy trade. I very readily promised to give no disturbance to her family, and soon dispatched a bargain on the usual terms.

I had not slept many nights in my new apartment before I began to inquire after my predecessors, and found my landlady, whose imagination is filled chiefly with her own affairs, very ready to give me information.

Curiosity, like all other desires, produces pain as well as pleasure. Before she began her narrative, I had heated my head with expectations of adventures and discoveries, of elegance in disguise, and learning in distress; and was somewhat mortified when I heard that the first tenant was a tailor, of whom nothing was remembered but that he complained of his room for want of light; and, after having lodged in it a month, and paid only a week's rent, pawned a piece of cloth which he was trusted to cut out, and was forced to make a precipitate retreat from this quarter of the town.

The next was a young woman newly arrived from the country, who lived for five weeks with great regularity, and became by frequent treats very much the favourite of the family, but at last received visits so frequently from a cousin in Cheapside, that she brought the reputation of the house into danger, and was therefore dismissed with good advice.

The room then stood empty for a fortnight: my landlady began to think she had judged hardly, and often wished for such another lodger. At last, an elderly man of a grave aspect read the bill, and bargained for the room at the very first price that was asked. He lived in close retirement, seldom went out till evening, and then returned early, sometimes cheerful, and at other times dejected. It was remarkable, that, whatever he purchased, he never had small money in his pocket; and, though cool and temperate on other occasions, was always vehement and stormy till he received his change. He paid his rent with great exactness, and seldom failed once a week to requite my

landlady's civility with a supper. At last, such is the fate
of human felicity, the house was alarmed at midnight by
the constable, who demanded to search the garrets. My
landlady assuring him that he had mistaken the door,
conducted him up stairs, where he found the tools of a
coiner; but the tenant had crawled along the roof to an
empty house, and escaped; much to the joy of my landlady, who declares him a very honest man, and wonders
why any body should be hanged for making money when
such numbers are in want of it. She however confesses
that she shall, for the future, always question the character
of those who take her garret without beating down the
price.

The bill was then placed again in the window, and the
poor woman was teased for seven weeks by innumerable
passengers, who obliged her to climb with them every hour
up five stories, and then disliked the prospect, hated the
noise of a publick street, thought the stairs narrow, objected
to a low ceiling, required the walls to be hung with fresher
paper, asked questions about the neighbourhood, could not
think of living so far from their acquaintance, wished the
windows had looked to the south rather than the west, told
how the door and chimney might have been better disposed, bid her half the price that she asked, or promised to
give her earnest the next day, and came no more.

At last, a short meagre man, in a tarnished waistcoat,
desired to see the garret, and, when he had stipulated for
two long shelves, and a large table, hired it at a low rate.
When the affair was completed, he looked round him
with great satisfaction, and repeated some words which the
woman did not understand. In two days he brought a
great box of books, took possession of his room, and
lived very inoffensively, except that he frequently disturbed

the inhabitants of the next floor by unseasonable noises. He was generally in bed at noon; but from evening to midnight he sometimes talked aloud with great vehemence, sometimes stamped as in rage, sometimes threw down his poker, then clattered his chairs, then sat down in deep thought, and again burst out into loud vociferation; sometimes he would sigh as oppressed with misery, and sometimes shake with convulsive laughter.   When he encountered any of the family, he gave way or bowed, but rarely spoke, except that as he went up stairs he often repeated,

"——Ὃς ὑπέρτατα δώματα ναίει."

" This habitant th' aërial regions boast :"

hard words, to which his neighbours listened so often that they learned them without understanding them.   What was his employment she did not venture to ask him, but at last heard a printer's boy inquire for the author.

My landlady was very often advised to beware of this strange man, who, though he was quiet for the present, might perhaps become outrageous in the hot months ; but, as she was punctually paid, she could not find any sufficient reason for dismissing him, till one night he convinced her, by setting fire to his curtains, that it was not safe to have an author for an inmate.

She had then for six weeks a succession of tenants, who left the house on Saturday, and, instead of paying their rent, stormed at their landlady.   At last she took in two sisters, one of whom had spent her little fortune in procuring remedies for a lingering disease, and was now supported and attended by the other: she climbed with difficulty to the apartment, where she languished eight weeks without impatience, or lamentation, except for the expense and fatigue which her sister suffered, and then calmly and contentedly expired. The sister followed her to the grave, paid the few debts which they had contracted, wiped away the tears of useless sorrow, and, returning to the business of common life, resigned to me the vacant habitation.

Such, Mr. Rambler, are the changes which have happened in the narrow space where my present fortune has fixed my residence. So true it is that amusement and instruction are always at hand for those who have skill and willingness to find them; and so just is the observation of Juvenal, that a single house will show whatever is done or suffered in the world.

I am, sir, &c.

Tuesday, October 29, 1751.

" *Nec pluteum cædi', nec demorsos sapit ungues.*" PERSIUS.

" No blood from bitten nails those poems drew ;
But churn'd, like spittle, from the lips they flew."

DRYDEN.

NATURAL historians assert that whatever is formed for long duration arrives slowly to its maturity. Thus the firmest timber is of tardy growth, and animals generally exceed each other in longevity, in proportion to the time between their conception and their birth.

The same observation may be extended to the offspring of the mind. Hasty compositions, however they please at first by flowery luxuriance, and spread in the sunshine of temporary favour, can seldom endure the change of seasons, but perish at the first blast of criticism, or frost of neglect. When Apelles was reproached with the paucity of his productions, and the incessant attention with which he retouched his pieces, he condescended to make no other answer than that *he painted for perpetuity.*

No vanity can more justly incur contempt and indignation than that which boasts of negligence and hurry. For who can bear with patience the writer who claims such superiority to the rest of his species, as to imagine that mankind are at leisure for attention to his extemporary sallies, and that posterity will reposite his casual effusions among the treasures of ancient wisdom?

Men have sometimes appeared of such transcendent abilities, that their slightest and most cursory performances excel all that labour and study can enable meaner intellects to compose; as there are regions of which the spontaneous products cannot be equalled in other soils by care and culture. But it is no less dangerous for any man to place himself in this rank of understanding, and fancy that he is born to be illustrious without labour, than to omit the cares of husbandry, and expect from his ground the blossoms of Arabia.

The greatest part of those who congratulate themselves upon their intellectual dignity, and usurp the privileges of genius, are men whom only themselves would ever have marked out as enriched by uncommon liberalities of nature, or entitled to veneration and immortality on easy terms. This ardour of confidence is usually found among those who, having not enlarged their notions by books or conversation, are persuaded, by the partiality which we all feel in our own favour, that they have reached the summit of excellence, because they discover none higher than themselves; and who acquiesce in the first thoughts that occur, because their scantiness of knowledge allows them little choice; and the narrowness of their views affords them no glimpse of perfection, of that sublime idea which human industry has from the first ages been vainly toiling to approach. They see a little, and believe that there is nothing beyond their sphere of vision, as the Patuecos of Spain, who inhabited a small valley, conceived the surrounding mountains to be the boundaries of the world. In proportion as perfection is more distinctly conceived, the pleasure of contemplating our own performances will be lessened ; it may therefore be observed, that they who most deserve praise are often afraid to decide in favour of their own performances ; they know how much is still wanting to their completion, and wait with anxiety and terrour the determination of the publick. "I please every one else," says Tully, " but never satisfy myself."

It has often been inquired, why, notwithstanding the advances of later ages in science, and the assistance which the infusion of so many new ideas has given us, we fall below the ancients in the art of composition. Some part of their superiority may be justly ascribed to the graces of their language, from which the most polished of the present European tongues are nothing more than barbarous degenerations. Some advantage they might gain merely by priority, which put them in possession of the most natural sentiments, and left us nothing but servile repetition or forced conceits. But the greater part of their praise seems to have been the just reward of modesty and labour. Their sense of human weakness confined them commonly to one study, which their knowledge of the extent of every science engaged them to prosecute with indefatigable diligence.

Among the writers of antiquity I remember none except Statius who ventures to mention the speedy production of his writings, either as an extenuation of his faults, or a proof of his facility. Nor did Statius, when he considered himself as a candidate for lasting reputation, think a closer attention unnecessary, but amidst all his pride and indigence, the two great hasteners of modern poems, employed twelve years upon the Thebaid, and thinks his claim to renown proportionate to his labour.

> " *Thebais, multa cruciata lima,*
> *Tentat, audaci fide, Mantuanæ*
> *Gaudia famæ.*"

> " Polish'd with endless toil, my lays
> At length aspire to Mantuan praise."

Ovid indeed apologizes in his banishment for the imperfection of his letters, but mentions his want of leisure to polish them, as an addition to his calamities; and was so far from imagining revisals and corrections unnecessary, that at his departure from Rome he threw his Metamorphoses into the fire, lest he should be disgraced by a book which he could not hope to finish.

It seems not often to have happened that the same writer aspired to reputation in verse and prose; and of those few that attempted such diversity of excellence, I know not that even one succeeded. Contrary characters they never imagined a single mind able to support, and therefore no man is recorded to have undertaken more than one kind of dramatick poetry.

What they had written, they did not venture in their first fondness to thrust into the world, but, considering the impropriety of sending forth inconsiderately that which cannot be recalled, deferred the publication, if not nine years, according to the direction of Horace, yet till their fancy was cooled after the raptures of invention and the glare of novelty had ceased to dazzle the judgment.

There were in those days no weekly or diurnal writers; *multa dies, & multa litura,* much time, and many rasures,

were considered as indispensable requisites; and that no
other method of attaining lasting praise has been yet
discovered, may be conjectured from the blotted manuscripts of Milton now remaining, and from the tardy
emission of Pope's compositions, delayed more than once
till the incidents to which they alluded were forgotten,
till his enemies were secure from his satire, and, what to
an honest mind must be more painful, his friends were
deaf to his encomiums.

To him, whose eagerness of praise hurries his productions
soon into the light, many imperfections are unavoidable,
even where the mind furnishes the materials, as well as
regulates their disposition, and nothing depends upon
search or information. Delay opens new veins of thought,
the subject dismissed for a time appears with a new train
of dependent images, the accidents of reading or conversation supply new ornaments or allusions, or mere
intermission of the fatigue of thinking enables the mind
to collect new force, and make new excursions. But all
those benefits came too late for him, who, when he was
weary with labour, snatched at the recompense, and gave
his work to his friends and his enemies as soon as impatience
and pride persuaded him to conclude it.

One of the most pernicious effects of haste is obscurity.
He that teems with a quick succession of ideas, and
perceives how one sentiment produces another, easily
believes that he can clearly express what he so strongly com-
prehends; he seldom suspects his thoughts of embarrassment, while he preserves in his own memory the series of
connection, or his diction of ambiguity, while only one sense
is present to his mind. Yet if he has been employed
on an abstruse or complicated argument, he will find, when
he has a while withdrawn his mind, and returns as a new

reader to his work, that he has only a conjectural glimpse of his own meaning, and that to explain it to those whom he desires to instruct, he must open his sentiments, disentangle his method, and alter his arrangement.

Authors and lovers always suffer some infatuation, from which only absence can set them free; and every man ought to restore himself to the full exercise of his judgment, before he does that which he cannot do improperly without injuring his honour and his quiet.

Saturday, November 23, 1751.

" ——*Naso suspendere adunco.*"   HOR.

" On me you turn the nose. ——"

THERE are many vexatious accidents and uneasy situ-ations which raise little compassion for the sufferer, and which no man but those whom they immediately distress can regard with seriousness. Petty mischiefs, that have no influence on futurity, nor extend their effects to the rest of life, are always seen with a kind of malicious pleasure. A mistake or embarrassment, which for the present moment fills the face with blushes, and the mind with confusion, will have no other effect upon those who observe it, than that of convulsing them with irresistible laughter. Some circumstances of misery are so powerfully ridiculous, that neither kindness nor duty can withstand them; they bear down love, interest, and reverence, and force the friend, the dependent, or the child, to give way to instantaneous motions of merriment.

Among the principal of comick calamities, may be reckoned the pain which an author, not yet hardened into insensibility, feels at the onset of a furious critick, whose age, rank, or fortune, gives him confidence to speak without reserve; who heaps one objection upon another, and obtrudes his remarks, and enforces his corrections, without tenderness or awe.

The author, full of the importance of his work, and anxious for the justification of every syllable, starts and kindles at the slightest attack; the critick, eager to establish his superiority, triumphing in every discovery of failure, and zealous to impress the cogency of his arguments, pursues him from line to line without cessation or remorse. The critick, who hazards little, proceeds with vehemence, impetuosity, and fearlessness; the author, whose quiet and fame, and life and immortality, are involved in the controversy, tries every art of subterfuge and defence; maintains modestly what he resolves never to yield, and yields unwillingly what cannot be maintained. The critick's purpose is to conquer, the author only hopes to escape; the critic therefore knits his brow, and raises his voice, and rejoices whenever he perceives any tokens of pain excited by the pressure of his assertions, or the point of his sarcasms. The author, whose endeavour is at once to mollify and elude his persecutor, composes his features and softens his accent, breaks the force of assault by retreat, and rather steps aside than flies or advances.

As it very seldom happens that the rage of extemporary criticism inflicts fatal or lasting wounds, I know not that the laws of benevolence entitle this distress to much sympathy. The diversion of baiting an author has the sanction of all ages and nations, and is more lawful than the sport of teasing other animals, because, for the most part, he comes voluntarily to the stake, furnished, as he imagines, by the patron powers of literature, with resistless weapons and impenetrable armour, with the mail of the boar of Erymanth, and the paws of the lion of Nemea.*

But the works of genius are sometimes produced by other motives than vanity; and he whom necessity or duty enforces to write, is not always so well satisfied with himself, as not to be discouraged by censorious impudence. It may therefore be necessary to consider, how they whom publication lays open to the insults of such as their obscurity secures against reprisals, may extricate themselves from unexpected encounters.

Vida, a man of considerable skill in the politicks of literature, directs his pupil wholly to abandon his defence, and, even when he can irrefragably refute all objections, to suffer tamely the exultations of his antagonist.

This rule may perhaps be just, when advice is asked, and severity solicited, because no man tells his opinion so freely as when he imagines it received with implicit veneration; and criticks ought never to be consulted, but while errors may yet be rectified or insipidity suppressed. But when the book has once been dismissed into the world, and can be no more retouched, I know not whether a very different conduct should not be prescribed, and whether firmness and spirit may not sometimes be of use to overpower arrogance and repel brutality. Softness, diffidence, and moderation, will often be mistaken for imbecility and dejection; they lure cowardice to the attack by the hopes of easy victory, and it will soon be found that he whom every man thinks he can conquer, shall never be at peace.

The animadversions of criticks are commonly such as

* Note XIV., Appendix.

may easily provoke the sedatest writer to some quickness of resentment and asperity of reply.* A man who by long consideration has familiarised a subject to his own mind, carefully surveyed the series of his thoughts, and planned all the parts of his composition into a regular dependence on each other, will often start at the sinistrous interpretations or absurd remarks of haste and ignorance, and wonder by what infatuation they have been led away from the obvious sense, and upon what peculiar principles of judgment they decide against him.

The eye of the intellect, like that of the body, is not equally perfect in all, nor equally adapted in any to all objects; the end of criticism is to supply its defects; rules are the instruments of mental vision, which may indeed assist our faculties when properly used, but produce confusion and obscurity by unskilful application.

Some seem always to read with the microscope of criticism, and employ their whole attention upon minute elegance, or faults scarcely visible to common observation. The dissonance of a syllable, the recurrence of the same sound, the repetition of a particle, the smallest deviation from propriety, the slightest defect in construction or arrangement, swell before their eyes into enormities. As they discern with great exactness, they comprehend but a narrow compass, and know nothing of the justness of the design, the general spirit of the performance, the artifice of connection, or the harmony of the parts; they never conceive how small a proportion that which they are busy in contemplating bears to the whole, or how the petty inaccuracies with which they are offended, are absorbed and lost in general excellence.

* Note XV., Appendix.

Others are furnished by criticism with a telescope. They see with great clearness whatever is too remote to be discovered by the rest of mankind, but are totally blind to all that lies immediately before them. They discover in every passage some secret meaning, some remote allusion, some artful allegory, or some occult imitation, which no other reader ever suspected; but they have no perception of the cogency of arguments, the force of pathetick sentiments, the various colours of diction, or the flowery embellishments of fancy; of all that engages the attention of others they are totally insensible, while they pry into worlds of conjecture, and amuse themselves with phantoms in the clouds.

In criticism, as in every other art, we fail sometimes by our weakness, but more frequently by our fault. We are sometimes bewildered by ignorance, and sometimes by prejudice; but we seldom deviate far from the right, but when we deliver ourselves up to the direction of vanity.

Saturday, November 30, 1751.

" Pars sanitatis velle sanari fuit."   SENECA,

" To yield to remedies is half the cure."

PYTHAGORAS is reported to have required from those whom he instructed in philosophy a probationary silence of five years. Whether this prohibition of speech extended to all the parts of this time, as seems generally to be supposed, or was to be observed only in the school or in the presence of their master, as is more probable, it was sufficient to discover the pupil's disposition; to try whether he was willing to pay the price of learning; or whether he was one of those whose ardour was rather violent than lasting, and who expected to grow wise on other terms than those of patience and obedience.

Many of the blessings universally desired, are very frequently wanted, because most men, when they should labour, content themselves to complain, and rather linger in a state in which they cannot be at rest, than improve their condition by vigour and resolution.

Providence has fixed the limits of human enjoyment by immoveable boundaries, and has set different gratifications at such a distance from each other, that no art or power can bring them together. This great law it is the business of every rational being to understand, that life may not pass away in an attempt to make contradictions consistent, to combine opposite qualities, and to unite things which the nature of their being must always keep asunder.

Of two objects tempting at a distance on contrary sides, it is impossible to approach one but by receding from the other; by long deliberation and dilatory projects, they may be both lost, but can never be both gained. It is, therefore, necessary to compare them, and, when we have determined the preference, to withdraw our eyes and our thoughts at once from that which reason directs us to reject. This is more necessary, if that which we are forsaking has the power of delighting the senses, or firing the fancy. He that once turns aside to the allurements of unlawful pleasure can have no security that he shall ever regain the paths of virtue.

The philosophick goddess of Boethius, having related the story of Orpheus, who, when he had recovered his wife from the dominions of death, lost her again by looking back upon her in the confines of light, concludes with a very elegant and forcible application. *Whoever you are that endeavour to elevate your minds to the illuminations of Heaven, consider yourselves as represented in this fable: for he that is once so far overcome as to turn back his eyes towards the infernal caverns, loses at the first sight all that influence which attracted him on high:*

> " Vos hæc fabula respicit,
> Quicunque in superum diem
> Mentem ducere quæritis.
>
> Nam qui Tartareum in specus
> Victus lumina flexerit,
>
> Quidquid præcipuum trahit,
> Perdit, dum videt inferos."

It may be observed in general, that the future is purchased by the present. It is not possible to secure distant or permanent happiness but by the forbearance of some immediate gratification. This is so evidently true with regard to the whole of our existence, that all the precepts of theology have no other tendency than to enforce a life of faith ; a life regulated not by our senses but our belief ; a life in which pleasures are to be refused for fear of invisible punishments, and calamities sometimes to be sought, and always endured, in hopes of rewards that shall be obtained in another state.

Even if we take into our view only that particle of our duration which is terminated by the grave, it will be found that we cannot enjoy one part of life beyond the common limitations of pleasure, but by anticipating some of the satisfaction which should exhilarate the following years. The heat of youth may spread happiness into wild luxuriance ; but the radical vigour requisite to make it perennial is exhausted, and all that can be hoped afterwards is languor and sterility.

The reigning error of mankind is, that we are not content with the conditions on which the goods of life are granted. No man is insensible of the value of knowledge, the advantages of health, or the convenience of plenty, but every day shows us those on whom the conviction is without effect.

Knowledge is praised and desired by multitudes whom her charms could never rouse from the couch of sloth; whom the faintest invitation of pleasure draws away from their studies; to whom any other method of wearing out the day is more eligible than the use of books, and who are more easily engaged by any conversation, than such as may rectify their notions or enlarge their comprehension.

Every man that has felt pain, knows how little all other comforts can gladden him to whom health is denied. Yet who is there does not sometimes hazard it for the enjoyment of an hour? All assemblies of jollity, all places of publick entertainment, exhibit examples of strength wasting in riot, and beauty withering in irregularity; nor is it easy to enter a house in which part of the family is not groaning in repentance of past intemperance, and part admitting disease by negligence, or soliciting it by luxury.

There is no pleasure which men of every age and sect have more generally agreed to mention with contempt, than the gratification of the palate; an entertainment so far removed from intellectual happiness, that scarcely the most shameless of the sensual herd have dared to defend it: yet even to this, the lowest of our delights, to this, though neither quick nor lasting, is health with all its activity and sprightliness daily sacrificed; and for this are half the miseries endured which urge impatience to call on death.

The whole world is put in motion by the wish for riches and the dread of poverty. Who then would not imagine that such conduct as will inevitably destroy what all are thus labouring to acquire, must generally be avoided? That he who spends more than he receives, must in time become indigent, cannot be doubted; but, how evident soever this consequence may appear, the spendthrift moves in the whirl of pleasure with too much rapidity to keep it before his eyes, and, in the intoxication of gaiety, grows every day poorer without any such sense of approaching ruin as is sufficient to wake him into caution.

Many complaints are made of the misery of life; and indeed it must be confessed that we are subject to calamities by which the good and bad, the diligent and slothful, the viligant and heedless, are equally afflicted. But surely, though some indulgence may be allowed to groans extorted by inevitable misery, no man has a right to repine at evils which, against warning, against experience, he deliberately and leisurely brings upon his own head; or to consider himself as debarred from happiness by such obstacles as resolution may break or dexterity may put aside.

Great numbers who quarrel with their condition, have wanted not the power but the will to obtain a better state. They have never contemplated the difference between good and evil sufficiently to quicken aversion, or invigorate desire; they have indulged a drowsy thoughtfulness or giddy levity; have committed the balance of choice to the management of caprice; and when they have long accustomed themselves to receive all that chance offered them, without examination, lament at last that they find themselves deceived.

Tuesday, December 24, 1751.

" *At vindicta bonum vita jucundius ipsa,*
  Nempe hoc indocti. ———
Chrysippus, non dicit idem, nec mite Thaletis
Ingenium, dulcique senex vicinus Hymetto,
Qui partem acceptæ sæva inter vincla Cicutæ
Accusatori nollet dare. ——*Quippe minuti*
Semper, et infirmi est animi, exiguique voluptas
Ultio."   JUV.

" *But O ! Revenge is sweet.*
  Thus think the crowd ; who, eager to engage,
  Take quickly fire, and kindle into rage.
  Not so mild Thales nor Chrysippus thought,
  Nor that good man who drank the pois'nous draught
  With mind serene, and could not wish to see
  His vile accuser drink as deep as he ;
  Exalted Socrates ! divinely brave !
  Injur'd he fell, and dying he forgave,
  Too noble for revenge ; which still we find
  The weakest frailty of a feeble mind."   DRYDEN.

NO vicious dispositions of the mind more obstinately
resist both the counsels of philosophy and the
injunctions of religion, than those which are complicated
with an opinion of dignity; and which we cannot dismiss
without leaving in the hands of opposition some advantage
iniquitously obtained, or suffering from our own prejudices
some imputation of pusillanimity.

For this reason, scarcely any law of our REDEEMER is
more openly transgressed, or more industriously evaded,
than that by which he commands his followers to forgive
injuries, and prohibits, under the sanction of eternal misery,

the gratification of the desire which every man feels to return pain upon him that inflicts it. Many who could have conquered their anger, are unable to combat pride, and pursue offences to extremity of vengeance, lest they should be insulted by the triumph of an enemy.

But certainly no precept could better become him, at whose birth *peace* was proclaimed *to the earth*. For, what would so soon destroy all the order of society, and deform life with violence and ravage, as a permission to every one to judge his own cause, and to apportion his own recompense for imagined injuries?

It is difficult for a man of the strictest justice not to favour himself too much, in the calmest moments of solitary meditation. Every one wishes for the distinctions for which thousands are wishing at the same time, in their own opinion, with better claims. He that, when his reason operates in its full force, can thus, by the mere prevalence of self-love, prefer himself to his fellow-beings, is very unlikely to judge equitably when his passions are agitated by a sense of wrong, and his attention wholly engrossed by pain, interest, or danger. Whoever arrogates to himself the right of vengeance, shows how little he is qualified to decide his own claims, since he certainly demands what he would think unfit to be granted to another.

Nothing is more apparent, than that, however injured or however provoked, some must at last be contented to forgive. For, it can never be hoped that he who first commits an injury will contentedly acquiesce in the penalty required: the same haughtiness of contempt, or vehemence of desire, that prompts the act of injustice, will more strongly incite its justification; and resentment can never so exactly balance the punishment with the fault, but there will remain an overplus of vengeance, which even he who condemns his first action will think himself entitled to retaliate. What then can ensue but a continual exacerbation of hatred, an unextinguishable feud, an incessant reciprocation of mischief, a mutual vigilance to entrap, and eagerness to destroy?

Since then the imaginary right of vengeance must be at last remitted, because it is impossible to live in perpetual hostility, and equally impossible that of two enemies, either should first think himself obliged by justice to submission, it is surely eligible to forgive early. Every passion is more easily subdued before it has been long accustomed to possession of the heart; every idea is obliterated with less difficulty, as it has been more slightly impressed, and less frequently renewed. He who has often brooded over his wrongs, pleased himself with schemes of malignity, and glutted his pride with the fancied supplications of humbled enmity, will not easily open his bosom to amity and reconciliation, or indulge the gentle sentiments of benevolence and peace.

It is easiest to forgive while there is yet little to be forgiven. A single injury may be soon dismissed from the memory; but a long succession of ill offices by degrees associates itself with every idea; a long contest involves so many circumstances, that every place and action will recall it to the mind; and fresh remembrance of vexation must still enkindle rage, and irritate revenge.

A wise man will make haste to forgive, because he knows the true value of time, and will not suffer it to pass away in unnecessary pain. He that willingly suffers the corrosions of inveterate hatred, and gives up his days and nights to the gloom of malice and perturbations of stratagem, cannot surely be said to consult his ease. Resentment is an union of sorrow with malignity, a combination of a passion which all endeavour to avoid, with a passion which all concur to detest. The man who retires to meditate mischief, and to exasperate his own rage; whose thoughts are employed only on means of distress and contrivances of ruin; whose mind never pauses from the remembrance of his own sufferings, but to indulge some hope of enjoying the calamities of another, may justly be numbered among the most miserable of human beings, among those who are guilty without reward, who have neither the gladness of prosperity, nor the calm of innocence.

Whoever considers the weakness both of himself and others, will not long want persuasives to forgiveness. We know not to what degree of malignity any injury is to be imputed; or how much its guilt, if we were to inspect the mind of him that committed it, would be extenuated by mistake, precipitance, or negligence : we cannot be certain how much more we feel than was intended to be inflicted, or how much we increase the mischief to ourselves by voluntary aggravations. We may charge to design the effects of accident; we may think the blow violent, only because we have made ourselves delicate and tender; we are on every side in danger of error and of guilt; which we are certain to avoid only by speedy forgiveness.

From this pacifick and harmless temper, thus propitious to others and ourselves, to domestick tranquillity and to social happiness, no man is withheld but by pride, by the fear of being insulted by his adversary, or despised by the world.

It may be laid down as an unfailing and universal axiom, that "all pride is abject and mean." It is always an ignorant, lazy, or cowardly acquiescence in a false appearance of excellence, and proceeds not from consciousness of our attainments, but insensibility of our wants.

Nothing can be great which is not right. Nothing which reason condemns can be suitable to the dignity of the human mind. To be driven by external motives from the path which our own heart approves; to give way to any thing but conviction; to suffer the opinion of others to rule our choice, or overpower our resolves; is to submit tamely to the lowest and most ignominious slavery, and to resign the right of directing our own lives.

The utmost excellence at which humanity can arrive, is a constant and determinate pursuit of virtue, without regard to present dangers or advantage; a continual reference of every action to the divine will; an habitual appeal to everlasting justice; and an unvaried elevation of the intellectual eye to the reward which perseverance only can obtain. But that pride which many, who presume to boast of generous sentiments, allow to regulate their measures, has nothing nobler in view than the approbation of men; of beings whose superiority we are under no obligation to acknowledge, and who, when we have courted them with the utmost assiduity, can confer no valuable or permanent reward; of beings who ignorantly judge of what they do not understand, or partially determine what they never have examined; and whose sentence is therefore of no weight till it has received the ratification of our own conscience.

He that can descend to bribe suffrages like these, at the price of his innocence; he that can suffer the delight of such acclamations to withhold his attention from the commands of the universal Sovereign, has little reason to congratulate himself upon the greatness of his mind: whenever he awakes to seriousness and reflection, he must become despicable in his own eyes, and shrink with shame from the remembrance of his cowardice and folly.

Of him that hopes to be forgiven, it is indispensably

required that he forgive. It is therefore superfluous to urge any other motive. On this great duty eternity is suspended ; and to him that refuses to practise it, the throne of mercy is inaccessible, and the SAVIOUR of the world has been born in vain.

Saturday, February 1, 1752.

> " *Multa ferunt anni venientes commoda secum,*
> *Multa recedentes adimunt.*——"   HOR.

> " The blessings flowing in with life's full tide
> Down with our ebb of life decreasing glide." FRANCIS.

BAXTER, in the narrative of his own life, has enumerated several opinions, which, though he thought them evident and incontestable at his first entrance into the world, time and experience disposed him to change.

Whoever reviews the state of his own mind from the dawn of manhood to its decline, and considers what he pursued or dreaded, slighted or esteemed, at different periods of his age, will have no reason to imagine such changes of sentiment peculiar to any station or character. Every man, however careless and inattentive, has conviction forced upon him ; the lectures of time obtrude themselves upon the most unwilling or dissipated auditor ; and, by comparing our past with our present thoughts, we perceive that we have changed our minds, though perhaps we cannot discover when the alteration happened, or by what causes it was produced.

This revolution of sentiments occasions a perpetual

contest between the old and young. They who imagine themselves entitled to veneration by the prerogative of longer life, are inclined to treat the notions of those whose conduct they superintend with superciliousness and contempt, for want of considering that the future and the past have different appearances ; that the disproportion will always be great between expectation and enjoyment, between new possession and satiety; that the truth of many maxims of age gives too little pleasure to be allowed till it is felt; and that the miseries of life would be increased beyond all human power of endurance, if we were to enter the world with the same opinions as we carry from it.

We naturally indulge those ideas that please us. HOPE will predominate in every mind, till it has been suppressed by frequent disappointments. The youth has not yet discovered how many evils are continually hovering about us, and when he is set free from the shackles of discipline, looks abroad into the world with rapture; he sees an elysian region open before him, so variegated with beauty, and so stored with pleasure, that his care is rather to accumulate good, than to shun evil; he stands distracted by different forms of delight, and has no other doubt, than which path to follow of those which all lead equally to the bowers of happiness.

He who has seen only the superficies of life believes every thing to be what it appears, and rarely suspects that external splendour conceals any latent sorrow or vexation. He never imagines that there may be greatness without safety, affluence without content, jollity without friendship, and solitude without peace. He fancies himself permitted to cull the blessings of every condition, and to leave its inconveniencies to the idle and the ignorant. He is

13

inclined to believe no man miserable but by his own fault, and seldom looks with much pity upon failings or miscarriages, because he thinks them willingly admitted, or negligently incurred.

It is impossible, without pity and contempt, to hear a youth of generous sentiments and warm imagination, declaring in the moment of openness and confidence, his designs and expectations; because long life is possible, he considers it as certain, and therefore promises himself all the changes of happiness, and provides gratifications for every desire. He is, for a time, to give himself wholly to frolick and diversion, to range the world in search of pleasure, to delight every eye, to gain every heart, and to be celebrated equally for his pleasing levities and solid attainments, his deep reflections and his sparkling repartees. He then elevates his views to nobler enjoyments, and finds all the scattered excellencies of the female world united in a woman, who prefers his addresses to wealth and titles; he is afterwards to engage in business, to dissipate difficulty, and overpower opposition; to climb, by the mere force of merit, to fame and greatness; and reward all those who countenanced his rise, or paid due regard to his early excellence. At last he will retire in peace and honour; contract his views to domestick pleasures; form the manners of children like himself; observe how every year expands the beauty of his daughters, and how his sons catch ardour from their father's history; he will give laws to the neighbourhood; dictate axioms to posterity; and leave the world an example of wisdom and happiness.

With hopes like these, he sallies jocund into life; to little purpose is he told, that the condition of humanity admits no pure and unmingled happiness; that the

exuberant gaiety of youth ends in poverty or disease;
that uncommon qualifications and contrarieties of excellence,
produce envy equally with applause ; that, whatever admiration and fondness may promise him, he must marry a
wife like the wives of others, with some virtues and some
faults, and be as often disgusted by her vices, as delighted
by her elegance ; that if he adventures into the circle
of action, he must expect to encounter men as artful, as
daring, as resolute as himself; that of his children, some
may be deformed, and others vicious ; some may disgrace
him by their follies, some offend him by their insolence,
and some exhaust him by their profusion. He hears all
this with obstinate incredulity, and wonders by what
malignity old age is influenced, that it cannot forbear to
fill his ears with predictions of misery.

Among other pleasing errours of young minds, is the
opinion of their own importance. He that has not yet
remarked how little attention his contemporaries can spare
from their own affairs, conceives all eyes turned upon
himself, and imagines every one that approaches him to be
an enemy or a follower, an admirer or a spy. He therefore
considers his fame as involved in the event of every action.
Many of the virtues and vices of youth proceed from this
quick sense of reputation. This it is that gives firmness
and constancy, fidelity and disinterestedness, and it is this
that kindles resentment for slight injuries, and dictates all
the principles of sanguinary honour.

But as time brings him forward into the world, he soon
discovers that he only shares fame or reproach with
innumerable partners; that he is left unmarked in the
obscurity of the crowd ; and that what he does, whether
good or bad, soon gives way to new objects of regard. He
then easily sets himself free from the anxieties of reputation,

and considers praise or censure as a transient breath, which, while he hears it, is passing away, without any lasting mischief or advantage.

In youth, it is common to measure right and wrong by the opinion of the world, and in age, to act without any measure but interest, and to lose shame without substituting virtue.

Such is the condition of life, that something is always wanting to happiness.* In youth, we have warm hopes, which are soon blasted by rashness and negligence, and great designs, which are defeated by inexperience. In age, we have knowledge and prudence without spirit to exert, or motives to prompt them; we are able to plan schemes, and regulate measures; but have not time remaining to bring them to completion.

Tuesday, February 18, 1752.

" ——*Sanctus haberi*
Promissique tenax dictis factisque mereris ?
Agnosco procerem."   JUV.

" Convince the world that you're devout and true ;
Be just in all you say, and all you do ;
Whatever be your birth, you're sure to be
A peer of the first magnitude to me."   STEPNEY.

BOYLE has observed, that the excellency of manufactures and the facility of labour would be much promoted, if the various expedients and contrivances which lie concealed in private hands, were by reciprocal communications made generally known ; for there are few operations

* Note XVI., Appendix.

that are not performed by one or other with some peculiar advantages, which, though singly of little importance, would, by conjunction and concurrence, open new inlets to knowledge, and give new powers to diligence.

There are, in like manner, several moral excellencies distributed among the different classes of a community. It was said by Cujacius, that he never read more than one book by which he was not instructed; and he that shall inquire after virtue with ardour and attention, will seldom find a man by whose example or sentiments he may not be improved.

Every profession has some essential and appropriate virtue, without which there can be no hope of honour or success, and which, as it is more or less cultivated, confers within its sphere of activity different degrees of merit and reputation. As the astrologers range the subdivisions of mankind under the planets which they suppose to influence their lives, the moralist may distribute them according to the virtues which they necessarily practise, and consider them as distinguished by prudence or fortitude, diligence or patience.

So much are the modes of excellence settled by time and place, that men may be heard boasting in one street of that which they would anxiously conceal in another. The grounds of scorn and esteem, the topicks of praise and satire, are varied according to the several virtues or vices which the course of life has disposed men to admire or abhor; but he who is solicitous for his own improvement must not be limited by local reputation, but select from every tribe of mortals their characteristical virtues, and constellate in himself the scattered graces which shine single in other men.

The chief praise to which a trader aspires is that of

punctuality,* or an exact and rigorous observance of commercial engagements ; nor is there any vice of which he so much dreads the imputation, as of negligence and instability.   This is a quality which the interest of mankind requires to be diffused through all the ranks of life, but which many seem to consider as a vulgar and ignoble virtue, below the ambition of greatness or attention of wit, scarcely requisite among men of gaiety and spirit, and sold at its highest rate when it is sacrificed to a frolick or a jest.

Every man has daily occasion to remark what vexations arise from this privilege of deceiving one another.   The active and vivacious have so long disdained the restraints of truth, that promises and appointments have lost their cogency, and both parties neglect their stipulations, because each concludes that they will be broken by the other.

Negligence is first admitted in small affairs, and strengthened by petty indulgences.   He that is not yet hardened by custom, ventures not on the violation of important engagements, but thinks himself bound by his word in cases of property or danger, though he allows himself to forget at what time he is to meet ladies in the Park, or at what tavern his friends are expecting him.

This laxity of honour would be more tolerable, if it could be restrained to the play-house, the ball-room, or the card-table ; yet even there it is sufficiently troublesome, and darkens those moments with expectation, suspense, and resentment, which are set aside for pleasure, and from which we naturally hope for unmingled enjoyment and total relaxation.   But he that suffers the slightest breach in his morality can seldom tell what shall enter it, or how wide it

* Note XVII., Appendix.

shall be made; when a passage is open, the influx of corruption is every moment wearing down opposition, and by slow degrees deluges the heart.

Aliger entered the world a youth of lively imagination, extensive views, and untainted principles. His curiosity incited him to range from place to place, and try all the varieties of conversation; his elegance of address and fertility of ideas gained him friends wherever he appeared; or at least he found the general kindness of reception always shown to a young man whose birth and fortune gave him a claim to notice, and who has neither by vice or folly destroyed his privileges. Aliger was pleased with this general smile of mankind, and was industrious to preserve it by compliance and officiousness, but did not suffer his desire of pleasing to vitiate his integrity. It was his established maxim, that a promise is never to be broken; nor was it without long reluctance that he once suffered himself to be drawn away from a festal engagement by the importunity of another company.

He spent the evening, as is usual in the rudiments of vice, in perturbation and imperfect enjoyment, and met his disappointed friends in the morning with confusion and excuses. His companions, not accustomed to such scrupulous anxiety, laughed at his uneasiness, compounded the offence for a bottle, gave him courage to break his word again, and again levied the penalty. He ventured the same experiment upon another society, and found them equally ready to consider it as a venal fault, always incident to a man of quickness and gaiety; till, by degrees, he began to think himself at liberty to follow the last invitation, and was no longer shocked at the turpitude of falsehood. He made no difficulty to promise his presence at distant places; and, if listlessness happened to creep upon him, would sit at home with great tranquillity, and has often sunk to sleep in a chair, while he held ten tables in continual expectations of his entrance.

It was so pleasant to live in perpetual vacancy, that he soon dismissed his attention as an useless incumbrance, and resigned himself to carelessness and dissipation, without any regard to the future or the past, or any other motive of action than the impulse of a sudden desire, or the attraction of immediate pleasure. The absent were immediately forgotten, and the hopes or fears felt by others had no influence upon his conduct. He was in speculation completely just, but never kept his promise to a creditor; he was benevolent, but always deceived those friends whom he undertook to patronize or assist; he was prudent, but suffered his affairs to be embarrassed for want of regulating his accounts at stated times. He courted a young lady, and, when the settlements were drawn, took a ramble into the country on the day appointed to sign them. He resolved to travel, and sent his chests on ship-board but delayed to follow them till he lost his passage. He was summoned as an evidence in a cause of great importance, and loitered on the way till the trial was past. It is said that when he had, with great expense, formed an interest in a borough, his opponents contrived, by some agents who knew his temper, to lure him away on the day of election.

His benevolence draws him into the commission of a thousand crimes, which others less kind or civil would escape. His courtesy invites application; his promises produce dependence; he has his pockets filled with petitions, which he intends some time to deliver and enforce, and his table covered with letters of request, with which he purposes to comply; but time slips imperceptibly away, while he is either idle or busy; his friends lose their opportunities, and charge upon him their miscarriages and calamities.

This character, however contemptible, is not peculiar to Aliger. They whose activity of imagination is often shifting the scenes of expectation, are frequently subject to such sallies of caprice as make all their actions fortuitous, destroy the value of their friendship, obstruct the efficacy of their virtues, and set them below the meanest of those that persist in their resolutions, execute what they design, and perform what they have promised.

Saturday, March 7, 1752.

"——*Propositi nondum pudet, atque eadem est mens,*
Ut bona summa putes, aliena vivere quadrâ."   JUV.

"But harden'd by affronts, and still the same,
   Lost to all sense of honour and of fame,
   Thou yet canst love to haunt the great man's board,
   And think no supper good but with a lord."   BOWLES.

WHEN Diogenes was once asked, what kind of wine he liked best, he answered, "That which is drunk at the cost of others."

Though the character of Diogenes has never excited any general zeal of imitation, there are many who resemble him in his taste of wine; many who are frugal, though not abstemious; whose appetites, though too powerful for reason, are kept under restraint by avarice; and to whom all delicacies lose their flavour, when they cannot be obtained but at their own expense.

Nothing produces more singularity of manners, and

inconstancy of life, than the conflict of opposite vices in the same mind. He that uniformly pursues any purpose, whether good or bad, has a settled principle of action ; and, as he may always find associates who are travelling the same way, is countenanced by example, and sheltered in the multitude ; but a man actuated at once by different desires must move in a direction peculiar to himself, and suffer that reproach which we are naturally inclined to bestow on those who deviate from the rest of the world, even without inquiring whether they are worse or better.

Yet this conflict of desires sometimes produces wonderful efforts. To riot in far-fetched dishes, or surfeit with unexhausted variety, and yet practise the most rigid economy, is surely an art which may justly draw the eyes of mankind upon them whose industry or judgment has enabled them to attain it. To him, indeed, who is content to break open the chests or mortgage the manors of his ancestors, that he may hire the ministers of excess at the highest price, gluttony is an easy science : yet we often hear the votaries of luxury boasting of the elegance which they owe to the taste of others ; relating with rapture the succession of dishes with which their cooks and caterers supply them ; and expecting their share of praise with the discoverers of arts and the civilizers of nations. But to shorten the way to convivial happiness, by eating without cost, is a secret hitherto in few hands, but which certainly deserves the curiosity of those whose principal employment is their dinner, and who see the sun rise with no other hope than that they shall fill their bellies before it sets.

Of them that have within my knowledge attempted this scheme of happiness, the greater part have been immediately obliged to desist ; and some, whom their first attempts flattered with success, were reduced by degrees to a few tables, from which they were at last chased to make way for others; and, having long habituated themselves to superfluous plenty, growled away their latter years in discontented competence.

None enter the regions of luxury with higher expectations than men of wit, who imagine that they shall never want a welcome to that company whose ideas they can enlarge, or whose imaginations they can elevate, and believe themselves able to pay for their wine with the mirth which it qualifies them to produce. Full of this opinion, they crowd with little invitation wherever the smell of a feast allures them, but are seldom encouraged to repeat their visits, being dreaded by the pert as rivals, and hated by the dull as disturbers of the company.

No man has been so happy in gaining and keeping the privilege of living at luxurious houses as Gulosulus, who, after thirty years of continual revelry, has now established, by uncontroverted prescription, his claim to partake of every entertainment, and whose presence they who aspire to the praise of a sumptuous table are careful to procure on a day of importance, by sending the invitation a fortnight before.

Gulosulus entered the world without any eminent degree of merit; but was careful to frequent houses where persons of rank resorted. By being often seen, he became in time known; and, from sitting in the same room, was suffered to mix in idle conversation, or assisted to fill up a vacant hour, when better amusement was not readily to be had. From the coffee-house he was sometimes taken away to dinner; and, as no man refuses the acquaintance of him whom he sees admitted to familiarity by others of equal dignity, when he had been met at a few tables, he with less difficulty found the way to more, till at last he was regularly expected to appear wherever preparations are made for a feast, within the circuit of his acquaintance.

When he was thus by accident initiated in luxury, he felt in himself no inclination to retire from a life of so much pleasure, and therefore very seriously considered how he might continue it. Great qualities, or uncommon accomplishments, he did not find necessary; for he had already seen that merit rather enforces respect than attracts fondness; and as he thought no folly greater than that of losing a dinner for any other gratification, he often congratulated himself, that he had none of that disgusting excellence which impresses awe upon greatness, and condemns its possessors to the society of those who are wise or brave, and indigent as themselves.

Gulosulus, having never allotted much of his time to books or meditation, had no opinion in philosophy or politicks, and was not in danger of injuring his interest by dogmatical positions, or violent contradiction. If a dispute arose, he took care to listen with earnest attention; and, when either speaker grew vehement and loud, turned towards him with eager quickness, and uttered a short phrase of admiration, as if surprised by such cogency of argument as he had never known before. By this silent concession, he generally preserved in either controvertist such a conviction of his own superiority, as inclined him rather to pity than irritate his adversary, and prevented those outrages which are sometimes produced by the rage of defeat, or petulance of triumph.

Gulosulus was never embarrassed but when he was required to declare his sentiments before he had been able to discover to which side the master of the house inclined; for it was his invariable rule to adopt the notions of those that invited him.

It will sometimes happen that the insolence of wealth breaks into contemptuousness, or the turbulence of wine requires a vent; and Gulosulus seldom fails of being singled out on such emergencies, as one on whom any experiment of ribaldry may be safely tried. Sometimes his lordship finds himself inclined to exhibit a specimen of raillery for the diversion of his guests, and Gulosulus always supplies him with a subject of merriment. But he has learned to consider rudeness and indignities as familiarities that entitle him to greater freedom: he comforts himself, that those who treat and insult him pay for their laughter, and that he keeps his money while they enjoy their jest.

His chief policy consists in selecting some dish from every course, and recommending it to the company, with an air so decisive, that no one ventures to contradict him. By this practice he acquires at a feast a kind of dictatorial authority; his taste becomes the standard of pickles and seasoning, and he is venerated by the professors of epicurism, as the only man who understands the niceties of cookery.

Whenever a new sauce is imported, or any innovation made in the culinary system, he procures the earliest intelligence, and the most authentick receipt; and, by communicating his knowledge under proper injunctions of secrecy, gains a right of tasting his own dish whenever it is prepared, that he may tell whether his directions have been fully understood.

By this method of life Gulosulus has so impressed on his imagination the dignity of feasting, that he has no other topick of talk, or subject of meditation. His calendar is a bill of fare; he measures the year by successive dainties. The only common places of his memory are his meals; and if you ask him at what time an event happened, he considers whether he heard it after a dinner of turbot or venison. He knows, indeed, that those who value themselves upon sense, learning, or piety, speak of him with contempt; but he considers them as wretches, envious or ignorant, who do not know his happiness, or wish to supplant him; and declares to his friends, that he is fully satisfied with his own conduct, since he has fed every day on twenty dishes, and yet doubled his estate.

Tuesday, March 10, 1752.

"*Solve senescentem mature sanus equum, ne
Peccet ad extremum ridendus.*"   Hor.

"The voice of reason cries with winning force,
Loose from the rapid car your aged horse,
Lest, in the race derided, left behind,
He drag his jaded limbs and burst his wind." Francis.

SUCH is the emptiness of human enjoyment, that we are always impatient of the present. Attainment is followed by neglect, and possession by disgust; and the malicious remark of the Greek epigrammatist on marriage may be applied to every other course of life, that its two days of happiness are the first and the last.

Few moments are more pleasing than those in which the mind is concerting measures for a new undertaking. From the first hint that wakens the fancy till the hour of actual execution, all is improvement and progress, triumph and felicity. Every hour brings additions to the original scheme, suggests some new expedient to secure success, or discovers consequential advantages not hitherto foreseen. While preparations are made, and materials accumulated, day glides after day through elysian prospects, and the heart dances to the song of hope.

Such is the pleasure of projecting, that many content themselves with a succession of visionary schemes, and wear out their allotted time in the calm amusement of contriving what they never attempt or hope to execute.

Others, not able to feast their imagination with pure ideas, advance somewhat nearer to the grossness of action, with great diligence collect whatever is requisite to their design, and, after a thousand researches and consultations, are snatched away by death, as they stand *in procinctu* waiting for a proper opportunity to begin.

If there were no other end of life, than to find some adequate solace for every day, I know not whether any condition could be preferred to that of the man who involves himself in his own thoughts, and never suffers experience to show him the vanity of speculation; for no sooner are notions reduced to practice, than tranquillity and confidence forsake the breast; every day brings its task, and often without bringing abilities to perform it: difficulties embarrass, uncertainty perplexes, opposition retards, censure exasperates, or neglect depresses. We proceed because we have begun; we complete our design that the labour already spent may not be in vain: but, as expectation gradually dies away, the gay smile of alacrity disappears, we are compelled to implore severer powers, and trust the event to patience and constancy.

When once our labour has begun, the comfort that enables us to endure it is the prospect of its end; for though in every long work there are some joyous intervals of self-applause, when the attention is recreated by unexpected facility, and the imagination soothed by incidental excellencies; yet the toil with which performance struggles after idea, is so irksome and disgusting, and so frequent is the necessity of resting below that perfection which we imagined within our reach, that seldom any man obtains more from his endeavours than a painful conviction of his defects, and a continual resuscitation of desires which he feels himself unable to gratify.

So certainly is weariness the concomitant of our undertakings, that every man, in whatever he is engaged, consoles himself with the hope of change; if he has made his way by assiduity to publick employment, he talks among his friends of the delight of retreat; if, by the necessity of solitary application, he is secluded from the world, he listens with a beating heart to distant noises, longs to mingle with living beings, and resolves to take hereafter his fill of diversions, or display his abilities on the universal theatre, and enjoy the pleasure of distinction and applause.

Every desire, however innocent, grows dangerous, as by long indulgence it becomes ascendant in the mind. When we have been much accustomed to consider any thing as capable of giving happiness, it is not easy to restrain our ardour, or to forbear some precipitation in our advances, and irregularity in our pursuits. He that has cultivated the tree, watched the swelling bud and opening blossom, and pleased himself with computing how much every sun and shower add to its growth, scarcely stays till the fruit has obtained its maturity, but defeats his own cares by eagerness to reward them. When we have diligently laboured for any purpose, we are willing to believe that we have attained it, and, because we have already done much, too suddenly conclude that no more is to be done.

All attraction is increased by the approach of the attracting body. We never find ourselves so desirous to finish, as in the latter part of our work, or so impatient of delay, as when we know that delay cannot be long. Thus unseasonable importunity of discontent may be partly imputed to languor and weariness, which must always oppress those more whose toil has been longer continued; but the greater part usually proceeds from frequent contemplation of that ease which is now considered as within reach, and which, when it has once flattered our hopes, we cannot suffer to be withheld.

In some of the noblest compositions of wit, the conclusion falls below the vigour and spirit of the first books; and as a genius is not to be degraded by the imputation of human failings, the cause of this declension is commonly sought in the structure of the work, and plausible reasons are given why in the defective part less ornament was necessary, or less could be admitted. But, perhaps, the author would have confessed, that his fancy was tired, and his perseverance broken; and he knew his design to be unfinished, but that, when he saw the end so near, he could no longer refuse to be at rest.

Against the instillitions of this frigid opiate, the heart should be secured by all the considerations which once concurred to kindle the ardour of enterprise. Whatever motive first incited action, has still greater force to stimulate perseverance; since he that might have lain still at first in blameless obscurity, cannot afterwards desist but with infamy and reproach. He, whom a doubtful promise of distant good could encourage to set difficulties at defiance, ought not to remit his vigour, when he has almost obtained his recompense. To faint or loiter, when only the last efforts are required, is to steer the ship through tempests, and abandon it to the winds in sight of land: it is to break the ground and scatter the seed, and at last to neglect the harvest.

14

The masters of rhetorick direct, that the most forcible arguments be produced in the latter part of an oration, lest they should be effaced or perplexed by supervenient images. This precept may be justly extended to the series of life. Nothing is ended with honour, which does not conclude better than it began. It is not sufficient to maintain the first vigour; for excellence loses its effect upon the mind by custom, as light after a time ceases to dazzle. Admiration must be continued by that novelty which first produced it, and how much soever is given, there must always be reason to imagine that more remains.

We not only are most sensible of the last impressions, but such is the unwillingness of mankind to admit transcendent merit, that, though it be difficult to obliterate the reproach of miscarriages by any subsequent achievement, however illustrious, yet the reputation raised by a long train of success may be finally ruined by a single failure; for weakness or error will be always remembered by that malice and envy which it gratifies.

For the prevention of that disgrace, which lassitude and negligence may bring at last upon the greatest performances, it is necessary to proportion carefully our labour to our strength. If the design comprises many parts, equally essential, and therefore not to be separated, the only time for caution is before we engage; the powers of the mind must be then impartially estimated, and it must be remembered, that not to complete the plan is not to have begun it; and that nothing is done, while any thing is omitted.

But if the task consists in the repetition of single acts, no one of which derives its efficacy from the rest, it may be attempted with less scruple, because there is always opportunity to retreat with honour. The danger is only, lest we expect from the world the indulgence with which most are disposed to treat themselves; and in the hour of listlessness imagine, that the diligence of one day will atone for the idleness of another, and that applause begun by approbation will be continued by habit.

He that is himself weary will soon weary the publick. Let him therefore lay down his employment, whatever it be, who can no longer exert his former activity or attention; let him not endeavour to struggle with censure, or obstinately infest the stage till a general hiss commands him to depart.*

* Note XVIII., Appendix.

THE ADVENTURER.

THE ADVENTURER.

1753.

[Dr. Hawkesworth, a friend and warm admirer of Dr. Johnson, started, towards the close of 1752, a new periodical, called the *Adventurer*. Johnson, at that time, was plunged in the deepest dejection, and though there can be little doubt, as Boswell says, that he gave Hawkesworth many valuable hints, it was not until the spring of the following year that he could be induced to take any personal share in the new undertaking. His first contribution, written in the shape of an imaginary letter, is dated significantly, "Fleet Prison." Johnson was, indeed, just then in the donjons of Giant Despair, for, as one of his friends at the time remarked, he seemed to have reached the meridian of his melancholy. His friendship with Dr. Hawkesworth was close and cordial, and Boswell believes that Johnson buried his wife in the churchyard of Bromley, Kent, because Hawkesworth lived in the little town.]

Saturday, April 28, 1753.

> " *Quicunque turpi fraude semel innotuit,*
> *Etiamsi vera dici, amittit fidem.*"   Phæd.

> " The wretch that often has deceiv'd,
> Though truth he speaks, is ne'er believ'd."

WHEN Aristotle was once asked, what a man could gain by uttering falsehoods? he replied, " Not to be credited when he shall tell the truth."

The character of a liar is at once so hateful and contemptible, that even of those who have lost their virtue it might be expected that from the violation of truth they should be restrained by their pride. Almost every other vice that disgraces human nature, may be kept in countenance by applause and association : the corrupter of virgin innocence sees himself envied by the men, and at least not detested by the women : the drunkard may easily unite with beings, devoted like himself to noisy merriments or silent insensibility, who will celebrate his victories over the novices of intemperance, boast themselves the companions of his prowess, and tell with rapture of the multitudes whom unsuccessful emulation has hurried to the grave : even the robber and the cut-throat have their followers, who admire their address and intrepidity, their stratagems of rapine, and their fidelity to the gang.

The liar, and only the liar, is invariably and universally despised, abandoned and disowned : he has no domestick consolations, which he can oppose to the censure of mankind ; he can retire to no fraternity, where his crimes may stand in the place of virtues ; but is given up to the hisses of the multitude, without friend and without apologist. It is the peculiar condition of falsehood, to be equally detested by the good and bad : "The devils," says Sir Thomas Brown, "do not tell lies to one another ; for truth is "necessary to all societies : nor can the society of hell "subsist without it."

It is natural to expect, that a crime thus generally detested should be generally avoided ; at least, that none should expose himself to unabated and unpitied infamy, without an adequate temptation ; and that to guilt so easily detected, and so severely punished, an adequate temptation would not readily be found.

Yet so it is, that in defiance of censure and contempt, truth is frequently violated ; and scarcely the most vigilant and unremitted circumspection will secure him that mixes with mankind, from being hourly deceived by men of whom it can scarcely be imagined, that they mean any injury to him or profit to themselves ; even where the subject of conversation could not have been expected to put the passions in motion, or to have excited either hope or fear, or zeal or malignity, sufficient to induce any man to put his reputation in hazard, however little he might value it, or to overpower the love of truth, however weak might be its influence.

The casuists have very diligently distinguished lies into their several classes, according to their various degrees of malignity : but they have, I think, generally omitted that which is most common, and, perhaps, not least mischievous ; which, since the moralists have not given it a name, I shall distinguish as the *lie* of *vanity*.

To vanity may justly be imputed most of the falsehoods, which every man perceives hourly playing upon his ear, and, perhaps, most of those that are propagated with success. To the lie of commerce, and the lie of malice, the motive is so apparent, that they are seldom negligently or implicitly received : suspicion is always watchful over the practices of interest ; and whatever the hope of gain, or desire of mischief, can prompt one man to assert, another is by reasons equally cogent incited to refute. But vanity pleases herself with such slight gratifications, and looks forward to pleasure so remotely consequential, that her practices raise no alarm, and her statagems are not easily discovered.

Vanity is, indeed, often suffered to pass unpursued by suspicion, because he that would watch her motions, can never be at rest : fraud and malice are bounded in their influence ; some opportunity of time and place is necessary to their agency ; but scarce any man is abstracted one moment from his vanity; and he, to whom truth affords no gratifications, is generally inclined to seek them in falsehoods.

It is remarked by Sir Kenelm Digby, " that every " man has a desire to appear superior to others, though " it were only in having seen what they have not " seen." Such an accidental advantage, since it neither implies merit, nor confers dignity, one would think should not be desired so much as to be counterfeited : yet even this vanity, trifling as it is, produces innumerable narratives, all equally false ; but more or less credible in proportion to the skill or confidence of the relater. How many may a man of diffusive conversation count among his acquaintances, whose lives have been signalized by numberless escapes ; who never cross the river but in a storm, or take a journey into the country without more adventures than befel the knights-errant of ancient times in pathless forests or enchanted castles ! How many must he know, to whom portents and prodigies are of daily occurrence ; and for whom nature is hourly working wonders invisible to every other eye, only to supply them with subjects of conversation !

Others there are that amuse themselves with the dissemination of falsehood, at greater hazard of detection and disgrace ; men marked out by some lucky planet for universal confidence and friendship, who have been consulted in every difficulty, intrusted with every secret, and summoned to every transaction : it is the supreme felicity of these men, to stun all companies with noisy information ; to still doubt, and overbear opposition, with certain knowledge or authentick intelligence. A liar of this kind, with a strong memory or brisk imagination, is often the oracle of an obscure club, and, till time discovers his impostures, dictates to his hearers with uncontrouled authority; for if a publick question be started, he was present at the debate; if a new fashion be mentioned, he was at court the first day of its appearance; if a new performance of literature draws the attention of the publick, he has patronised the author, and seen his work in manuscript; if a criminal of eminence be condemned to die, he often predicted his fate, and endeavoured his reformation : and who that lives at a distance from the scene of action, will dare to contradict a man, who reports from his own eyes and ears, and to whom all persons and affairs are thus intimately known ?

This kind of falsehood is generally successful for a time, because it is practised at first with timidity and caution : but the prosperity of the liar is of short duration; the reception of one story is always an incitement to the forgery of another less probable; and he goes on to triumph over tacit credulity, till pride or reason rises up against him, and his companions will no longer endure to see him wiser than themselves.

It is apparent, that the inventors of all these fictions intend some exaltation of themselves, and are led off by the pursuit of honour from their attendance upon truth : their narratives always imply some consequence in favour of their courage, their sagacity, or their activity, their familiarity with the learned, or their reception among the great; they are always bribed by the present pleasure of seeing themselves superior to those that surround them, and receiving the homage of silent attention and envious admiration.

But vanity is sometimes excited to fiction by less visible gratifications : the present age abounds with a race of liars who are content with the consciousness of falsehood, and whose pride is to deceive others without any gain or glory to themselves. Of this tribe it is the supreme pleasure to remark a lady in the playhouse or the park, and to publish, under the character of a man suddenly enamoured, an advertisement in the news of the next day, containing a minute description of her person and her dress. From this artifice, however, no other effect can be expected, than perturbations which the writer can never see, and conjectures of which he never can be informed: some mischief, however, he hopes he has done; and to have done mischief, is of some importance. He sets his invention to work again, and produces a narrative of a robbery or a murder, with all the circumstances of time and place accurately adjusted. This is a jest of greater effect and longer duration: if he fixes his scene at a proper distance, he may for several days keep a wife in terror for her husband, or a mother for her son; and please himself with reflecting, that by his abilities and address some addition is made to the miseries of life.

There is, I think, an ancient law of Scotland, by which leasing-making was capitally punished. I am, indeed, far from desiring to increase in this kingdom the number of executions; yet I cannot but think, that they who destroy the confidence of society, weaken the credit of intelligence, and interrupt the security of life; harrass the delicate with shame, and perplex the timorous with alarms; might very properly be awakened to a sense of their crimes, by denunciations of a whipping-post or pillory: since many are so insensible of right and wrong, that they have no standard of action but the law; nor feel guilt, but as they dread punishment.*

* Note XIX., Appendix.

Saturday, May 25, 1758.

" Damnant quod non intelligunt."   Cic.

" They condemn what they do not understand."

E URIPIDES, having presented Socrates with the writings
    of Heraclitus, a philosopher famed for involution and
obscurity, inquired afterwards his opinion of their merit.
"What I understand," said Socrates, "I find to be
"excellent; and, therefore, believe that to be of equal
"value which I cannot understand."

The reflection of every man who reads this passage will
suggest to him the difference between the practice of
Socrates, and that of modern criticks. Socrates, who had,
by long observation upon himself and others, discovered the
weakness of the strongest, and the dimness of the most
enlightened intellect, was afraid to decide hastily in his own
favour, or to conclude that an author had written without
meaning, because he could not immediately catch his
ideas; he knew that the faults of books are often more
justly imputable to the reader, who sometimes wants
attention, and sometimes penetration; whose understanding is often obstructed by prejudice, and often dissipated
by remissness; who comes sometimes to a new study,
unfurnished with knowledge previously necessary; and
finds difficulties insuperable, for want of ardour sufficient to
encounter them.

Obscurity and clearness are relative terms: to some
readers scarce any book is easy, to others not many are
difficult: and surely they, whom neither any exuberant

praise bestowed by others, nor any eminent conquests over stubborn problems, have entitled to exalt themselves above the common orders of mankind, might condescend to imitate the candour of Socrates; and where they find incontestible proofs of superior genius, be content to think that there is justness in the connection which they cannot trace, and cogency in the reasoning which they cannot comprehend.

This diffidence is never more reasonable than in the perusal of the authors of antiquity; of those whose works have been the delight of ages, and transmitted as the great inheritance of mankind from one generation to another: surely, no man can, without the utmost arrogance, imagine that he brings any superiority of understanding to the perusal of these books which have been preserved in the devastation of cities, and snatched up from the wreck of nations; which those who fled before barbarians have been careful to carry off in the hurry of migration, and of which barbarians have repented the destruction. If in books thus made venerable by the uniform attestation of successive ages, any passages shall appear unworthy of that praise which they have formerly received, let us not immediately determine, that they owed their reputation to dulness or bigotry; but suspect at least that our ancestors had some reasons for their opinions, and that our ignorance of those reasons make us differ from them.

It often happens that an author's reputation is endangered in succeeding times, by that which raised the loudest applause among his contemporaries: nothing is read with greater pleasure than allusions to recent facts, reigning opinions, or present controversies; but when facts are forgotten, and controversies extinguished, these favourite touches lose all their graces; and the author in his descent to posterity must be left to the mercy of chance, without any power of ascertaining the memory of those things, to which he owed his luckiest thoughts and his kindest reception.

On such occasions every reader should remember the diffidence of Socrates, and repair by his candour the injuries of time; he should impute the seeming defects of his author to some chasm of intelligence, and suppose that the sense which is now weak was once forcible, and the expression which is now dubious formerly determinate.

How much the mutilation of ancient history has taken away from the beauty of poetical performances, may be conjectured from the light which a lucky commentator sometimes effuses, by the recovery of an incident that had been long forgotten: thus, in the third book of Horace, Juno's denunciations against those that should presume to raise again the walls of Troy, could for many ages please only by splendid images and swelling language, of which no man discovered the use or propriety, till Le Fevre, by showing on what occasion the Ode was written, changed wonder to rational delight. Many passages yet undoubtedly remain in the same author, which an exacter knowledge of the incidents of his time would clear from objections. Among these I have always numbered the following lines:

> " *Aurum per medios ire satellites,*
> *Et perrumpere amat saxa, potentius*
> *Ictu fulmineo. Concidit Auguris*
> *Argivi domus ob lucrum*
> *Demersa excidio. Diffidit urbium*
> *Portas vir Macedo, et subruit æmulos*
> *Reges muneribus. Munera navium*
> *Sævos illaqueant duces.*"

> " Stronger than thunder's winged force,
> All-powerful gold can spread its course,

> Thro' watchful guards its passage make,
> And loves thro' solid walls to break :
> From gold the overwhelming woes,
> That crush'd the Grecian augur rose ;
> Philip with gold thro' cities broke,
> And rival monarchs felt his yoke ;
> *Captains of ships to gold are slaves,*
> *Tho' fierce as their own winds and waves."*
>
>   FRANCIS.

The close of this passage by which every reader is now
disappointed and offended, was probably the delight of the
Roman court: it cannot be imagined, that Horace, after
having given to gold the force of thunder, and told of its
power to storm cities and to conquer kings, would have
concluded his account of its efficacy with its influence
over naval commanders, had he not alluded to some fact
then current in the mouths of men, and therefore more
interesting for a time than the conquests of Philip. Of the
like kind may be reckoned another stanza in the same
book :

> " ——*Jussa coram non sine conscio*
> *Surgit marito, seu vocat* institor
> *Seu* navis Hispanæ magister
> *Dedecorum pretiosus emptor."*

> " The conscious husband bids her rise,
> *When some rich factor courts her charms,*
> Who calls the wanton to his arms,
> And, prodigal of wealth and fame,
> Profusely buys the costly shame."   FRANCIS.

He has little knowledge of Horace who imagines that the
factor, or the Spanish merchant, are mentioned by chance :
there was undoubtedly some popular story of an intrigue,
which those names recalled to the memory of his reader.

The flame of his genius in other parts, though somewhat

dimmed by time, is not totally eclipsed; his address and judgment yet appear, though much of the spirit and vigour of his sentiment is lost: this has happened to the twentieth Ode of the first book ;

> " *Vile potabis modicis Sabinum*
> *Cantharis, Græcà quod ego ipse testâ*
> *Conditum levi ; datus in theatro*
> *Cùm tibi plausus,*
> *Chare Mæcenas eques. Ut paterni*
> *Fluminis ripæ, simul et jocosa*
> *Redderet laudes tibi Vaticani*
> *Montis imago.*"

> " A poet's beverage humbly cheap,
> (Should great Mæcenas be my guest)
> The vintage of the Sabine grape,
> But yet in sober cups shall crown the feast !
> 'Twas rack'd into a Grecian cask,
> Its rougher juice to melt away ;
> I seal'd it too—a pleasing task !
> With annual joy to mark the glorious day,
> When in applausive shouts thy name
> Spread from the theatre around,
> Floating on thy own Tiber's stream,
> And Echo, playful nymph, return'd the sound."

FRANCIS.

We here easily remark the intermixture of a happy compliment with an humble invitation; but certainly are less delighted than those, to whom the mention of the applause bestowed upon Mæcenas, gave occasion to recount the actions or words that produced it.

Two lines which have exercised the ingenuity of modern criticks, may, I think, be reconciled to the judgment, by an easy supposition : Horace thus addresses Agrippa ;

15

" *Scriberis Varfio ortis, et hostium*
  Victor, Mæonii carminis alite."

"Varius, a *swan of Homer's wing,*
  Shall brave Agrippa's conquests sing."

That Varius should be called "A bird of Homeric song,"
appears so harsh to modern ears, that an emendation of the
text has been proposed : but surely the learning of the
ancients had been long ago obliterated, had every man
thought himself at liberty to corrupt the lines which he did
not understand. If we imagine that Varius had been by
any of his contemporaries celebrated under the appellation
of Musarum Ales, the swan of the Muses, the language of
Horace becomes graceful and familiar ; and that such a
compliment was at least possible, we know from the
transformation feigned by Horace of himself.

The most elegant compliment that was paid to Addison,
is of this obscure and perishable kind ;

" When panting Virtue her last efforts made,
  You brought your CLIO to the Virgin's aid."

These lines must please as long as they are understood ;
but can be understood only by those that have observed
Addison's signatures in the *Spectator.*

The nicety of these minute allusions I shall exemplify by
another instance, which I take this occasion to mention,
because, as I am told, the commentators have omitted it.
Tibullus addresses Cynthia in this manner :

" *Te spectem, suprema mihi cùm venerit hora,*
  Te teneam moriens deficiente manu."

" Before my closing eyes dear Cynthia stand,
  Held weakly by my fainting trembling hand."

To these lines Ovid thus refers in his elegy on the death of Tibullus:

> " *Cynthia decedens, felicius, inquit, amata*
> *Sum tibi; vixisti dum tuus ignis eram,*
> *Cui Nemesis, quid, ait, tibi sunt mea damna dolori?*
> *Me tenuit moriens deficiente manu.*"

> " Blest was my reign, retiring Cynthia cry'd:
> Nor till he left my breast, Tibullus dy'd.
> Forbear, said Nemesis, my loss to moan,
> The fainting trembling hand was mine alone."

The beauty of this passage, which consists in the appropriation made by Nemesis of the line originally directed to Cynthia, had been wholly imperceptible to succeeding ages, had chance, which has destroyed so many greater volumes, deprived us likewise of the poems of Tibullus.

Tuesday, August 28, 1753.

> " *Qui cupit optatam cursu contingere metam,*
> *Multa tulit fecitque puer.*" Hor.

> " The youth, who hopes th' Olympick prize to gain,
> All arts must try, and every toil sustain." Francis.

IT is observed by Bacon, that " reading makes a full " man, conversation a ready man, and writing an exact " man."

As Bacon attained to degrees of knowledge scarcely ever attained by any other man, the directions which he gives for study have certainly a just claim to our regard; for who can teach an art with so great authority, as he that has practised it with undisputed success?

Under the protection of so great a name, I shall, therefore, venture to inculcate to my ingenious contemporaries, the necessity of reading, the fitness of consulting other understandings than their own, and of considering the sentiments and opinions of those who, however neglected in the present age, had in their own times, and many of them a long time afterwards, such reputation for knowledge and acuteness as will scarcely ever be attained by those that despise them.

An opinion has of late been, I know not how, propagated amongst us, that libraries are filled only with useless lumber; that men of parts stand in need of no assistance; and that to spend life in poring upon books, is only to imbibe prejudices, to obstruct and embarrass the powers of nature, to cultivate memory at the expense of judgment, and to bury reason under a chaos of indigested learning.

Such is the talk of many who think themselves wise, and of some who are thought wise by others; of whom part probably believe their own tenets, and part may be justly suspected of endeavouring to shelter their ignorance in multitudes, and of wishing to destroy that reputation which they have no hopes to share. It will, I believe, be found invariably true, that learning was never decried by any learned man; and what credit can be given to those, who venture to condemn that which they do not know?

If reason has the power ascribed to it by its advocates, if so much is to be discovered by attention and meditation, it is hard to believe, that so many millions, equally participating of the bounties of nature with ourselves, have been for ages upon ages meditating in vain: if the wits of the present time expect the regard of posterity, which will then inherit the reason which is now thought superior to instruction, surely they may allow themselves to be instructed by the reason of former generations. When, therefore, an author declares, that he has been able to learn nothing from the writings of his predecessors, and such a declaration has been lately made, nothing but a degree of arrogance unpardonable in the greatest human understanding, can hinder him from perceiving that he is raising prejudices against his performance ; for with what hopes of success can he attempt that in which greater abilities have hitherto miscarried ? or with what peculiar force does he suppose himself invigorated, that difficulties hitherto invincible should give way before him.

Of those whom Providence has qualified to make any additions to human knowledge, the number is extremely small ; and what can be added by each single mind, even of this superior class, is very little : the greatest part of mankind must owe all their knowledge, and all must owe far the larger part of it, to the information of others.   To understand the works of celebrated authors, to comprehend their systems, and retain their reasonings, is a task more than equal to common intellects ; and he is by no means to be accounted useless or idle, who has stored his mind with acquired knowledge, and can detail it occasionally to others who have less leisure or weaker abilities.

Perseus has justly observed, that knowledge is nothing to him who is not known by others to possess it : to the scholar himself it is nothing with respect either to honour or advantage, for the world cannot reward those qualities which are concealed from it ; with respect to others it is nothing, because it affords no help to ignorance or error.

It is with justice, therefore, that in an accomplished character, Horace unites just sentiments with the power of expressing them ; and he that has once accumulated learning, is next to consider, how he shall most widely diffuse and most agreeably impart it.

A ready man is made by conversation. He that buries himself among his manuscripts "besprent," as Pope expresses it, "with learned dust," and wears out his days and nights in perpetual research and solitary meditation, is too apt to lose in his elocution what he adds to his wisdom ; and when he comes into the world, to appear overloaded with his own notions, like a man armed with weapons which he cannot wield. He has no facility of inculcating his speculations, of adapting himself to the various degrees of intellect which the accidents of conversation will present ; but will talk to most unintelligibly, and to all unpleasantly.

I was once present at the lectures of a profound philosopher, a man really skilled in the science which he professed, who having occasion to explain the terms *opacum* and *pellucidum*, told us, after some hesitation, that *opacum* was, as one might say, *opake*, and that *pellucidum* signified *pellucid*. Such was the dexterity with which this learned reader facilitated to his auditors the intricacies of science ; and so true is it, that a man may know what he cannot teach.

Boerhaave* complains, that the writers who have treated of chymistry before him, are useless to the greater part of students, because they presuppose their readers to have such degrees of skill as are not often to be found. Into the same error are all men apt to fall, who have familiarized any subject to themselves in solitude : they discourse as if they thought every other man had been employed in the same enquiries ; and expect that short hints and obscure allusions

---

* Note XX., Appendix.

will produce in others the same train of ideas which they excite in themselves.

Nor is this the only inconvenience which the man of study suffers from a recluse life. When he meets with an opinion that pleases him, he catches it up with eagerness; looks only after such arguments as tend to his confirmation; or spares himself the trouble of discussion, and adopts it with very little proof; indulges it long without suspicion, and in time unites it to the general body of his knowledge, and treasures it up among incontestible truths : but when he comes into the world among men who, arguing upon dissimilar principles, have been led to different conclusions, and being placed in various situations, view the same object on many sides; he finds his darling position attacked, and himself in no condition to defend it : having thought always in one train, he is in the state of a man who having fenced with the same master, is perplexed and amazed by a new posture of his antagonist; he is entangled in unexpected difficulties, he is harrassed by sudden objections, he is unprovided with solutions or replies; his surprize impedes his natural powers of reasoning, his thoughts are scattered and confounded, and he gratifies the pride of airy petulence with an easy victory.

It is difficult to imagine, with what obstinacy truths which one mind perceives almost by intuition, will be rejected by another; and how many artifices must be practised, to procure admission for the most evident propositions into understandings frighted by their novelty, or hardened against them by accidental prejudice; it can scarcely be conceived, how frequently, in these extemporaneous controversies, the dull will be subtle, and the acute absurd; how often stupidity will elude the force of argument, by involving itself in its own gloom; and mistaken ingenuity will weave artful fallacies, which reason can scarcely find means to disentangle.

In these encounters the learning of the recluse usually fails him: nothing but long habit and frequent experiments can confer the power of changing a position into various forms, presenting it in different points of view, connecting it with known and granted truths, fortifying it with intelligible arguments, and illustrating it by apt similitudes; and he, therefore, that has collected his knowledge in solitude, must learn its application by mixing with mankind.

But while the various opportunities of conversation invite us to try every mode of argument, and every art of recommending our sentiments, we are frequently betrayed to the use of such as are not in themselves strictly defensible: a man heated in talk, and eager of victory, takes advantage of the mistakes or ignorance of his adversary, lays hold of concessions to which he knows he has no right, and urges proofs likely to prevail in his opponent, though he knows himself that they have no force: thus the severity of reason is relaxed, many topicks are accumulated, but without just arrangement or distinction; we learn to satisfy ourselves with such ratiocination as silences others; and seldom recall to a close examination, that discourse which has gratified our vanity with victory and applause.

Some caution, therefore, must be used lest copiousness and facility be made less valuable by inaccuracy and confusion. To fix the thoughts by writing, and subject them to frequent examinations and reviews, is the best method of enabling the mind to detect its own sophisms, and keep it on guard against the fallacies which it practises on others: in conversation we naturally diffuse our thoughts, and in writing we contract them; method is the excellence of writing, and unconstraint the grace of conversation.

To read, write, and converse in due proportions, is therefore, the business of a man of letters. For all these there is not often equal opportunity; excellence, therefore, is not often attainable; and most men fail in one or other of the ends proposed, and are full without readiness, or ready without exactness. Some deficiency must be forgiven all, because all are men; and more must be allowed to pass uncensured in the greater part of the world, because none can confer upon himself abilities, and few have the choice of situations proper for the improvement of those which nature has bestowed: it is however, reasonable, to have *perfection* in our eye; that we may always advance towards it, though we know it never can be reached.

Tuesday, October 2, 1753.

" ——*Dulcique animos novitate tenebo.*" OVID.

" And with sweet novelty your soul detain."

IT is often charged upon writers, that with all their pretensions to genius and discoveries, they do little more than copy one another; and that compositions intruded upon the world with the pomp of novelty, contain only tedious repetitions of common sentiments, or at best exhibit a transposition of known images, and give a new appearance to truth only by some slight difference of dress and decoration.

The allegation of resemblance between authors, is indisputably true; but the image of plagiarism, which is raised upon it, is not to be allowed with equal readiness. A coincidence of sentiment may easily happen without any communication, since there are many occasions in which all reasonable men will nearly think alike. Writers of all ages have had the same sentiments, because they have in all ages had the same objects of speculation; the interests and passions, the virtues and vices of mankind, have been diversified in different times, only by unessential and casual varieties; and we must, therefore, expect in the works of all those who attempt to describe them, such a likeness as we find in the pictures of the same person drawn in different periods of his life.

not the most rocious terary rime

It is necessary, therefore, that before an author be charged with plagiarism, one of the most reproachful, though, perhaps, not the most atrocious of literary crimes, the subject on which he treats should be carefully considered. We do not wonder, that historians, relating the same facts, agree in their narration; or that authors, delivering the elements of science, advance the same theorems, and lay down the same definitions; yet it is not wholly without use to mankind, that books are multiplied, and different authors lay out their labours on the same subject; for there will always be some reason why one should on particular occasions or to particular persons, be preferable to another; some will be clear where others are obscure, some will please by their style and others by their method, some by their embellishments and others by their simplicity, some by closeness and others by diffusion.

The same indulgence is to be shewn to the writers of morality: right and wrong are immutable: and those, therefore, who teach us to distinguish them, if they all teach us right, must agree with one another. The relations of social life, and the duties resulting from them, must be the same at all times and in all nations: some petty differences may be, indeed, produced, by forms of government or arbitrary customs; but the general doctrine can receive no alteration.

Yet it is not to be desired, that morality should be considered as interdicted to all future writers: men will always be tempted to deviate from their duty, and will, therefore, always want a monitor to recall them; and a new book often seizes the attention of the publick, without any other claim than that it is new. There is likewise in composition, as in other things, a perpetual vicissitude of fashion; and truth is recommended at one time to regard, by appearances which at another would expose it to neglect; the author, therefore, who has judgment to discern the taste of his contemporaries, and skill to gratify it, will have always an opportunity to deserve well of mankind, by conveying instruction to them in a grateful vehicle.

There are likewise many modes of composition, by which a moralist may deserve the name of an original writer: he may familiarize his system by dialogues after the manner of the ancients, or subtilize it into a series of syllogistic arguments: he may enforce his doctrine by seriousness and solemnity, or enliven it by sprightliness and gaiety; he may deliver his sentiments in naked precepts, or illustrate them by historical examples; he may detain the studious by the artful concatenation of a continued discourse, or relieve the busy by short strictures, and unconnected essays.

To excel in any of these forms of writing will require a particular cultivation of the genius: whoever can attain to excellence, will be certain to engage a set of readers, whom no other method would have equally allured; and he that communicates truth with success, must be numbered among the first benefactors to mankind.

The same observation may be extended likewise to the passions : their influence is uniform, and their effects nearly the same in every human breast : a man loves and hates, desires and avoids, exactly like his neighbour ; resentment and ambition, avarice and indolence, discover themselves by the same symptoms in minds distant a thousand years from one another.

Nothing, therefore, can be more unjust, than to charge an author with plagiarism, merely because he assigns to every cause its natural effect ; and makes his personages act, as others in like circumstances have always done. There are conceptions in which all men will agree, though each derives them from observation : whoever has been in love, will represent a lover impatient of every idea that interrupts his meditations on his mistress, retiring to shades and solitude, that he may muse without disturbance on the approaching happiness, or associating himself with some friend that flatters his passion, and talking away the hours of absence upon his darling subject. Whoever has been so unhappy as to have felt the miseries of long-continued hatred, will, without any assistance from ancient volumes, be able to relate how the passions are kept in perpetual agitation, by the recollection of injury and meditations of revenge : how the blood boils at the name of the enemy, and life is worn away in contrivances of mischief.

Every other passion is alike simple and limited, if it be considered only with regard to the breast which it inhabits ; the anatomy of the mind, as that of the body, must perpetually exhibit the same appearances ; and though by the continued industry of successive inquirers, new movements will be from time to time discovered, they can effect only the minuter parts, and are commonly of more curiosity than importance.

It will now be natural to inquire, by what arts are the writers of the present and future ages to attract the notice and favour of mankind. They are to observe the alterations which time is always making in the modes of life, that they may gratify every generation with a picture of themselves. Thus love is uniform, but courtship is perpetually varying; the different arts of gallantry, which beauty has inspired, would of themselves be sufficient to fill a volume; sometimes balls and serenades, sometimes tournaments and adventures, have been employed to melt the hearts of ladies, who in another century have been sensible of scarce any other merit than that of riches, and listened only to jointures and pin-money. Thus the ambitious man has at all times been eager of wealth and power; but these hopes have been gratified in some countries by supplicating the people, and in others by flattering the prince: honour in some states has been only the reward of military achievements, in others it has been gained by noisy turbulence and popular clamours. Avarice has worn a different form, as she actuated the usurer of Rome, and the stock-jobber of England; and idleness itself, how little soever inclined to the trouble of invention, has been forced from time to time to change its amusements, and contrive different methods of wearing out the day.

Here then is the fund, from which those who study mankind may fill their compositions with an inexhaustible variety of images and illusions; and he must be confessed to look with little attention upon scenes thus perpetually changing, who cannot catch some of the figures before they are made vulgar by reiterated descriptions.

It has been discovered by Sir Isaac Newton, that the distinct and primogenial colours are only seven; but every eye can witness, that from various mixtures, in various proportions, infinite diversifications of tints may be produced. In like manner, the passions of the mind, which put the world in motion, and produce all the bustle and eagerness of the busy crowds that swarm upon the earth : the passions, from whence arise all the pleasures and pains that we see and hear of, if we analyse the mind of man, are very few ; but those few agitated and combined, as external causes shall happen to operate, and modified by prevailing opinions, and accidental caprices, make such frequent alterations on the surface of life, that the show, while we are busied in delineating it, vanishes from the view, and a new set of objects succeed, doomed to the same shortness of duration with the former : thus curiosity may always find employment, and the busy part of mankind will furnish the contemplative with the materials of speculation to the end of time.

The complaint, therefore, that all topicks are preoccupied, is nothing more than the murmur of ignorance or idleness, by which some discourage others and some themselves ; the mutability of mankind will always furnish writers with new images, and the luxuriance of fancy may always embellish them with new decorations.

Saturday, October 27, 1753.

" ——*Quid tam dextro pede concipis, ut te
Conatus non pæniteat votique peracti ?*"   Juv.

" What in the conduct of our life appears
So well design'd, so luckily begun,
But, when we have our wish, we wish undone."
                                        DRYDEN.

To the ADVENTURER.

SIR,

I HAVE been for many years a trader in London. My beginning was narrow, and my stock small; I was, therefore, a long time brow-beaten and despised by those, who having more money thought they had more merit than myself. I did not, however, suffer my resentment to instigate me to any mean arts of supplantation, nor my eagerness of riches to betray me to any indirect methods of gain; I pursued my business with incessant assiduity, supported by the hope of being one day richer than those who contemned me; and had, upon every annual review of my books, the satisfaction of finding my fortune increased beyond my expectation.

In a few years my industry and probity were fully recompensed, my wealth was really great, and my reputation for wealth still greater. I had large warehouses crowded with goods, and considerable sums in the publick funds; I was caressed upon the Exchange by the most eminent merchants; became the oracle of the common council;

was solicited to engage in all commercial undertakings; was flattered with the hopes of becoming in a short time one of the directors of a wealthy company, and, to complete my mercantile honours, enjoyed the expensive happiness of fining for sheriff.

Riches you know, easily produce riches: when I had arrived to this degree of wealth, I had no longer any obstruction or opposition to fear; new acquisitions were hourly brought within my reach, and I continued for some years longer to heap thousands upon thousands.

At last I resolved to complete the circle of a citizen's prosperity by the purchase of an estate in the country, and to close my life in retirement. From the hour that this design entered my imagination, I found the fatigues of my employment every day more oppressive, and persuaded myself that I was no longer equal to perpetual attention, and that my health would soon be destroyed by the torment and distraction of extensive business. I could image to myself no happiness, but in vacant jollity and uninterrupted leisure; nor entertain my friends with any other topick, than the vexation and uncertainty of trade, and the happiness of rural privacy.

But notwithstanding these declarations, I could not at once reconcile myself to the thoughts of ceasing to get money; and though I was every day inquiring for a purchase, I found some reason for rejecting all that were offered me; and, indeed, had accumulated so many beauties and conveniences in my idea of the spot where I was finally to be happy, that, perhaps, the world might have been travelled over, without discovery of a place which would not have been defective in some particular.

Thus I went on still talking of retirement, and still refusing to retire; my friends began to laugh at my delays, and

I grew ashamed to trifle longer with my own inclinations ; an estate was at length purchased, I transferred my stock to a prudent young man who had married my daughter, went down into the country, and commenced lord of a spacious manor.

Here for some time I found happiness equal to my expectation. I reformed the old house according to the advice of the best architects, I threw down the walls of the garden, and enclosed it with palisades, planted long avenues of trees, filled a greenhouse with exotick plants, dug a new canal, and threw the earth into the old moat.

The fame of these expensive improvements brought in all the country to see the show. I entertained my visitors with great liberality, led them round my gardens, showed them my apartments, laid before them plans for new decorations, and was gratified by the wonder of some and the envy of others.

I was envied ; but how little can one man judge of the condition of another ! The time was now coming in which affluence and splendour could no longer make me pleased with myself. I had built till the imagination of the architect was exhausted ; I had added one convenience to another, till I knew not what more to wish or to design ; I had laid out my gardens, planted my park, and completed my water-works ; and what remained now to be done ? what, but to look up to turrets, of which when they were once raised I had no further use, to range over apartments where time was tarnishing the furniture, to stand by the cascade of which I scarcely now perceived the sound, and to watch the growth of woods that must give their shade to a distant generation.

In this gloomy inactivity, is every day begun and ended : the happiness that I have been so long procuring is now at

16

an end, because it has been procured; I wander from room
to room till I am weary of myself; I ride out to a
neighbouring hill in the centre of my estate, from whence
all my lands lie in prospect round me ; I see nothing that I
have not seen before, and return home disappointed, though
I knew that I had nothing to expect.

In my happy days of business I had been accustomed to
rise early in the morning; and remember the time when I
grieved that the night came so soon upon me, and obliged
me for a few hours to shut out affluence and prosperity. I
now seldom see the rising sun, but to " tell him," with the
fallen angel, " how I hate his beams."   I awake from sleep
as to languor or imprisonment, and have no employment for
the first hour but to consider by what art I shall rid myself
of the second.   I protract the breakfast as long as I can,
because when it is ended I have no call for my attention,
till I can with some degree of decency grow impatient for
my dinner.   If I could dine all my life, I should be happy ;
I eat not because I am hungry, but because I am idle : but,
alas ! the time quickly comes when I can eat no longer ;
and so ill does my constitution second my inclination, that
I cannot bear strong liquors : seven hours must then be
endured before I shall sup ; but supper comes at last, the
more welcome as it is in a short time succeeded by sleep.

Such, Mr. Adventurer, is the happiness, the hope of
which seduced me from the duties and pleasures of a
mercantile life.* I shall be told by those who read my
narrative, that there are many means of innocent amusement, and many schemes of useful employment, which I do
not appear ever to have known ; and that nature and art
have provided pleasures, by which, without the drudgery of

* Note XXI., Appendix.

settled business, the active may be engaged, the solitary soothed, and the social entertained.

These arts, Sir, I have tried. When first I took possession of my estate, in conformity to the taste of my neighbours, I bought guns and nets, filled my kennel with dogs and my stable with horses: but a little experience showed me, that these instruments of rural felicity would afford me few gratifications. I never shot but to miss the mark, and to confess the truth, was afraid of the fire of my own gun. I could discover no musick in the cry of the dogs, nor could divest myself of pity for the animal whose peaceful and inoffensive life was sacrificed to our sport. I was not, indeed, always at leisure to reflect upon her danger; for my horse, who had been bred to the chase, did not always regard my choice either of speed or way, but leaped hedges and ditches at his own discretion, and hurried me along with the dogs, to the great diversion of my brother sportsmen. His eagerness of pursuit once incited him to swim a river; and I had leisure to resolve in the water, that I would never hazard my life again for the destruction of a hare.

I then ordered books to be procured, and by the direction of the vicar had in a few weeks a closet elegantly furnished. You will perhaps, be surprised when I shall tell you, that when once I had ranged them according to their sizes, and piled them up in regular gradations, I had received all the pleasure which they could give me. I am not able to excite in myself any curiosity after events which have been long passed, and in which I can therefore have no interest; I am utterly unconcerned to know whether Tully or Demosthenes excelled in oratory, whether Hannibal lost Italy by his own negligence or the corruption of his countrymen. I have no skill in controversial learning, nor can conceive why so many volumes should have been written upon questions, which I have lived so long and so happily without understanding. I once resolved to go through the volumes relating to the office of justice of the peace, but found them so crabbed and intricate, that in less than a month I desisted in despair, and resolved to supply my deficiencies by paying a competent salary to a skilful clerk.

I am naturally inclined to hospitality, and for some time kept up a constant intercourse of visits with the neighbouring gentlemen : but thought they are easily brought about me by better wine than they can find at any other house, I am not much relieved by their conversation ; they have no skill in commerce or the stocks, and I have no knowledge of the history of families or the factions of the country ; so that when the first civilities are over, they usually talk to one another, and I am left alone in the midst of the company. Though I cannot drink myself, I am obliged to encourage the circulation of the glass ; their mirth grows more turbulent and obstreperous ; and before their merriment is at an end, I am sick with disgust, and, perhaps, reproached with my sobriety, or by some sly insinuations insulted as a cit.

Such, Mr. Adventurer, is the life to which I am condemned by a foolish endeavour to be happy by imitation ; such is the happiness to which I pleased myself with approaching, and which I considered as the chief end of my cares and my labours. I toiled year after year with cheerfulness, in expectation of the happy hour in which I might be idle : the privilege of idleness is attained, but has not brought with it the blessing of tranquillity.

I am,
Yours, &c.,
MERCATOR.

Tuesday, November 27, 1753.

"―――― *Quæ non fecimus ipsi
Vix ea nostra voco.*" OVID.

" The deeds of long descended ancestors
Are but by grace of imputation ours." DRYDEN.

THE evils inseparably annexed to the present condition
of man, are so numerous and afflictive, that it has
been, from age to age, the task of some to bewail, and of
others to solace them ; and he, therefore, will be in danger
of seeing a common enemy, who shall attempt to depreciate
the few pleasures and felicities which nature has allowed us.

Yet I will confess, that I have sometimes employed my
thoughts in examining the pretensions that are made to
happiness, by the splendid and envied condition of life ;
and have not thought the hour unprofitably spent, when I
have detected the imposture of counterfeit advantages, and
found disquiet lurking under false appearances of gayety and
greatness.

It is asserted by a tragick poet, that " est miser nemo
"nisi comparatus," "no man is miserable, but as he is com-
" pared with others happier than himself :" this position is
not strictly and philosophically true. He might have said,
with rigorous propriety, that no man is happy but as he is
compared with the miserable ; for such is the state of this
world, that we find it absolute misery, but happiness only
comparative ; we may incur as much pain as we can possibly
endure, though we never can obtain as much happiness as
we might possibly enjoy.

Yet it is certain likewise, that many of our miseries are merely comparative : we are often made unhappy, not by the presence of any real evil, but by the absence of some fictitious good ; of something which is not required by any real want of nature, which has not in itself any power of gratification, and which neither reason nor fancy would have prompted us to wish, did we not see it in the possession of others.

For a mind diseased with vain longings after unattainable advantages, no medicine can be prescribed, but an impartial inquiry into the real worth of that which is so ardently desired. It is well known, how much the mind, as well as the eye, is deceived by distance ; and, perhaps, it will be found, that of many imagined blessings it may be doubted, whether he that wants or possesses them has more reason to be satisfied with his lot.

The dignity of high birth and long extraction, no man to whom nature has denied it, can confer upon himself ; and, therefore, it deserves to be considered, whether the want of that which can never be gained, may not easily be endured. It is true, that if we consider the triumph and delight with which most of those recount their ancestors, who have ancestors to recount, and the artifices by which some who have risen to unexpected fortune endeavour to insert them-selves into an honourable stem, we shall be inclined to fancy that wisdom or virtue may be had by inheritance, or that all the excellencies of a line of progenitors are accumu-lated on their descendants. Reason, indeed, will soon inform us, that our estimation of birth is arbitrary and capricious, and that dead ancestors can have no influence but upon imagination : let it then be examined, whether one dream may not operate in the place of another : whether he that owes nothing to forefathers, may not

receive equal pleasure from the consciousness of owing all
to himself; whether he may not, with a little meditation,
find it more honourable to found than to continue a family,
and to gain dignity than transmit it; whether, if he receives
no dignity from the virtues of his family, he does not likewise escape the danger of being disgraced by their crimes;
and whether he that brings a new name into the world, has
not the convenience of playing the game of life without a
stake, and opportunity of winning much though he has
nothing to lose.

There is another opinion concerning happiness, which
approaches much more nearly to universality, but which
may, perhaps, with equal reason be disputed. The pretensions to ancestral honours many of the sons of earth easily
see to be ill-grounded; but all agree to celebrate the
advantage of hereditary riches, and to consider those as
the minions of fortune, who are wealthy from their cradles,
whose estate is "res non parta labore sed relicta:" "the
"acquisition of another, not of themselves;" and whom a
father's industry has dispensed from a laborious attention to
arts or commerce, and left at liberty to dispose of life as
fancy shall direct them.

If every man were wise and virtuous, capable to discern
the best use of time, and resolute to practise it; it might be
granted, I think, without hesitation, that total liberty would
be a blessing; and that it would be desirable to be left at
large to the exercise of religious and social duties, without
the interruption of importunate avocations.

But since felicity is relative, and that which is the means
of happiness to one man may be to another the cause of
misery, we are to consider, what state is best adapted to
human nature in its present degeneracy and frailty. And,
surely, to far the greater number it is highly expedient, that

they should by some settled scheme of duties be rescued from the tyranny of caprice, that they should be driven on by necessity through the paths of life with their attention confined to a stated task, that they may be less at leisure to deviate into mischief at the call of folly.

When we observe the lives of those whom an ample inheritance has let loose to their own direction, what do we discover that can excite our envy? Their time seems not to pass with much applause from others, or satisfaction to themselves: many squander their exuberance of fortune in luxury and debauchery, and have no other use of money than to inflame their passions, and riot in a wide range of licentiousness; others less criminal indeed, but surely, not much to be praised, lie down to sleep, and rise up to trifle, are employed every morning in finding expedients to rid themselves of the day, chace pleasure through all the places of publick resort, fly from London to Bath, and from Bath to London, without any other reason for changing place, but that they go in quest of company as idle and as vagrant as themselves, always endeavouring to raise some new desire that they may have something to pursue, to rekindle some hope which they know will be disappointed, changing one amusement for another which a few months will make equally insipid, or sinking into langour and disease for want of something to actuate their bodies or exhilarate their minds.

Whoever has frequented those places, where idlers assemble to escape from solitude, knows that this is generally the state of the wealthy; and from this state it is no great hardship to be debarred. No man can be happy in total idleness: he that should be condemned to lie torpid and motionless, "would fly for recreation," says South, "to the "mines and the galleys;" and it is well, when nature or fortune find employment for those, who would not have known how to procure it for themselves.

He whose mind is engaged by the acquisition or improvement of a fortune, not only escapes the insipidity of indifference, and the tediousness of inactivity, but gains enjoyments wholly unknown to those, who live lazily on the toil of others; for life affords no higher pleasure than that of surmounting difficulties, passing from one step of success to another, forming new wishes, and seeing them gratified. He that labours in any great or laudable undertaking, has his fatigues first supported by hope, and afterwards rewarded by joy; he is always moving to a certain end, and when he has attained it, an end more distant invites him to a new pursuit.

It does not, indeed, always happen, that diligence is fortunate; the wisest schemes are broken by unexpected accidents; the most constant perseverance sometimes toils through life without a recompense; but labour, though unsuccessful, is more eligible than idleness; he that prosecutes a lawful purpose by lawful means, acts always with the approbation of his own reason; he is animated through the course of his endeavours by an expectation which, though not certain, he knows to be just: and is at last comforted in his disappointment, by the consciousness that he has not failed by his own fault.

That kind of life is most happy which affords us most opportunities of gaining our own esteem; and what can any man infer in his own favour from a condition to which, however prosperous, he contributed nothing, and which the vilest and weakest of the species would have obtained by the same right, had he happened to be the son of the same father.

To strive with difficulties, and to conquer them, is the

highest human felicity ; the next is to strive, and deserve to
conquer ; but he whose life has passed without a contest,
and who can boast neither success nor merit, can survey
himself only as a useless filler of existence ; and if he is
content with his own character, must owe his satisfaction to
insensibility.

Thus it appears that the satirist advised rightly, when he
directed us to resign ourselves to the hands of Heaven, and
to leave to superior powers the determination of our lot :

> " *Permittes ipsis expendere Numinibus, quid*
> *Conveniat nobis, rebusque sit u ile nostris :*
> *Carior est illis homo quam sibi.* '

> " Intrust thy fortune to the pow'rs above :
> Leave them to manage for thee, and to grant
> What their unerring wisdom sees thee want.
> In goodness as in greatness they excel :
> Ah ! that we lov'd ourselves but half so well." DRYDEN.

What state of life admits most happiness, is uncertain ;
but that uncertainty ought to repress the petulance of
comparison, and silence the murmurs of discontent.

Tuesday, December 11, 1753.

" *Scribmus indocti doctique.*"   HOR.

" All dare to write, who can or cannot read."

THEY who have attentively considered the history of
mankind, know that every age has its peculiar
character. At one time, no desire is felt but for military
honours ; every summer affords battles and sieges, and the
world is filled with ravage, bloodshed, and devastation : this

sanguinary fury at length subsides, and nations are divided into factions, by controversies about points that will never be decided. Men then grow weary of debate and altercation, and apply themselves to the arts of profit; trading companies are formed, manufactures improved, and navigation extended; and nothing is any longer thought on, but the increase and preservation of property, the artificers of getting money, and the pleasures of spending it.

The present age, if we consider chiefly the state of our own country, may be styled with great propriety *The age of Authors;* for, perhaps, there never was a time in which men of all degrees of ability, of every kind of education, of every profession and employment, were posting with ardour so general to the press. The province of writing was formerly left to those, who by study, or the appearance of study, were supposed to have gained knowledge unattainable by the busy part of mankind; but in these enlightened days, every man is qualified to instruct every other man: and he that beats the anvil, or guides the plough, not content with supplying corporal necessities, amuses himself in the hours of leisure with providing intellectual pleasures for his countrymen.

It may be observed, that of this, as of other evils, complaints have been made by every generation: but though it may, perhaps, be true, that at all times more have been willing than have been able to write, yet there is no reason for believing, that the dogmatical legions of the present race were ever equalled in number by any former period; for so widely is spread the itch of literary praise, that almost every man is an author, either in act or in purpose; has either bestowed his favours on the publick, or withholds them, that they may be more seasonably offered, or made more worthy of acceptance.

In former times, the pen, like the sword, was considered as consigned by nature to the hands of men ! the ladies contented themselves with private virtues and domestick excellence ; and a female writer, like a female warriour, was considered as a kind of eccentric being, that deviated, however illustriously, from her due sphere of motion, and was, therefore, rather to be gazed at with wonder, than countenanced by imitation.   But as the times past are said to have been a nation of Amazons, who drew the bow and wielded the battle-axe, formed encampments and wasted nations ; the revolution of years has now produced a generation of Amazons of the pen, who with the spirit of their predecessors have set masculine tyranny at defiance, asserted their claim to the regions of science, and seemed resolved to contest the usurpations of virility.

Some, indeed, there are of both sexes, who are authors only in desire, but have not yet attained the power of executing their intentions ; whose performances have not arrived at bulk sufficient to form a volume, or who have not the confidence, however impatient, of nameless obscurity, to solicit openly the assistance of the printer.   Among these are the innumerable correspondents of publick papers, who are always offering assistance which no man will receive, and suggesting hints that are never taken, and who complain loudly of the perverseness and arrogance of authors, lament their insensibility of their own interest, and fill the coffeehouses with dark stories of performances by eminent hands, which have been offered and rejected.

To what cause this universal eagerness of writing can be properly ascribed, I have not yet been able to discover.   It is said, that every art is propagated in proportion to the rewards conferred upon it ; a position from which a stranger would naturally infer, that literature was now blessed with patronage far transcending the candour or munificence of the Augustine age, that the road to greatness was open to none but authors, and that by writing alone riches and honour were to be obtained.

But since it is true, that writers like other competitors, are very little disposed to favour one another, it is not to be expected, that at a time when every man writes, any man will patronize; and accordingly, there is not one that I can recollect at present who professes the least regard for the votaries of science, invites the addresses of learned men, or seems to hope for reputation from any pen but his own.

The cause, therefore, of this epidemical conspiracy for the destruction of paper, must remain a secret: nor can I discover, whether we owe it to the influences of the constellations, or the intemperature of seasons: whether the long continuance of the wind at any single point, or intoxicating vapours exhaled from the earth, have turned our nobles and our peasants, our soldiers and traders, our men and women, all into wits, philosophers, and writers.

It is, indeed, of more importance to search out the cure than the cause of this intellectual malady; and he would deserve well of his country, who, instead of amusing himself with conjectural speculations, should find means of persuading the peer to inspect his steward's accounts, or repair the rural mansion of his ancestors, who could replace the tradesman behind his counter, and send back the farmer to the mattock and the flail.

General irregularities are known in time to remedy themselves. By the constitution of ancient Egypt, the priesthood was continually increasing, till at length there was no people beside themselves: the establishment was then dissolved, and the number of priests was reduced and limited. Thus amongst us, writers will, perhaps, be multiplied, till no readers will be found, and then the ambition of writing must necessarily cease.

But as it will be long before the cure is thus gradually effected, and the evil should be stopped, if it be possible, before it rises to so great a height, I could wish that both sexes would fix their thoughts upon some salutary considerations, which might repress their ardour for that reputation which not one of many thousands is fated to obtain.

Let it be deeply impressed, and frequently recollected, that he who has not obtained the proper qualifications of an author, can have no excuse for the arrogance of writing, but the power of imparting to mankind something necessary to be known. A man uneducated or unlettered may sometimes start a useful thought, or make a lucky discovery, or obtain by chance some secret of nature, or some intelligence of facts, of which the most enlightened mind may be ignorant, and which it is better to reveal, though by a rude and unskilful communication, than to lose for ever by suppressing it.

But few will be justified by this plea ; for of the innumerable books and pamphlets that have overflowed the nation, scarce one has made any addition to real knowledge, or contained more than a transposition of common sentiments and a repetition of common phrases.

It will be naturally inquired, when the man who feels an inclination to write, may venture to suppose himself properly qualified ; and, since every man who is inclined to think well of his own intellect, by what test he may try his abilities, without hazarding the contempt or resentment of the publick.

The first qualification of a writer, is a perfect knowledge of the subject which he undertakes to treat ; since we cannot teach what we do not know, nor can properly undertake to

instruct others while we are ourselves in want of instruction.
The next requisite is, that he be master of the language in
which he delivers his sentiments ; if he treats of science and
demonstration, that he has attained a style clear, pure,
nervous, and expressive; if his topicks be probable and
persuasory, that he be able to recommend them by the
superaddition of elegance and imagery, to display the
colours of varied diction, and pour forth the music of
modulated periods.

If it be again inquired, upon what principles any man shall
conclude that he wants these powers, it may be readily
answered, that no end is attained but by the proper means :
he only can rationally presume that he understands a
subject, who has read and compared the writers that have
hitherto discussed it, familiarized their aguments to himself
by long meditation, consulted the foundations of different
systems, and separated truth from errour by a rigorous
examination.

In like manner, he only has a right to suppose that he
can express his thoughts, whatever they are, with perspicuity
or elegance, who has carefully perused the best authors,
accurately noted their diversities of style, diligently selected
the best modes of diction, and familiarized them by long
habits of attentive practice.

No man is a rhetorician or philosopher by chance. He
who knows that he undertakes to write on questions which
he has never studied, may without hesitation determine, that
he is about to waste his own time and that of his reader,
and expose himself to the derision of those whom he aspires
to instruct: he that without forming his style by the study
of the best models, hastens to obtrude his compositions on
the publick, may be certain, that whatever hope or flattery
may suggest, he shall shock the learned ear with barbarisms,

and contribute wherever his works shall be received, to the depravation of taste and the corruption of language.

<hr>

Saturday, December 29, 1753.

<hr>

" —— *Ultima semper*
Expectanda dies homini, dicique beatus
Ante obitum nemo supremaque funera debet."   OVID.

" But no frail man, however great or high,
Can be concluded blest before he die."   ADDISON.

THE numerous miseries of human life have extorted in all ages an universal complaint. The wisest of men terminated all his experiments in search of happiness, by the mournful confession, that "all is vanity;" and the ancient patriarchs lamented, that "the days of their pilgrimage were "few and evil."

There is, indeed, no topick on which it is more superfluous to accumulate authorities, nor any assertion of which our own eyes will more easily discover, or our sensations more frequently impress the truth, than, that misery is the lot of man, that our present state is a state of danger and infelicity.

When we take the most distant prospect of life, what does it present us but a chaos of unhappiness, a confused and tumultuous scene of labour and contest, disappointment and defeat? If we view past ages in the reflection of history, what do they offer to our meditation but crimes and calamities? One year is distinguished by a famine, another by an earthquake; kingdoms are made desolate, sometimes by wars, and sometimes by pestilence; the peace of the world is interrupted at one time by the caprices of a tyrant, at another by the rage of a conqueror. The memory is stored only with vicissitudes of evil; and the happiness, such as it is, of one part of mankind, is found to arise commonly from sanguinary success, from victories which confer upon them the power, not so much of improving life by any new enjoyment, as of inflicting misery on others, and gratifying their own pride by comparative greatness.

But by him that examines life with a more close attention, the happiness of the world will be found still less than it appears. In some intervals of publick prosperity, or to use terms more proper, in some intermissions of calamity, a general diffusion of happiness may seem to overspread a people; all is triumph and exultation, jollity and plenty; there are no publick fears and dangers, and "no complainings in the streets." But the condition of individuals is very little mended by this general calm: pain and malice and discontent still continue their havock; the silent depredation goes incessantly forward: and the grave continues to be filled by the victims of sorrow.

He that enters a gay assembly, beholds the cheerfulness displayed in every countenance, and finds all sitting vacant and disengaged, with no other attention than to give or to receive pleasure, would naturally imagine, that he had reached at last the metropolis of felicity, the place sacred to gladness of heart, from whence all fear and anxiety were irreversibly excluded. Such, indeed, we may often find to be the opinion of those, who from a lower station look up to the pomp and gayety which they cannot reach: but who is there of those who frequent luxurious assemblies, that will not confess his own uneasiness, or cannot recount the

17

vexations and distresses that prey upon the lives of his gay companions.

The world, in its best state, is nothing more than a larger assembly of beings, combining to counterfeit happiness which they do not feel, employing every art and contrivance to embellish life, and to hide their real condition from the eyes of one another.

The species of happiness most obvious to the observation of others, is that which depends upon the goods of fortune; yet even this is often fictitious. There is in the world more poverty than is generally imagined; not only because many whose possessions are large have desires still larger, and many measure their wants by the gratifications which others enjoy: but great numbers are pressed by real necessities which it is their chief ambition to conceal, and are forced to purchase the appearance of competence and cheerfulness at the expence of many comforts and conveniencies of life.

Many, however, are confessedly rich, and many more are sufficiently removed from all danger of real poverty: but it has been long ago remarked, that money cannot purchase quiet; the highest of mankind can promise themselves no exemption from that discord or suspicion, by which the sweetness of domestick retirement is destroyed; and must always be even more exposed, in the same degree as they are elevated above others, to the treachery of dependents, the calumny of defamers, and the violence of opponents.

Affliction is inseparable from our present state; it adheres to all the inhabitants of this world, in different proportions indeed, but with an allotment which seems very little regulated by our own conduct. It has been the boast of some swelling moralists, that every man's fortune was in his own power, that prudence supplied the place of all other divinities, and that happiness is the unfailing consequence of virtue. But, surely, the quiver of Omnipotence is stored with arrows, against which the shield of human virtue, however adamantine it has been boasted, is held up in vain : we do not always suffer by our crimes ; we are not always protected by our innocence.

A good man is by no means exempt from the danger of suffering by the crimes of others ; even his goodness may raise him enemies of implacable malice and restless per-severance : the good man has never been warranted by Heaven from the treachery of friends, the disobedience of children, or the dishonesty of a wife ; he may see his cares made useless by profusion, his instructions defeated by perverseness, and his kindness rejected by ingratitude ; he may languish under the infamy of false accusations, or perish reproachfully by an unjust sentence.

A good man is subject, like other mortals, to all the influences of natural evil ; his harvest is not spared by the tempest, nor his cattle by the murrain ; his house flames like others in a conflagration ; nor have his ships any peculiar power of resisting hurricanes : his mind, however elevated, inhabits a body subject to innumerable casualties, of which he must always share the dangers and the pains ; he bears about him the seeds of disease, and may linger away a great part of his life under the tortures of the gout or stone ; at one time groaning with insufferable anguish, at another dissolved in listlessness and languor.

From this general and indiscriminate distribution of misery, the moralists have always derived one of their strongest moral arguments for a future state ; for since the common events of the present life happen alike to the good and bad, it follows from the justice of the Supreme Being, that there must be another state of existence, in which a just retribution shall be made, and every man shall be happy and miserable according to his works.

The .miseries of life may, perhaps, afford some proof of a future state, compared as well with the mercy as the justice of God. It is scarcely to be imagined that infinite benevolence would create a being capable of enjoying so much more than is here to be enjoyed, and qualified by nature to prolong pain by remembrance, and anticipate it by terrour, if he was not designed for something nobler and better than a state, in which many of his faculties can serve only for his torment; in which he is to be importuned by desires that never can be satisfied, to feel many evils which he had no power to avoid, and to fear many which he shall never feel: there will surely come a time, when every capacity of happiness shall be filled, and none shall be wretched but by his own fault.

In the mean time, it is by affliction chiefly that the heart of man is purified, and that the thoughts are fixed upon a better state. Prosperity, allayed and imperfect as it is, has power to intoxicate the imagination, to fix the mind upon the present scene, to produce confidence and elation, and to make him who enjoys affluence and honours forget the hand by which they were bestowed. It is seldom that we are otherwise, than by affliction, awakened to a sense of our own imbecility, or taught to know how little all our acquisitions can conduce to safety or to quiet; and how justly we may ascribe to the superintendence of a higher power, those blessings which in the wantonness of success we considered as the attainments of our policy or courage.

Nothing confers so much ability to resist the temptations that perpetually surround us, as an habitual consideration of the shortness of life, and the uncertainty of those pleasures that solicit our pursuit; and this consideration can be inculcated only by affliction. "O Death! how bitter is the "remembrance of thee, to a man that lives at ease in his "possessions!" If our present state were one continued succession of delights, or one uniform flow of calmness and tranquillity, we should never willingly think upon its end; death would then surely surprise us as "a thief in the night;" and our task of duty would remain unfinished, till "the night came when no man can work."

While affliction thus prepares us for felicity, we may console ourselves under its pressures, by remembering, that they are no particular marks of Divine displeasure; since all the distresses of persecution have been suffered by those, "of whom the world was not worthy; and the Redeemer of "Mankind himself was a man of sorrows and acquainted "with grief."

Tuesday, February 26, 1754.

"Τι δ ἔρεξα." PYTH.

"What have I been doing?"

AS man is a being very sparingly furnished with the power of prescience, he can provide for the future only by considering the past; and as futurity is all in which he has any real interest, he ought very diligently to use the only means by which he can be enabled to enjoy it, and frequently to revolve the experiments which he has hitherto made upon life, that he may gain wisdom from his mistakes, and caution from his miscarriages.

Though I do not so exactly conform to the precepts of

Pythagoras, as to practise every night this solemn recollection, yet I am not so lost in dissipation as wholly to omit it; nor can I forbear sometimes to inquire of myself, in what employment my life has passed away. Much of my time has sunk into nothing, and left no trace by which it can be distinguished; and of this I now only know, that it was once in my power, and might once have been improved.*

Of other parts of life, memory can give some account; at some hours I have been gay, and at others serious; I have sometimes mingled in conversation, and sometimes meditated in solitude; one day has been spent in consulting the ancient sages, and another in writing *Adventurers.*

At the conclusion of any undertaking, it is usual to compute the loss and profit. As I shall soon cease to write *Adventurers,* I could not forbear lately to consider what has been the consequence of my labours; and whether I am to reckon the hours laid out in these compositions, as applied to a good and laudable purpose, or suffered to fume away in useless evaporations.

That I have intended well, I have the attestation of my own heart: but good intentions may be frustrated when they are executed without suitable skill, or directed to an end unattainable in itself.

Some there are who leave writers very little room for self-congratulation; some who affirm, that books have no influence upon the publick, that no age was ever made better by its authors, and that to call upon mankind to correct their manners, is like *Xerxes,* to scourge the wind, or shackle the torrent.

* Note XXII., Appendix.

This opinion they pretend to support by unfailing experience. The world is full of fraud and corruption, rapine or malignity; interest is the ruling motive of mankind, and every one is endeavouring to increase his own stores of happiness by perpetual accumulations, without reflecting upon the numbers whom his superfluity condemns to want: in this state of things a book or morality is published, in which charity and benevolence are strongly enforced; and it is proved beyond opposition, that men are happy in proportion as they are virtuous, and rich as they are liberal. The book is applauded, and the author is preferred; he imagines his applause deserved, and receives less pleasure from the acquisition of reward than the consciousness of merit. Let us look again upon mankind: interest is still the ruling motive, and the world is yet full of fraud and corruption, malevolence and rapine.

The difficulty of confuting this assertion, arises merely from its generality and comprehension : to overthrow it by a detail of distinct facts, requires a wider survey of the world than human eyes can take; the progress of reformation is gradual and silent, as the extension of evening shadows; we know that they were short at noon, and are long at sunset, but our senses were not able to discern their increase: we know of every civil nation, that it was once savage, and how was it reclaimed but by precept and admonition?

Mankind are universally corrupt, but corrupt in different degrees; as they are universally ignorant, yet with greater or less irradiations of knowledge. How has knowledge or virtue been increased and preserved in one place beyond another; but by diligent inculcation and rational inforcement?

Books of morality are daily written, yet its influence is still little in the world; so the ground is annually ploughed, and yet multitudes are in want of bread. But, surely, neither the labours of the moralist nor of the husbandman are vain; let them for a while neglect their tasks, and their usefulness will be known; the wickedness that is now frequent would become universal, the bread that is now scarce would wholly fail.

The power, indeed, of every individual is small, and the consequence of his endeavours imperceptible in a general prospect of the world. Providence has given no man ability to do much, that something be left for every man to do. The business of life is carried on by a general co-operation; in which the part of any single man can be no more distinguished, than the effect of a particular drop when the meadows are floated by a summer shower: yet every drop increases the inundation, and every hand adds to the happiness or misery of mankind.

That a writer, however zealous or eloquent, seldom works a visible effect upon cities or nations, will readily be granted. The book which is read most, is read by few, compared with those that read it not; and of those few, the greater part peruse it with dispositions that very little favour their own improvement.

It is difficult to enumerate the several motives which procure to books the honour of perusal: spite, vanity, and curiosity, hope and fear, love and hatred, every passion which incites to any other action serves at one time or other to stimulate a reader.

Some are fond to take a celebrated volume into their hands, because they hope to distinguish their penetration, by finding faults which have escaped the publick; others eagerly buy it in the first bloom of reputation, that they may join the chorus of praise, and not lag, as *Falstaff* terms it, in " the rearward of the fashion."

Some read for style, and some for argument; one has little care about the sentiment, he observes only how it is expressed; another regards not the conclusion, but is diligent to mark how it is inferred: they read for other purposes than the attainment of practical knowledge; and are no more likely to grow wise by an examination of a treatise of moral prudence than an architect to inflame his devotion by considering attentively the proportions of a temple.

Some read that they may embellish their conversation, or shine in dispute; some that they may not be detected in ignorance, or want the reputation of literary accomplishments: but the most general and prevalent reason of study is the impossibility of finding another amusement equally cheap or constant, equally independent on the hour or the weather.* He that wants money to follow the chase of pleasure through her yearly circuit, and is left at home when the gay world rolls to *Bath* or *Tunbridge;* he whose gout compels him to hear from his chamber the rattle of chariots transporting happier beings to plays or assemblies, will be forced to seek in books a refuge from himself.

The author is not wholly useless, who provides innocent amusements for minds like these. There are, in the present state of things, so many more instigations to evil, than incitements to good, that he who keeps men in a neutral state, may be justly considered as a benefactor to life.

But, perhaps, it seldom happens, that study terminates in mere pastime. Books have always a secret influence on the understanding; we cannot at pleasure obliterate ideas: he

* Note XXIII., Appendix.

that reads books of science, though without any fixed
desire of improvement, will grow more knowing; he that
entertains himself with moral or religious treatises, will
imperceptibly advance in goodness; the ideas which are
often offered to the mind, will at last find a lucky moment
when it is disposed to receive them.

It is, therefore, urged without reason, as a discouragement to writers, that there are already books sufficient in
the world; that all the topicks of persuasion have been
discussed, and every important question clearly stated and
justly decided; and that, therefore, there is no room to
hope that pigmies should conquer where heroes have been
defeated, or that the petty copiers of the present time should
advance the great work of reformation, which their predecessors were forced to leave unfinished.

Whatever be the present extent of human knowledge, it
is not only finite, and therefore in its own nature capable of
increase; but so narrow, that almost every understanding
may, by a diligent application of its powers, hope to enlarge
it. It is, however, not necessary, that a man should forbear
to write, till he has discovered some truth unknown before;
he may be sufficiently useful, by only diversifying the
surface of knowledge, and luring the mind by a new appearance to a second view of those beauties which it had passed
over inattentively before. Every writer may find intellects
correspondent to his own, to whom his expressions are
familiar and his thoughts congenial; and, perhaps, truth is
often more successfully propagated by men of moderate
abilities, who, adopting the opinions of others, have no care
but to explain them clearly, than by subtle speculatists and
curious searchers, who exact from their readers powers
equal to their own, and if their fabricks of science be
strong, take no care to make them accessible.

For my part, I do not regret the hours which I have laid out in these little compositions. That the world has grown apparently better, since the publication of the *Adventurer*, I have not observed; but am willing to think, that many have been affected by single sentiments, of which it is their business to renew the impression; that many have caught hints of truth, which it is now their duty to pursue; and that those who have received no improvement, have wanted not opportunity but intention to improve.

Saturday, March 2, 1754.

> "*Quid purè tranquillet? honos, an dulce lucellum,*
> *An secretum iter, et fallentis semita vitæ?*" HOR.

> "Whether the tranquil mind and pure,
> Honours or wealth our bliss insure;
> Or down through life unknown to stray,
> Where lonely leads the silent way." FRANCIS.

HAVING considered the importance of authors to the welfare of the publick, I am led by a natural train of thought, to reflect on their condition with regard to themselves; and to inquire what degree of happiness or vexation is annexed to the difficult and laborious employment of providing instruction or entertainment for mankind.

In estimating the pain or pleasure of any particular state, every man, indeed, draws his decisions from his own breast, and cannot with certainty determine, whether other minds are affected by the same causes in the same manner. Yet by this criterion we must be content to judge, because no other can be obtained ; and, indeed, we have no reason to think it very fallacious, for excepting here and there an anomalous mind, which either does not feel like others, or dissembles its sensibility, we find men unanimously concur in attributing happiness or misery to particular conditions, as they agree in acknowledging the cold of winter and the heat of autumn.

If we apply to authors themselves for an account of their state, it will appear very little to deserve envy ; for they have in all ages been addicted to complaint. The neglect of learning, the ingratitude of the present age, and the absurd preference by which ignorance and dulness often obtain favour and rewards, have been from age to age topicks of invective ; and few have left their names to posterity, without some appeal to future candour from the perverseness and malice of their own times.

I have nevertheless, been often inclined to doubt, whether authors, however querulous, are in reality more miserable than their fellow mortals. The present life is to all a state of infelicity ; every man, like an author, believes himself to merit more than he obtains, and solaces the present with the prospect of the future ; others, indeed, suffer those disappointments in silence, of which the writer complains, to show how well he has learnt the art of lamentation.

There is at least one gleam of felicity, of which few writers have missed the enjoyment : he whose hopes have so far overpowered his fears, as that he has resolved to stand forth a candidate for fame, seldom fails to amuse himself, before his appearance, with pleasing scenes of affluence or honour ; while his fortune is yet under the regulation of fancy, he easily models it to his wish, suffers no thoughts of criticks or rivals to intrude upon his mind, but counts over the bounties of patronage, or listens to the voice of praise.

Some there are, that talk very luxuriously of the second period of an author's happiness, and tell of the tumultuous raptures of invention, when the mind riots in imagery; and the choice stands suspended between different sentiments.

These pleasures, I believe, may sometimes be indulged to those, who come to a subject of disquisition with minds full of ideas, and with fancies so vigorous, as easily to excite, select, and arrange them. To write is, indeed, no unpleasing employment, when one sentiment readily produces another, and both ideas and expressions present themselves at the first summons: but such happiness, the greatest genius does not always obtain; and common writers know it only to such a degree, as to credit its possibility. Composition is, for the most part, an effort of slow diligence and steady perseverance, to which the mind is dragged by necessity or resolution, and from which the attention is every moment starting to more delightful amusements.

It frequently happens, that a design which, when considered at a distance, gave flattering hopes of facility, mocks us in the execution with unexpected difficulties; the mind which, while it considered it in the gross, imagined itself amply furnished with materials, finds sometimes an unexpected barrenness and vacuity, and wonders whither all those ideas are vanished, which a little before seemed struggling for emission.

Sometimes many thoughts present themselves; but so confused and unconnected, that they are not without difficulty reduced to method, or concatenated in a regular and dependent series: the mind falls at once into a labyrinth, of which neither the beginning nor end can be discovered, and toils and struggles without progress or extrication.

It is asserted by Horace, that "if matter be once got " together, words will be found with very little difficulty ; " a position which, though sufficiently plausible to be inserted in poetical precepts, is by no means strictly and philo- sophically true. If words were naturally and necessarily consequential to sentiments, it would always follow, that he who has most knowledge must have most eloquence, and that every man would clearly express what he fully under- stood : yet we find, that to think, and discourse, are often the qualities of different persons : and many books might surely be produced, where just and noble sentiments are degraded and obscured by unsuitable diction.

Words, therefore, as well as things, claim the care of an author. Indeed of many authors, and those not useless or contemptible, words are almost the only care : many make it their study, not so much to strike out new sentiments, as to recommend those which are already known to more favourable notice by fairer decorations : but every man, whether he copies or invents, whether he delivers his own thoughts or those of another, has often found himself deficient in the power of expression, big with ideas which he could not utter, obliged to ransack his memory for terms adequate to his conceptions, and at last unable to impress upon his reader the image existing in his own mind.

It is one of the common distresses of a writer, to be within a word of a happy period, to want only a single epithet to give amplification its full force, to require only a correspondent term in order to finish a paragraph with elegance, and make one of its members answer to the other: but these deficiencies cannot always be supplied : and after a long study and vexation, the passage is turned anew, and the web unwoven that was so nearly finished.

But when thoughts and words are collected and adjusted, and the whole composition at last concluded, it seldom gratifies the author when he comes coolly and deliberately to review it, with the hopes which had been excited in the fury of the performance : novelty always captivates the mind ; as our thoughts rise fresh upon us, we readily believe them just and original, which, when the pleasure of production is over, we find to be mean and common, or borrowed from the works of others, and supplied by memory rather than invention.

But though it should happen that the writer finds no such faults in his performance, he is still to remember, that he looks upon it with partial eyes : and when he considers how much men who could judge of others with great exactness, have often failed of judging of themselves, he will be afraid of deciding too hastily in his own favour, or of allowing himself to contemplate with too much complacence, treasure that has not yet been brought to the test, nor passed the only trial that can stamp its value.

From the publick, and only from the publick, is he to await a confirmation of his claim, and a final justification of self-esteem ; but the publick is not easily persuaded to favour an author. If mankind were left to judge for themselves, it is reasonable to imagine, that of such writings, at least, as describe the movements of the human passions, and of which every man carries the archetype within him, a just opinion would be formed ; but whoever has remarked the fate of books, must have found it governed by other causes, than general consent arising from general conviction. If a new performance happens not to fall into the hands of some who have courage to tell, and authority to propagate their opinion, it often remains long in obscurity, and perishes unknown and unexamined. A few, a very few, commonly constitute the taste of the time ;* the judgment which they had once pronounced, some are too lazy to discuss, and some too timorous to contradict : it may however be, I think, observed, that their power is greater to depress than exalt, as mankind are more credulous of censure than of praise.

This perversion of the publick judgment is not to be rashly numbered amongst the miseries of an author : since it commonly serves, after miscarriage, to reconcile him to himself. Because the world has sometimes passed an unjust sentence, he readily concludes the sentence unjust by which his performance is condemned ; because some have been exalted above their merits by partiality, he is sure to ascribe the success of a rival, not to the merit of his work, but the zeal of his patrons. Upon the whole, as the author seems to share all the common miseries of life, he appears to partake likewise of its lenitives and abatements.

* Note XXIV., Appendix.

THE IDLER.

THE IDLER.

1758–1760.

———+◦+———

[DR. JOHNSON began the *Idler* on the 15th of April 1758, in a
Saturday newspaper called the *Universal Chronicle*, or *Weekly Gazette;*
the last number appeared on the 5th of April 1760. Out of the hundred and three essays of which the *Idler* consists, Johnson wrote all
but twelve. Boswell remarks that the *Idler* is "evidently the work of
the same mind which produced the *Rambler*, but has less body and
more spirit. . . . . Johnson describes the miseries of idleness, with the
lively sensations of one who has felt them ; and in his private memo-
randums while engaged in it, we find, 'This year I hope to learn
diligence.' Many of these excellent essays were written as hastily as
an ordinary letter. Mr. Langton remembers Johnson, when on a visit
at Oxford, asking him one evening when the post went out ; and on
being told in about half-an-hour, he exclaimed, 'Then we shall do very
well.' He upon this instantly sat down and finished an *Idler*, which it
was necessary should be in London the next day."—(Boswell's *Life of
Johnson*, vol. i., 330.) "The *Idlers* were inserted in the *Universal
Chronicle* on the plea that the 'occurrences of the week were not
sufficient to fill the columns;' but they at once became its chief attraction, and Johnson had, in January 1759, to prepare an advertisement,
warning the publishers of other papers who had, 'with so little regard
to justice or decency,' reprinted them into their own columns without
permission or acknowledgment ; that the 'time of impunity was at an
end.' 'Whoever,' he said, 'shall, without our leave, lay the hand of
rapine upon our pages, is to expect that we shall vindicate our due by

the means which justice prescribes, and which are warranted by the immemorial prescriptions of honourable trade.'"—(*English Newspapers: Chapters in the History of Journalism.* By II. R. Fox Bourne. Vol. i., p. 144.)]

Saturday, April 15, 1758.*

" *Vacui sub umbra*
Lusimus."   HOR.

THOSE who attempt periodical essays seem to be often stopped in the beginning, by the difficulty of finding a proper title.   Two writers, since the time of the *Spectator*, have assumed his name, without any pretensions to lawful inheritance; an effort was once made to revive the *Tatler*; and the strange appellations by which other papers have been called, show that the authors were distressed like the natives of America, who come to the Europeans to beg a name.

It will be easily believed of the Idler, that if his title had required any search, he never would have found it.   Every mode of life has its conveniencies.   The Idler, who habituates himself to be satisfied with what he can most easily obtain, not only escapes labours which are often fruitless, but sometimes succeeds better than those who despise all that is within their reach, and think every thing more valuable as it is harder to be acquired.

If similitude of manners be a motive to kindness, the Idler may flatter himself with universal patronage.   There

---

* Originally published in *The Universal Chronicle, or Weekly Gazette*, a newspaper projected by Mr. John Newbery.

is no single character under which such numbers are comprised. Every man is, or hopes to be, an Idler. Even those who seem to differ most from us are hastening to increase our fraternity; as peace is the end of war, so to be idle is the ultimate purpose of the busy.

There is perhaps no appellation by which a writer can better denote his kindred to the human species. It has been found hard to describe man by an adequate definition. Some philosophers have called him a reasonable animal; but others have considered reason as a quality of which many creatures partake. He has been termed likewise a laughing animal; but it is said that some men have never laughed. Perhaps man may be more properly distinguished as an idle animal; for there is no man who is not sometimes idle. It is at least a definition from which none that shall find it in this paper can be excepted; for who can be more idle than the reader of the *Idler?*

That the definition may be complete, idleness must be not only the general but the peculiar characteristic of man; and perhaps man is the only being that can properly be called idle, that does by others what he might do himself, or sacrifices duty or pleasure to the love of ease.

Scarcely any name can be imagined from which less envy or competition is to be dreaded. The Idler has no rivals or enemies. The man of business forgets him; the man of enterprise despises him; and though such as tread the same track of life fall commonly into jealousy and discord, Idlers are always found to associate in peace; and he who is most famed for doing nothing, is glad to meet another as idle as himself.

What is to be expected from this paper, whether it will be uniform or various, learned or familiar, serious or gay, political or moral, continued or interrupted, it is hoped that no reader will inquire. That the Idler has some scheme, cannot be doubted; for to form schemes is the Idler's privilege. But though he has many projects in his head, he is now grown sparing of communication, having observed, that his hearers are apt to remember what he forgets himself; that his tardiness of execution exposes him to the encroachments of those who catch a hint and fall to work; and that very specious plans, after long contrivance and pompous displays, have subsided in weariness without a trial, and without miscarriage have been blasted by derision.

Something the Idler's character may be supposed to promise. Those that are curious after diminutive history, who watch the revolutions of families, and the rise and fall of characters either male or female, will hope to be gratified by this paper; for the Idler is always inquisitive and seldom retentive. He that delights in obloquy and satire, and wishes to see clouds gathering over any reputation that dazzles him with its brightness, will snatch up the *Idler's* essays with a beating heart. The Idler is naturally censorious; those who attempt nothing themselves think every thing easily performed, and consider the unsuccesful always as criminals.

I think it necessary to give notice, that I make no contract, nor incur any obligation. If those who depend on the Idler for intelligence and entertainment should suffer the disappointment which commonly follows ill-placed expectations, they are to lay the blame only to themselves.

Yet hope is not wholly to be cast away. The Idler, though sluggish, is yet alive, and may sometimes be stimulated to vigour and activity. He may descend into profoundness, or tower into sublimity; for the diligence of an Idler is rapid and impetuous, as ponderous bodies forced into velocity move with violence proportionate to their weight.

But these vehement exertions of intellect cannot be frequent, and he will therefore gladly receive help from any correspondent who shall enable him to please without his own labour. He excludes no style, he prohibits no subject; only let him that writes to the Idler remember, that his letters must not be long; no words are to be squandered in declarations of esteem, or confessions of inability; conscious dulness has little right to be prolix, and praise is not so welcome to the Idler as quiet.

Saturday, April 22, 1758.

" *Toto vix quater anno*
Membranam."   Hor.

M ANY positions are often on the tongue, and seldom in the mind; there are many truths which every human being acknowledges and forgets. It is generally known, that he who expects much will be often disappointed; yet disappointment seldom cures us of expectation, or has any other effect than that of producing a moral sentence or peevish exclamation. He that embarks in the voyage of life, will always wish to advance rather by the impulse of the wind than the strokes of the oar; and many founder in the passage, while they lie waiting for the gale that is to waft them to their wish.

It will naturally be suspected that the Idler has lately suffered some disappointment, and that he does not talk thus gravely for nothing. No man is required to betray his own secrets. I will, however, confess, that I have now been a writer almost a week, and have not yet heard a single word of praise, nor received one hint from any correspondent.

Whence this negligence proceeds I am not able to discover. Many of my predecessors have thought themselves obliged to return their acknowledgments in the second paper, for the kind reception of the first; and, in a short time, apologies have become necessary to those ingenious gentlemen and ladies, whose performances, though in the highest degree elegant and learned, have been unavoidably delayed.

What then will be thought of me, who, having experienced no kindness, have no thanks to return; whom no gentleman or lady has yet enabled to give any cause of discontent, and who have therefore no opportunity of showing how skilfully I can pacify resentment, extenuate negligence, or palliate rejection?

I have long known that splendour of reputation is not to be counted among the necessaries of life, and therefore shall not much repine if praise be withheld till it is better deserved. But surely I may be allowed to complain, that, in a nation of authors, not one has thought me worthy of notice after so fair an invitation.

At the time when the rage of writing has seized the old and young, when the cook warbles her lyricks in the kitchen, and the thrasher vociferates his heroicks in the barn; when our traders deal out knowledge in bulky volumes, and our girls forsake their samplers to teach kingdoms wisdom; it may seem very unnecessary to draw any more from their proper occupations, by affording new opportunities of literary fame.

I should be indeed unwilling to find that, for the sake of corresponding with the *Idler*, the smith's iron had cooled on the anvil, or the spinster's distaff stood unemployed. I solicit only the contributions of those who have already devoted themselves to literature, or, without any determinate intention, wander at large through the expanse of life, and wear out the day in hearing at one place what they utter at another.

Of these, a great part are already writers. One has a friend in the country upon whom he exercises his powers ; whose passions he raises and depresses ; whose understanding he perplexes with paradoxes, or strengthens by argument ; whose admiration he courts, whose praises he enjoys ; and who serves him instead of a senate or a theatre ; as the young soldiers in the Roman camp learned the use of their weapons by fencing against a post in the place of an enemy.

Another has his pockets filled with essays and epigrams, which he reads from house to house to select parties, and which his acquaintances are daily entreating him to withhold no longer from the impatience of the publick.

If among these any one is persuaded, that, by such preludes of composition, he has qualified himself to appear in the open world, and is yet afraid of those censures which they who have already written, and they who cannot write, are equally ready to fulminate against publick pretenders to fame, he may, by transmitting his performances to the *Idler*, make a cheap experiment of his abilities, and enjoy the pleasure of success without the hazard of miscarriage.

Many advantages not generally known arise from this method of stealing on the publick. The standing author of the paper is always the object of critical malignity.

Whatever is mean will be imputed to him, and whatever is excellent be ascribed to his assistants. It does not much alter the event, that the author and his correspondents are equally unknown; for the author, whoever he be, is an individual of whom every reader has some fixed idea, and whom he is therefore unwilling to gratify with applause; but the praises given to his correspondents are scattered in the air, none can tell on whom they will light, and therefore none are unwilling to bestow them.

He that is known to contribute to a periodical work, needs no other caution than not to tell what particular pieces are his own; such secrecy is indeed very difficult; but if it can be maintained, it is scarcely to be imagined at how small an expence he may grow considerable.

A person of quality, by a single paper, may engross the honour of a volume. Fame is indeed dealt with a hand less and less bounteous through the subordinate ranks, till it descends to the professed author, who will find it very difficult to get more than he deserves; but every man who does not want it, or who needs not value it, may have liberal allowances; and, for five letters in the year sent to the *Idler*, of which perhaps only two are printed, will be promoted to the first rank of writers by those who are weary of the present race of wits,* and wish to sink them into obscurity before the lustre of a name not yet known enough to be detested.

* Note XXV., Appendix.

Saturday, July 15, 1758.

WHEN Diogenes received a visit in his tub from Alexander the Great, and was asked, according to the ancient forms of royal courtesy, what petition he had to offer; "I have nothing," said he, "to ask, but that you would remove to the other side, that you may not, by intercepting the sunshine, take from me what you cannot give me."

Such was the demand of Diogenes from the greatest monarch of the earth; which those who have less power than Alexander may, with yet more propriety, apply to themselves. He that does much good, may be allowed to do sometimes a little harm. But if the opportunities of beneficence be denied by fortune, innocence should at least be vigilantly preserved.

It is well known, that time once past never returns; and that the moment which is lost is lost for ever. Time therefore ought, above all other kinds of property, to be free from invasion; and yet there is no man who does not claim the power of wasting that time which is the right of others.

This usurpation is so general, that a very small part of the year is spent by choice; scarcely any thing is done when it is intended, or obtained when it is desired. Life is continually ravaged by invaders; one steals away an hour, and another a day; one conceals the robbery by hurrying us into business, another by lulling us with amusement; the depredation is continued through a thousand vicissitudes of tumult and tranquillity, till, having lost all, we can lose no more.

This waste of the lives of men has been very frequently charged upon the Great, whose followers linger from year to year in expectations, and die at last with petitions in their hands. Those who raise envy will easily incur censure. I know not whether statesmen and patrons do not suffer more reproaches than they deserve, and may not rather themselves complain, that they are given up a prey to pretensions without merit, and to importunity without shame.

The truth is, that the inconveniences of attendance are more lamented than felt. To the greater number solicitation is its own reward. To be seen in good company, to talk of familiarities with men of power, to be able to tell the freshest news, to gratify an inferior circle with predictions of increase or decline of favour, and to be regarded as a candidate for high offices, are compensations more than equivalent to the delay of favours, which perhaps he that begs them has hardly confidence to expect.

A man conspicuous in a high station, who multiplies hopes that he may multiply dependants, may be considered as a beast of prey, justly dreaded, but easily avoided; his den is known, and they who would not be devoured need not approach it. The great danger of the waste of time is from caterpillars and moths, who are not resisted, because they are not feared, and who work on with unheeded mischiefs and invisible encroachments.

He whose rank or merit procures him the notice of mankind must give up himself, in a great measure, to the convenience or humour of those who surround him. Every man who is sick of himself will fly to him for relief; he that wants to speak will require him to hear; and he that wants to hear will expect him to speak. Hour passes after hour, the noon succeeds to morning, and the evening to noon, while a thousand objects are forced upon his attention, which he rejects as fast as they are offered, but which the custom of the world requires to be received with appearance of regard.

If we will have the kindness of others, we must endure their follies. He who cannot persuade himself to withdraw from society, must be content to pay a tribute of his time to a multitude of tyrants; to the loiterer, who makes appointments which he never keeps; to the consulter, who asks advice which he never takes; to the boaster, who blusters only to be praised; to the complainer, who whines only to be pitied; to the projector, whose happiness is to entertain his friends with expectations which all but himself know to be vain; to the economist, who tells of bargains and settlements; to the politician, who predicts the fate of battles and breach of alliances; to the usurer, who compares the different funds; and to the talker, who talks only because he loves to be talking.

To put every man in possession of his own time, and rescue the day from this succession of usurpers, is beyond my power, and beyond my hope. Yet, perhaps, some stop might be put to this unmerciful persecution, if all would seriously reflect, that whoever pays a visit that is not desired, or talks longer than the hearer is willing to attend, is guilty of an injury which he cannot repair, and takes away that which he cannot give.

Saturday, September 23, 1758.

LIFE has no pleasure higher or nobler than that of friendship. It is painful to consider, that this sublime enjoyment may be impaired or destroyed by innumerable causes, and that there is no human possession of which the duration is less certain.

Many have talked, in very exalted language, of the perpetuity of friendship, of invincible constancy, and unalienable kindness ; and some examples have been seen of men who have continued faithful to their earliest choice, and whose affection has predominated over changes of fortune and contrariety of opinion.

But these instances are memorable, because they are rare.   The friendship which is to be practised or expected by common mortals, must take its rise from mutual pleasure, and must end when the power ceases of delighting each other.

Many accidents therefore may happen, by which the ardour of kindness will be abated, without criminal baseness or contemptible inconstancy on either part.   To give pleasure is not always in our power ; and little does he know himself, who believes that he can be always able to receive it.

Those who would gladly pass their days together may be separated by the different course of their affairs ; and friendship, like love, is destroyed by long absence, though it may be increased by short intermissions.   What we have missed long enough to want it, we value more when it is regained ; but that which has been lost till it is forgotten, will be found at last with little gladness, and with still less if a substitute has supplied the place. A man deprived of the companion to whom he used to open his bosom, and with whom he shared the hours of leisure and merriment, feels the day at first hanging heavy on him ; his difficulties oppress and his doubts distract him ; he sees time come and go without his wonted gratification, and all is sadness within, and solitude about him. But this uneasiness never lasts long ; necessity produces expedients, new amusements are discovered, and new conversation is admitted.

No expectation is more frequently disappointed, than that which naturally arises in the mind from the prospect of meeting an old friend after long separation. We expect the attraction to be revived, and the coalition to be renewed ; no man considers how much alteration time has made in himself, and very few inquire what effect it has had upon others. The first hour convinces them, that the pleasure which they have formerly enjoyed is for ever at an end ; different scenes have made different impressions ; the opinions of both are changed ; and that similitude of manners and sentiment is lost, which confirmed them both in the approbation of themselves.

Friendship is often destroyed by opposition of interest, not only by the ponderous and visible interest which the desire of wealth and greatness forms and maintains, but by a thousand secret and slight competitions, scarcely known to the mind upon which they operate. There is scarcely any man without some favourite trifle which he values above greater attainments, some desire of petty praise which he cannot patiently suffer to be frustrated. This minute ambition is sometimes crossed before it is known, and sometimes defeated by wanton petulance : but such attacks are seldom made without the loss of friendship ; for, whoever has once found the vulnerable part will always be feared, and the resentment will burn on in secret, of which shame hinders the discovery.

This, however, is a slow malignity, which a wise man will obviate as inconsistent with quiet, and a good man will repress as contrary to virtue; but human happiness is sometimes violated by some more sudden strokes.

A dispute begun in jest upon a subject which a moment before was on both parts regarded with careless indifference, is continued by the desire of conquest, till vanity kindles into rage, and opposition rankles into enmity. Against this hasty mischief I know not what security can be obtained : men will be sometimes surprised into quarrels; and though they might both hasten to reconciliation, as soon as their tumult had subsided, yet two minds will seldom be found together, which can at once subdue their discontent, or immediately enjoy the sweets of peace, without remember-ing the wounds of the conflict.

Friendship has other enemies. Suspicion is always hardening the cautious, and disgust repelling the delicate. Very slender differences will sometimes part those whom long reciprocation of civility or beneficence has united. Lonelove and Ranger retired into the country to enjoy the company of each other, and returned in six weeks cold and petulant; Ranger's pleasure was to walk in the fields, and Lonelove's to sit in a bower; each had complied with the other in his turn, and each was angry that compliance had been exacted.

The most fatal disease of friendship is gradual decay, or dislike hourly increased by causes too slender for complaint, and too numerous for removal.*—Those who are angry may be reconciled; those who have been injured may receive a recompense: but when the desire of pleasing and willingness to be pleased is silently diminished, the renovation of friendship is hopeless; as, when the vital powers sink into langour, there is no longer any use of the physician.

Saturday, November 11, 1758.

THE desires of man increase with his acquisitions; every step which he advances brings something within his view, which he did not see before, and which, as soon as he sees it, he begins to want. Where necessity ends, curiosity begins; and no sooner are we supplied with every thing that nature can demand, than we sit down to contrive artificial appetites.

By this restlessness of mind, every populous and wealthy city is filled with innumerable employments, for which the greater part of mankind is without a name; with artificers, whose labour is exerted in producing such petty conveniences, that many shops are furnished with instruments of which the use can hardly be found without inquiry, but which he that once knows them quickly learns to number among necessary things.

Such is the diligence with which, in countries completely civilized, one part of mankind labours for another, that wants are supplied faster than they can be formed, and the idle and luxurious find life stagnate for want of some desire to keep it in motion. This species of distress furnishes a new set of occupations; and multitudes are busied, from day to day, in finding the rich and the fortunate something to do.

It is very common to reproach those artists as useless, who produce only such superfluities as neither accommodate the body nor improve the mind ; and of which no other effect can be imagined, than that they are the occasions of spending money and consuming time.

But this censure will be mitigated, when it is seriously considered, that money and time are the heaviest burdens of life, and that the unhappiest of all mortals are those who have more of either than they know how to use. To set himself free from these incumbrances, one hurries to New-market ; another travels over Europe ; one pulls down his house and calls architects about him ; another buys a seat in the country, and follows his hounds over hedges and through rivers ; one makes collections of shells ; and another searches the world for tulips and carnations.

He is surely a publick benefactor who finds employment for those to whom it is thus difficult to find it for themselves. It is true, that this is seldom done merely from generosity or compassion ; almost every man seeks his own advantage in helping others ; and therefore it is too common for mercenary officiousness to consider rather what is grateful than what is right.

We all know that it is more profitable to be loved than esteemed ; and ministers of pleasure will always be found, who study to make themselves necessary, and to supplant those who are practising the same arts.

One of the amusements of idleness is reading without the fatigue of close attention ; and the world therefore swarms with writers whose wish is not to be studied, but to be read.

No species of literary men has lately been so much multiplied as the writers of news. Not many years ago the

nation was content with one gazette; but now we have not
only in the metropolis papers for every morning and every
evening, but almost every large town has its weekly historian,
who regularly circulates his periodical intelligence, and fills
the villages of his district with conjectures on the events of
war, and with debates on the true interest of Europe.

To write news in its perfection requires such a combination
of qualities, that a man completely fitted for the task is
not always to be found. In Sir Henry Wotton's jocular
definition, "An ambassador is said to be a man of virtue
sent abroad to tell lies for the advantage of his country; a
news-writer is a man without virtue, who writes lies at home
for his own profit." To these compositions is required
neither genius nor knowledge, neither industry nor sprightliness; but contempt of shame and indifference to truth are
absolutely necessary. He who by a long familiarity with
infamy has obtained these qualities, may confidently tell
to-day what he intends to contradict to-morrow; he may
affirm fearlessly what he knows that he shall be obliged to
recant, and may write letters from Amsterdam or Dresden
to himself.

In a time of war the nation is always of one mind, eager
to hear something good of themselves and ill of the enemy.
At this time the task of news-writers is easy; they have
nothing to do but to tell that a battle is expected, and
afterwards that a battle has been fought, in which we and
our friends, whether conquering or conquered, did all, and
our enemies did nothing.

Scarcely any thing awakens attention like a tale of cruelty.
The writer of news never fails in the intermission of action
to tell how the enemies murdered children and ravished
virgins; and, if the scene of action be somewhat distant,
scalps half the inhabitants of a province.

Among the calamities of war may be justly numbered the diminution of the love of truth, by the falsehoods which interest dictates and credulity encourages. A peace will equally leave the warrior and relater of wars destitute of employment; and I know not whether more is to be dreaded from the streets filled with soldiers accustomed to plunder, or from garrets filled with scribblers accustomed to lie.*

Saturday, November 18, 1758.

MANY moralists have remarked, that pride has of all human vices the widest dominion, appears in the greatest multiplicity of forms, and lies hid under the greatest variety of disguises; of disguises, which, like the moon's *veil of brightness*, are both its *lustre and its shade*, and betray it to others, though they hide it from ourselves.

It is not my intention to degrade pride from this pre-eminence of mischief; yet I know not whether idleness may not maintain a very doubtful and obstinate competition.

There are some that profess idleness in its full dignity, who call themselves the *Idle*, as Busiris in the play calls himself the *Proud;* who boast that they do nothing, and thank their stars that they have nothing to do; who sleep every night till they can sleep no longer, and rise only that exercise may enable them to sleep again; who prolong the reign of darkness by double curtains, and never see the sun but to *tell him how they hate his beams;* whose whole labour is to vary the posture of indolence, and whose day

* Note XXVI., Appendix.

differs from their night but as a couch or chair differs from a bed.

These are the true and open votaries of Idleness, for whom she weaves the garlands of poppies, and into whose cup she pours the waters of oblivion; who exist in a state of unruffled stupidity, forgetting and forgotten; who have long ceased to live, and at whose death the survivors can only say, that they have ceased to breathe.

But idleness predominates in many lives where it is not suspected; for, being a vice which terminates in itself, it may be enjoyed without injury to others; and it is therefore not watched like fraud, which endangers property; or like pride, which naturally seeks its gratifications in another's inferiority. Idleness is a silent and peaceful quality, that neither raises envy by ostentation, nor hatred by opposition; and therefore nobody is busy to censure or detect it.

As pride sometimes is hid under humility, idleness is often covered by turbulence and hurry. He that neglects his known duty and real employment, naturally endeavours to crowd his mind with something that may bar out the remembrance of his own folly, and does any thing but what he ought to do with eager diligence, that he may keep himself in his own favour.

Some are always in a state of preparation, occupied in previous measures, forming plans, accumulating materials, and providing for the main affair. These are certainly under the secret power of idleness. Nothing is to be expected from the workman whose tools are for ever to be sought. I was once told by a great master, that no man ever excelled in painting, who was eminently curious about pencils and colours.

There are others to whom idleness dictates another

expedient, by which life may be passed unprofitably away without the tediousness of many vacant hours. The art is, to fill the day with petty business, to have always something in hand which may raise curiosity, but not solicitude, and keep the mind in a state of action, but not of labour.

This art has for many years been practised by my old friend Sober* with wonderful success. Sober is a man of strong desires and quick imagination, so exactly balanced by the love of ease, that they can seldom stimulate him to any difficult undertaking; they have however so much power, that they will not suffer him to lie quite at rest; and though they do not make him sufficiently useful to others, they make him at least weary of himself.

Mr. Sober's chief pleasure is conversation: there is no end of his talk or his attention; to speak or to hear is equally pleasing; for he still fancies that he is teaching or learning something, and is free for the time from his own reproaches.

But there is one time at night when he must go home, that his friends may sleep; and another time in the morning, when all the world agrees to shut out interruption.† These are the moments of which poor Sober trembles at the thought. But the misery of these tiresome intervals he has many means of alleviating. He has persuaded himself, that the manual arts are undeservedly overlooked; he has observed in many trades the effects of close thought, and just ratiocination. From speculation he proceeded to practice, and supplied himself with the tools of a carpenter, with which he mended his coal-box very successfully, and which he still continues to employ, as he finds occasion.

* Note XXVII., Appendix.   † Note XXVIII., Appendix.

He has attempted at other times the crafts of shoe-maker, tinman, plumber, and potter; in all these arts he has failed, and resolves to qualify himself for them by better information. But his daily amusement is chemistry. He has a small furnace, which he employs in distillation, and which has long been the solace of his life. He draws oils and waters, and essences and spirits, which he knows to be of no use; sits and counts the drops as they come from his retort, and forgets that, whilst a drop is falling, a moment flies away.

Poor Sober! I have often teased him with reproof, and he has often promised reformation; for no man is so much open to conviction as the Idler, but there is none on whom it operates so little. What will be the effect of this paper I know not; perhaps he will read it and laugh, and light the fire in his furnace; but my hope is, that he will quit his trifles, and betake himself to rational and useful diligence.

Saturday, December 23, 1758.

THE great differences that disturb the peace of mankind are not about ends, but means. We have all the same general desires; but how those desires shall be accomplished will for ever be disputed. The ultimate purpose of government is temporal, and that of religion is eternal, happiness. Hitherto we agree; but here we must part, to try, according to the endless varieties of passion and understanding combined with one another, every possible form of government, and every imaginable tenet of religion.

We are told by Cumberland that *rectitude*, applied to action or contemplation, is merely metaphorical ; and that as a *right* line describes the shortest passage from point to point, so a *right* action effects a good design by the fewest means ; and so likewise a *right* opinion is that which connects distant truths by the shortest train of intermediate propositions.

To find the nearest way from truth to truth, or from purpose to effect, not to use more instruments where fewer will be sufficient, not to move by wheels and levers what will give way to the naked hand, is the great proof of a healthful and vigorous mind, neither feeble with helpless ignorance, nor over-burdened with unwieldly knowledge.

But there are men who seem to think nothing so much the characteristick of a genius, as to do common things in an uncommon manner ; like Hudibras, to *tell the clock by algebra ;* or like the lady in Dr. Young's satires, *to drink tea by stratagem;* to quit the beaten track only because it is known, and take a new path, however crooked or rough, because the straight was found out before.

Every man speaks and writes with intent to be understood ; and it can seldom happen but he that understands himself, might convey his notions to another, if, content to be understood, he did not seek to be admired ; but when once he begins to contrive how his sentiments may be received, not with most ease to his reader, but with most advantage to himself, he then transfers his consideration from words to sounds, from sentences to periods, and, as he grows more elegant, becomes less intelligible.

It is difficult to enumerate every species of authors whose labours counteract themselves ; the man of exuberance and copiousness, who diffuses every thought through so many diversities of expression, that it is lost like water in a mist ; the ponderous dictator of sentences, whose notions are delivered in the lump, and are, like uncoined bullion, of more weight than use ; the liberal illustrator, who shows by examples and comparisons what was clearly seen when it was first proposed ; and the stately son of demonstration, who proves with mathematical formality what no man has yet pretended to doubt.

There is a mode of style for which I know not that the masters of oratory have yet found a name ; a style by which the most evident truths are so obscured, that they can no longer be perceived, and the most familiar propositions so disguised that they cannot be known. Every other kind of eloquence is the dress of sense ; but this is the mask by which a true master of his art will so effectually conceal it, that a man will as easily mistake his own positions, if he meets them thus transformed, as he may pass in a masquerade his nearest acquaintance.

This style may be called the *terrific*,* for its chief intention is to terrify and amaze ; it may be termed the *repulsive*, for its natural effect is to drive away the reader ; or it may be distinguished, in plain English, by the denomination of the *bugbear style*, for it has more terrour than danger, and will appear less formidable as it is more nearly approached.

A mother tells her infant, that *two and two make four ;* the child remembers the proposition, and is able to count four to all the purpose of life, till the course of his education brings him among philosophers, who fright him from his former knowledge, by telling him, that four is a certain aggregate of units ; that all numbers being only the repetition

* Note XXIX., Appendix.

of an unit, which, though not a number itself, is the parent, root, or original of all number, *four* is the denomination assigned to a certain number of such repetitions. The only danger is, lest, when he first hears these dreadful sounds, the pupil should run away : if he has but the courage to stay till the conclusion, he will find that, when speculation has done its worst, two and two still make four.

An illustrious example of this species of eloquence may be found in *Letters concerning Mind.** The author begins by declaring, that *the sorts of things are things that now are, have been, and shall be, and the th'ngs that strictly* are. In this position, except the last clause, in which he uses something of the scholastick language, there is nothing but what every man has heard, and imagines himself to know. But who would not believe that some wonderful novelty is presented to his intellect, when he is afterwards told in the true *bugbear* style, that *the* ares, *in the former sense, are things that lie between the* have-beens *and* shall-bes. *The* have-beens *are things that are past ; the* shall-bes *are things that are to come ; and. the things that* are, in the latter sense, *are things that have not been, nor shall be, nor stand in the midst of such as are before them, or shall be after them. The things that have been, and shall be, have respect to present, past, and future. Those likewise that now* are *have moreover place ; that, for instance, which is here, that which is to the east, that which is to the west.*

All this, my dear reader, is very strange ; but though it be strange, it is not new : survey these wonderful sentences again, and they will be found to contain nothing more than very plain truths, which, till this author arose, had always been delivered in plain language.

* By John Petvin. Published in London in 1750.

Saturday, January 27, 1759.

THE following letter relates to an affliction perhaps not necessary to be imparted to the publick ; but I could not persuade myself to suppress it, because I think I know the sentiments to be sincere, and I feel no disposition to provide for this day any other entertainment.

MR. IDLER,

Notwithstanding the warnings of philosophers, and the daily examples of losses and misfortunes which life forces upon our observation, such is the absorption of our thoughts in the business of the present day, such the resignation of our reason to empty hopes of future felicity, or such our unwillingness to foresee what we dread, that every calamity comes suddenly upon us, and not only presses us as a burthen, but crushes as a blow.

There are evils which happen out of the common course of nature, against which it is no reproach not to be provided. A flash of lightning intercepts the traveller in his way ; the concussion of an earthquake heaps the ruins of cities upon their inhabitants. But other miseries time brings, though silently yet visibly, forward by its even lapse, which yet approach us unseen because we turn our eyes away, and seize us unresisted because we could not arm ourselves against them but by setting them before us.

That it is vain to shrink from what cannot be avoided, and to hide that from ourselves which must some time be found, is a truth which we all know, but which all neglect, and perhaps none more than the speculative reasoner, whose thoughts are always from home, whose eye wanders over life, whose fancy dances over meteors of happiness kindled by itself, and who examines every thing rather than his own state.

Nothing is more evident than that the decays of age must terminate in death ; yet there is no man, says Tully, who does not believe that he may yet live another year ; and there is none who does not, upon the same principle, hope another year for his parent or his friend : but the fallacy will be in time detected ; the last year, the last day must come.[*] It has come, and is passed. The life which made my own life pleasant is at an end, and the gates of death are shut upon my prospects.

The loss of a friend upon whom the heart was fixed, to whom every wish and endeavour tended, is a state of dreary desolation, in which the mind looks abroad impatient of itself, and finds nothing but emptiness and horrour. The blameless life, the artless tenderness, the pious simplicity, the modest resignation, the patient sickness, and the quiet death, are remembered only to add value to the loss, to aggravate regret for what cannot be amended, to deepen sorrow for what cannot be recalled.

These are the calamities by which Providence gradually disengages us from the love of life. Other evils fortitude may repel, or hope may mitigate ; but irreparable privation leaves nothing to exercise resolution or flatter expectation. The dead cannot return, and nothing is left us here but languishment and grief.

Yet such is the course of nature, that whoever lives long must outlive those whom he loves and honours. Such is the condition of our present existence, that life must one time lose its associations, and every inhabitant of the earth

* Note XXX., Appendix.

must walk downward to the grave alone and unregarded, without any partner of his joy or grief, without any interested witness of his misfortunes or success.

Misfortune, indeed, he may yet feel; for where is the bottom of the misery of man? But what is success to him that has none to enjoy it? Happiness is not found in self-contemplation; it is perceived only when it is reflected from another.

We know little of the state of departed souls, because such knowledge is not necessary to a good life. Reason deserts us at the brink of the grave, and can give no further intelligence. Revelation is not wholly silent. *There is joy in the angels of Heaven over one sinner that repenteth ;* and surely this joy is not incommunicable to souls disentangled from the body, and made like angels.

Let hope therefore dictate, what revelation does not confute, that the union of souls may still remain; and that we who are struggling with sin, sorrow, and infirmities, may have our part in the attention and kindness of those who have finished their course, and are now receiving their reward.

These are the great occasions which force the mind to take refuge in religion: when we have no help in ourselves, what can remain but that we look up to a higher and a greater Power? and to what hope may we not raise our eyes and hearts, when we consider that the greatest POWER is the BEST?

Surely there is no man who, thus afflicted, does not seek succour in the *Gospel,* which has brought *life and immortality to light.* The precepts of Epicurus, who teaches us to endure what the laws of the universe make necessary, may silence but not content us. The dictates of Zeno, who commands us to look with indifference on external things, may dispose us to conceal our sorrow, but cannot assuage it. Real alleviation of the loss of friends, and rational tranquillity in the prospect of our own dissolution, can be received only from the promises of Him in whose hands are life and death, and from the assurance of another and better state, in which all tears will be wiped from the eyes, and the whole soul shall be filled with joy. Philosophy may infuse stubbornness, but Religion only can give patience.

I am, &c.*

Saturday, February 10, 1759.

THE natural advantages which arise from the position of the earth which we inhabit with respect to the other planets, afford much employment to mathematical speculation ; by which it has been discovered, that no other conformation of the system could have given such commodious distributions of light and heat, or imparted fertility and pleasure to so great a part of a revolving sphere.

It may be perhaps observed by the moralist, with equal reason, that our globe seems particularly fitted for the residence of a being, placed here only for a short time, whose task is to advance himself to a higher and happier state of existence, by unremitted vigilance of caution, and activity of virtue.

The duties required of man are such as human nature does not willingly perform, and such as those are inclined to delay who yet intend some time to fulfil them. It was therefore necessary that this universal reluctance should be

---

* This paper was written by Dr. Johnson on the death of his mother. He wrote " Rasselas " in order to defray the expenses of her funeral, and to pay a few small debts she left.

counteracted, and the drowsiness of hesitation wakened into resolve ; that the danger of procrastination should be always in view, and the fallacies of security be hourly detected.

To this end all the appearances of nature uniformly conspire. Whatever we see on every side reminds us of the lapse of time and the flux of life. The day and night succeed each other, the rotation of seasons diversifies the year ; the sun rises, attains the meridian, declines, and sets ; and the moon every night changes its form.

The day has been considered as an image of the year, and the year as the representation of life. The morning answers to the spring, and the spring to childhood and youth ; the noon corresponds to the summer, and the summer to the strength of manhood. The evening is an emblem of autumn, and autumn of declining life. The night with its silence and darkness shows the winter, in which all the powers of vegetation are benumbed ; and the winter points out the time when life shall cease, with its hopes and pleasures.

He that is carried forward, however swiftly, by a motion equable and easy, perceives not the change of place but by the variation of objects. If the wheel of life, which rolls thus silently along, passed on through undistinguishable uniformity, we should never mark its approaches to the end of the course. If one hour were like another ; if the passage of the sun did not shew that the day is wasting ; if the change of seasons did not impress upon us the flight of the year ; quantities of duration equal to days and years would glide unobserved. If the parts of time were not variously coloured, we should never discern their departure or succession, but should live thoughtless of the past, and careless of the future, without will, and perhaps without power, to compute the periods of life, or to compare the time which is already lost with that which may probably remain.

But the course of time is so visibly marked, that it is observed even by the birds of passage, and by nations who have raised their minds very little above animal instinct: there are human beings whose language does not supply them with words by which they can number five; but I have read of none that have not names for day and night, for summer and winter.

Yet it is certain that these admonitions of nature, however forcible, however importunate, are too often vain; and that many who mark with such acccuracy the course of time, appear to have little sensibility of the decline of life. Every man has something to do which he neglects; every man has faults to conquer which he delays to combat.

So little do we accustom ourselves to consider the effects of time, that things necessary and certain often surprise us like unexpected contingencies. We leave the beauty in her bloom, and, after an absence of twenty years, wonder, at our return, to find her faded. We meet those whom we left children, and can scarcely persuade ourselves to treat them as men. The traveller visits in age those countries through which he rambled in his youth, and hopes for merriment at the old place. The man of business, wearied with unsatisfactory prosperity, retires to the town of his nativity, and expects to play away the last years with the companions of his childhood, and recover youth in the fields where he once was young.

From this inattention, so general and so mischievous, let it be every man's study to exempt himself. Let him that desires to see others happy make haste to give while his gift can be enjoyed, and remember that every moment of delay takes something from the value of his benefaction.

And let him who purposes his own happiness reflect, that while he forms his purpose the day rolls on, and *the night cometh when no man can work.* *

Saturday, March 10, 1759.

To the Idler.

Mr. Idler,

I AM the unfortunate wife of a city wit, and cannot but think that my case may deserve equal compassion with any of those which have been represented in your paper.

I married my husband within three months after the expiration of his apprenticeship; we put our money together, and furnished a large and splendid shop, in which he was for five years and a half diligent and civil. The notice which curiosity or kindness commonly bestows on beginners, was continued by confidence and esteem; one customer, pleased with his treatment and his bargain, recommended another; and we were busy behind the counter from morning to night.

Thus every day increased our wealth and our reputation. My husband was often invited to dinner openly on the Exchange by hundred thousand pounds men : and whenever I went to any of the halls, the wives of the aldermen made me low courtesies. We always took up our notes before the day, and made all considerable payments by draughts upon our banker.

You will easily believe that I was well enough pleased with my condition; for what happiness can be greater than

* Note XXXI., Appendix.

20

that of growing every day richer and richer? I will not deny that, imagining myself likely to be in a short time the sheriff's lady, I broke off my acquaintance with some of my neighbours; and advised my husband to keep good company, and not to be seen with men that were worth nothing.

In time he found that ale agreed with his constitution, and went every night to drink his pint at a tavern, where he met with a set of critics, who disputed upon the merit of the different theatrical performers. By these idle fellows he was taken to the play, which at first he did not seem much to heed; for he owned, that he very seldom knew what they were doing, and that, while his companions would let him alone, he was commonly thinking on his last bargain.

Having once gone, however, he went again and again, though I often told him that three shillings were thrown away: at last he grew uneasy if he missed a night, and importuned me to go with him. I went to a tragedy which they called Macbeth; and, when I came home, told him that I could not bear to see men and women make themselves such fools, by pretending to be witches and ghosts, generals and kings, and to walk in their sleep when they were as much awake as those who looked at them. He told me that I must get higher notions, and that a play was the most rational of all entertainments, and most proper to relax the mind after the business of the day.

By degrees he gained knowledge of some of the players, and, when the play was over, very frequently treated them with suppers; for which he was admitted to stand behind the scenes.

He soon began to lose some of his morning hours in the same folly, and was for one winter very diligent in his attendance on the rehearsals; but of this species of idleness he grew weary, and said that the play was nothing without the company.

His ardour for the diversion of the evening increased; he bought a sword, and paid five shillings a night to sit in the boxes; he went sometimes into a place which he calls the Green-room, where all the wits of the age assemble; and, when he had been there, could do nothing for two or three days, but repeat their jests, or tell their disputes.

He has now lost his regard for every thing but the play-house; he invites, three times a week, one or other to drink claret, and talk of the drama. His first care in the morning is to read the play-bills; and, if he remembers any lines of the tragedy which is to be represented, walks about the shop repeating them so loud, and with such strange gestures, that the passengers gather round the door.

His greatest pleasure when I married him was to hear the situation of his shop commended, and to be told how many estates have been got in it by the same trade; but of late he grows peevish at any mention of business, and delights in nothing so much as to be told that he speaks like Mossop.

Among his new associates he has learned another language, and speaks in such a strain that the neighbours cannot understand him. If a customer talks longer than he is willing to hear, he will complain that he has been excruciated with unmeaning verbosity; he laughs at the letters of his friends for their tameness of expression, and often declares himself weary of attending to the *minutiæ* of a shop.

It is well for me that I know how to keep a book, for of late he is scarcely ever in the way. Since one of his friends told him that he had a genius for tragick poetry, he has locked himself in an upper room six or seven hours a day; and when I carry him any paper to be read or signed, I hear him talking vehemently to himself, sometimes of love and beauty, sometimes of friendship and virtue, but more frequently of liberty and his country.

I would gladly, Mr. Idler, be informed what to think of a shopkeeper who is incessantly talking about liberty; a word which, since his acquaintance with polite life, my husband has always in his mouth: he is on all occasions afraid of our liberty. What can the man mean? I am sure he has liberty enough: it were better for him and me if his liberty was lessened.

He has a friend, whom he calls a critick, that comes twice a week to read what he is writing. This critick tells him that his piece is a little irregular, but that some detached scenes will shine prodigiously, and that in the character of Bombulus he is wonderfully great. My scribbler then squeezes his hand, calls him the best of friends, thanks him for his sincerity, and tells him that he hates to be flattered. I have reason to believe that he seldom parts with his dear friend without lending him two guineas, and I am afraid that he gave bail for him three days ago.

By this course of life our credit as traders is lessened; and I cannot forbear to reflect, that my husband's honour as a wit is not much advanced, for he seems to be always the lowest of the company, and is afraid to tell his opinion till the rest have spoken. When he was behind his counter, he used to be brisk, active, and jocular, like a man that knew what he was doing, and did not fear to look another in the face; but, among wits and criticks, he is timorous and awkward, and hangs down his head at his own table. Dear Mr. Idler, persuade him, if you can, to return once more to his native element. Tell him that his wit will never make him rich, but that there are places where riches will always make a wit.

                    I am, Sir, etc.,
                              DEBORAH GINGER.

Saturday, June 9, 1759.

CRITICISM is a study by which men grow important and formidable at a very small expense. The power of invention has been conferred by nature upon few, and the labour of learning those sciences which may by mere labour be obtained is too great to be willingly endured; but every man can exert such judgment as he has upon the works of others; and he whom nature has made weak, and idleness keeps ignorant, may yet support his vanity by the name of a Critick.

I hope it will give comfort to great numbers who are passing through the world in obscurity, when I inform them how easily distinction may be obtained. All the other powers of literature are coy and haughty, they must be long courted, and at last are not always gained; but Criticism is a goddess easy of access and forward of advance, who will meet the slow, and encourage the timorous; the want of meaning she supplies with words, and the want of spirit she recompenses with malignity.

This profession has one recommendation peculiar to itself, that it gives vent to malignity without real mischief.

No genius was ever blasted by the breath of criticks.* The poison which, if confined, would have burst the heart, fumes away in empty isses, and malice is set at ease with very little danger to merit. The Critick is the only man whose triumph is without another's pain, and whose greatness does not rise upon another's ruin.

To a study at once so easy and so reputable, so malicious and so harmless, it cannot be necessary to invite my readers by a long or laboured exhortation; it is sufficient, since all would be Criticks if they could, to shew by one eminent example that all can be Criticks if they will.

Dick Minim, after the common course of puerile studies, in which he was no great proficient, was put apprentice to a brewer, with whom he had lived two years, when his uncle died in the city, and left him a large fortune in the stocks. Dick had for six months before used the company of the lower players, of whom he had learned to scorn a trade, and, being now at liberty to follow his genius, he resolved to be a man of wit and humour. That he might be properly initiated in his new character, he frequented the coffee-houses near the theatres, where he listened very diligently, day after day, to those who talked of language and sentiments, and unities and catastrophes, till, by slow degrees, he began to think that he understood something of the stage, and hoped in time to talk himself.

But he did not trust so much to natural sagacity as wholly to neglect the help of books. When the theatres were shut, he retired to Richmond with a few select writers, whose opinions he impressed upon his memory by unwearied diligence; and, when he returned with other wits to the town, was able to tell, in very proper phrases, that

* Note XXXII., Appendix.

the chief business of art is to copy nature ; that a perfect writer is not to be expected, because genius decays as judgment increases ; that the great art is the art of blotting ; and that, according to the rule of Horace, every piece should be kept nine years.

Of the great authors he now began to display the characters, laying down as an universal position, that all had beauties and defects. His opinion was, that Shakespeare, committing himself wholly to the impulse of nature, wanted that correctness which learning would have given him ; and that Jonson, trusting to learning, did not sufficiently cast his eyes on nature. He blamed the stanzas of Spenser, and could not bear the hexameters of Sidney. Denham and Waller he held the first reformers of English numbers ; and thought that if Waller could have obtained the strength of Denham, or Denham the sweetness of Waller, there had been nothing wanting to complete a poet. He often expressed his commiseration of Dryden's poverty, and his indignation at the age which suffered him to write for bread ; he repeated with rapture the first lines of All for Love, but wondered at the corruption of taste which could bear anything so unnatural as rhyming tragedies. In Otway he found uncommon powers of moving the passions, but was disgusted by his general negligence, and blamed him for making a conspirator his hero ; and never concluded his disquisition, without remarking how happily the sound of the clock is made to alarm the audience. Southern would have been his favourite, but that he mixes comick with tragick scenes, intercepts the natural course of the passions, and fills the mind with a wild confusion of mirth and melancholy. The versification of Rowe he thought too melodious for the stage, and too little varied in different passions. He made it the great fault of Congreve, that all his persons were wits, and that he always wrote with more art than nature. He considered Cato rather as a poem than play, and allowed Addison to be the complete master of allegory and grave humour, but paid no great deference to him as a critick. He thought the chief merit of Prior was in his easy tales and lighter poems, though he allowed that his Solomon had many noble sentiments elegantly expressed. In Swift he discovered an inimitable vein of irony, and an easiness which all would hope and few would attain. Pope he was inclined to degrade from a poet to a versifier, and thought his numbers rather luscious than sweet. He often lamented the neglect of Phædra and Hippolitus, and wished to see the stage under better regulations.

These assertions passed commonly uncontradicted; and if now and then an opponent started up, he was quickly repressed by the [suffrages] of the company, and Minim went away from every dispute with elation of heart and increase of confidence.

He now grew conscious of his abilities, and began to talk of the present state of dramatick poetry; wondered what had become of the comick genius which supplied our ancestors with wit and pleasantry, and why no writer could be found that durst now venture beyond a farce. He saw no reason for thinking that the vein of humour was exhausted, since we live in a country where liberty suffers every character to spread itself to its utmost bulk, and which therefore produces more originals than all the rest of the world together. Of tragedy he concluded business to be the soul, and yet often hinted that love predominates too much upon the modern stage.

He was now an acknowledged critick, and had his own seat in a coffee-house, and headed a party in the pit. Minim has more vanity than ill-nature, and seldom desires to do much mischief; he will perhaps murmur a little in the ear of him that sits next him, but endeavours to influence the audience to favour, by clapping when an actor exclaims, "Ye gods!" or laments the misery of his country.

By degrees he was admitted to rehearsals; and many of his friends are of opinion, that our present poets are indebted to him for their happiest thoughts: by his contrivance the bell was wrung twice in Barbarossa, and by his persuasion the author of Cleone concluded his play without a couplet; for what can be more absurd, said Minim, than that part of a play should be ryhmed, and part written in blank verse? and by what acquisition of faculties is the speaker, who never could find rhymes before, enabled to rhyme at the conclusion of an act?

He is the great investigator of hidden beauties, and is particularly delighted when he finds "the sound an echo to the sense." He has read all our poets with particular attention to this delicacy of versification, and wonders at the supineness with which their works have been hitherto perused, so that no man has found the sound of a drum in this distich:

> "When pulpit, drum ecclesiastick,
> Was beat with fist instead of a stick;"

and that the wonderful lines upon honour and a bubble have hitherto passed without notice:

> "Honour is like the glossy bubble,
> Which cost philosophers such trouble;
> Where, one part crack'd, the whole does fly,
> And wits are crack'd to find out why."

In these verses, says Minim, we have two striking

accommodations of the sound to the sense. It is impossible to utter the first two lines emphatically without an act like that which they describe ; *bubble* and *trouble* causing a momentary inflation of the cheeks by the retention of the breath, which is afterwards forcibly emitted, as in the practice of *blowing bubbles.* But the greatest excellence is in the third line, which is *crack'd* in the middle to express a crack, and then shivers into monosyllables. Yet has this diamond lain neglected with common stones, and among the innumerable admirers of Hudibras, the observation of this superlative passage has been reserved for the sagacity of Minim.

Saturday, June 15, 1759.

M R. MINIM had now advanced himself to the zenith of critical reputation ; when he was in the pit, every eye in the boxes was fixed upon him : when he entered his coffee-house, he was surrounded by circles of candidates, who passed their noviciate of literature under his tuition : his opinion was asked by all who had no opinion of their own, and yet loved to debate and decide ; and no composition was supposed to pass in safety to posterity, till it had been secured by Minim's approbation.

Minim professes great admiration of the wisdom and munificence by which the academies of the continent were raised ; and often wishes for some standard of taste, for some tribunal, to which merit may appeal from caprice, prejudice, and malignity. He has formed a plan for an academy of criticism, where every work of imagination may be read before it is printed and which shall authoritatively direct the theatres what pieces to receive or reject, to exclude or to revive.

Such an institution would, in Dick's opinion, spread the fame of English literature over Europe, and make London the metropolis of elegance and politeness, the place to which the learned and ingenious of all countries would repair for instruction and improvement, and where nothing would any longer be applauded or endured that was not conformed to the nicest rules, and finished with the highest elegance.

Till some happy conjunction of the planets shall dispose our princes or ministers to make themselves immortal by such an academy, Minim contents himself to preside four nights in a week in a critical society selected by himself, where he is heard without contradiction, and whence his judgment is disseminated through the great vulgar and the small.

When he is placed in the chair of criticism, he declares loudly for the noble simplicity of our ancestors, in opposition to the petty refinements and ornamental luxuriance. Sometimes he is sunk in despair, and perceives false delicacy daily gaining ground, and sometimes brightens his countenance with a gleam of hope, and predicts the revival of the true sublime. He then fulminates his loudest censures against the monkish barbarity of rhyme; wonders how beings that pretend to reason can be pleased with one line always ending like another; tells how unjustly and unnaturally sense is sacrificed to sound; how often the best thoughts are mangled by the necessity of confining or extending them to the dimensions of a couplet; and rejoices that genius has, in our days, shaken off the shackles which had encumbered it so long. Yet he allows that rhyme may sometimes be borne, if the lines be often broken, and the pauses judiciously diversified.

From blank verse he makes an easy transition to Milton, whom he produces as an example of the slow advance of lasting reputation.   Milton is the only writer in whose books Minim can read for ever without weariness.   What cause it is that exempts this pleasure from satiety he has long and diligently inquired, and believes it to consist in the perpetual variation of the numbers, by which the ear is gratified and the attention awakened.   The lines that are commonly thought rugged and unmusical, he conceives to have been written to temper the melodious luxury of the rest, or to express things by a proper cadence: for he scarcely finds a verse that has not this favourite beauty ; he declares that he could shiver in a hot-house when he reads that

> " the ground
> Burns frore, and cold performs th' effect of fire ; "

and that, when Milton bewails his blindness, the verse,

> " So thick a drop serene has quenched these orbs,"

has, he knows not how, something that strikes him with an obscure sensation like that which he fancies would be felt from the sound of darkness.

Minim is not so confident of his rules of judgment as not very eagerly to catch new light from the name of the author. He is commonly so prudent as to spare those whom he cannot resist, unless, as will sometimes happen, he finds the publick combined against them.   But a fresh pretender to fame he is strongly inclined to censure, till his own honour requires that he commend him.   Till he knows the success of a composition, he intrenches himself in general terms ; there are some new thoughts and beautiful passages, but there is likewise much which he would have advised the author to expunge. He has several favourite epithets, of which he never settled the meaning, but which are very commodiously applied to books which he has not read, or cannot understand. One is *manly*, another is *dry*, another *stiff*, and another *flimsy;* sometimes he discovers delicacy of style, and sometimes meets with *strange expressions.*

He is never so great, nor so happy, as when a youth of promising parts is brought to receive his directions for the prosecution of his studies. He then puts on a very serious air; he advises the pupil to read none but the best authors, and, when he finds one congenial to his own mind, to study his beauties, but avoid his faults; and, when he sits down to write, to consider how his favourite author would think at the present time on the present occasion. He exhorts him to catch those moments when he finds his thoughts expanded and his genius exalted, but to take care lest imagination hurry him beyond the bounds of nature. He holds diligence the mother of success; yet enjoins him, with great earnestness, not to read more than he can digest, and not to confuse his mind by pursuing studies of contrary tendencies. He tells him, that every man has his genius, and that Cicero could never be a poet. The boy retires illuminated, resolves to follow his genius, and to think how Milton would have thought: and Minim feasts upon his own beneficence till another day brings another pupil.

Saturday, August 25, 1759.

DICK SHIFTER was born in Cheapside, and, having passed reputably through all the classes of St. Paul's school, has been for some years a student in the Temple. He is of opinion, that intense application dulls the faculties, and thinks it necessary to temper the severity of the law by books that engage the mind, but do not fatigue it. He has therefore made a copious collection of plays, poems, and romances, to which he has recourse when he fancies himself tired with statutes and reports; and he seldom inquires very nicely whether he is weary or idle.

Dick has received from his favourite authors very strong impressions of a country life; and though his furthest excursions have been to Greenwich on one side, and Chelsea on the other, he has talked for several years, with great pomp of language and elevation of sentiments, about a state too high for contempt and too low for envy, about homely quiet and blameless simplicity, pastoral delights and rural innocence.

His friends who had estates in the country, often invited him to pass the summer among them, but something or other had always hindered him; and he considered, that to reside in the house of another man was to incur a kind of dependence inconsistent with that laxity of life which he had imaged as the chief good.

This summer he resolved to be happy, and procured a lodging to be taken for him at a solitary house, situated about thirty miles from London, on the banks of a small river, with corn-fields before it, and a hill on each side covered with wood. He concealed the place of his retirement, that none might violate his obscurity ; and promised himself many a happy day when he should hide himself among the trees, and contemplate the tumults and vexations of the town.

He stepped into the post-chaise with his heart beating and his eyes sparkling, was conveyed through many varieties of delightful prospects, saw hills and meadows, corn-fields and pasture, succeed each other, and for four hours charged none of his poets with fiction or exaggeration. He was now within six miles of happiness ; when, having never felt so much agitation before, he began to wish his journey at an end, and the last hour was passed in changing his posture, and quarrelling with his driver.

An hour may be tedious, but cannot be long. He at length alighted at his new dwelling, and was received as he expected ; he looked round upon the hills and rivulets, but his joints were stiff and his muscles sore, and his first request was to see his bed-chamber.

He rested well, and ascribed the soundness of his sleep to the stillness of the country. He expected from that time nothing but nights of quiet and days of rapture, and, as soon as he had risen, wrote an account of his new state to one of his friends in the Temple.

" DEAR FRANK,

" I never pitied thee before. I am now as I could wish every man of wisdom and virtue to be, in the regions of calm content and placid meditation ; with all the beauties of nature soliciting my notice, and all the diversities of pleasure courting my acceptance ; the birds are chirping in the hedges, and the flowers blooming in the mead ; the breeze is whistling in the wood, and the sun dancing on the water.

I can now say, with truth, that a man, capable of enjoying the purity of happiness, is never more busy than in his hours of leisure, nor ever less solitary than in a place of solitude.

"I am, dear Frank, etc."

When he had sent away his letter, he walked into the wood with some inconvenience, from the furze that pricked his legs, and the briers that scratched his face. He at last sat down under a tree, and heard with great delight a shower, by which he was now wet, rattling among the branches: This, said he, is the true image of obscurity; we hear of troubles and commotions, but never feel them.

His amusement did not overpower the calls of nature, and he therefore went back to order his dinner. He knew that the country produces whatever is eaten or drunk, and, imagining that he was now at the source of luxury, resolved to indulge himself with dainties which he supposed might be procured at a price next to nothing, if any price at all was expected; and intended to amaze the rusticks with his generosity, by paying more than they would ask. Of twenty dishes which he named, he was amazed to find that scarcely one was to be had; and heard, with astonishment and indignation, that all the fruits of the earth were sold at a higher price than in the streets of London.

His meal was short and sullen; and he retired again to his tree, to inquire how dearness could be consistent with abundance, or how fraud could be practised by simplicity. He was not satisfied with his own speculations, and, returning home early in the evening, went a while from window to window, and found that he wanted something to do.

He inquired for a newspaper, and was told that farmers never minded news, but that they could send for it from the ale-house. A messenger was dispatched, who ran away at full speed, but loitered an hour behind the hedges, and at last coming back with his feet purposely bemired, instead of expressing the gratitude which Mr. Shifter expected for the bounty of a shilling, said, that the night was wet, and the way dirty, and he hoped that his worship would not think it much to give him half a crown.

Dick now went to bed with some abatement of his expectations; but sleep, I know not how, revives our hopes, and rekindles our desires. He rose early in the morning, surveyed the landscape, and was pleased. He walked out, and passed from field to field, without observing any beaten path, and wondered that he had not seen the shepherdesses dancing, nor heard the swains piping to their flocks.

At last he saw some reapers and harvest-women at dinner. Here, said he, are the true Arcadians, and advanced courteously towards them, as afraid of confusing them by the dignity of his presence. They acknowledged his superiority by no other token than that of asking him for something to drink. He imagined that he had now purchased the privilege of discourse, and began to descend to familiar questions, endeavouring to accommodate his discourse to the grossness of rustick understandings. The clowns soon found that he did not know wheat from rye, and began to despise him; one of the boys, by pretending to shew him a bird's nest, decoyed him into a ditch; and one of the wenches sold him a bargain.

This walk had given him no great pleasure; but he hoped to find other rusticks less coarse of manners, and less mischievous of disposition. Next morning he was accosted by an attorney, who told him that, unless he made farmer Dobson satisfaction for trampling his grass, he had orders to indict him. Shifter was offended, but not terrified; and, telling the attorney that he was himself a lawyer, talked so volubly of pettyfoggers and barraters, that he drove him away.

Finding his walks thus interrupted, he was inclined to ride, and, being pleased with the appearance of a horse that was grazing in a neighbouring meadow, inquired the owner; who warranted him sound, and would not sell him but that he was too fine for a plain man.   Dick paid down the price, and, riding out to enjoy the evening, fell with his new horse into a ditch; they got out with difficulty, and, as he was going to mount again, a countryman looked at the horse, and perceived him to be blind.   Dick went to the seller, and demanded back his money; but was told, that a man who rented his ground must do the best for himself; that his landlord had his rent though the year was barren; and that, whether horses had eyes or no, he should sell them to the highest bidder.

Shifter now began to be tired with rustick simplicity, and on the fifth day took possession again of his chambers, and bade farewel to the regions of calm content and placid meditation.

Saturday, October 13, 1759.

I HAVE passed the summer in one of these places to which a mineral spring gives the idle and luxurious an annual reason for resorting, whenever they fancy themselves offended by the heat of London.   What is the true motive of this periodical assembly, I have never yet been able to discover.   The greater part of the visitants neither feel diseases nor fear them. What pleasure can be expected more than the variety of the journey, I know not; for the numbers are too great for privacy, and too small for diversion. As each is known to be a spy upon the rest, they all live in continual restraint; and having but a narrow range for censure, they gratify its cravings by preying on one another.

But every condition has some advantages. In this confinement, a smaller circle affords opportunities for more exact observation. The glass that magnifies its object contracts the sight to a point; and the mind must be fixed upon a single character to remark its minute peculiarities. The quality or habit which passes unobserved in the tumult of successive multitudes, becomes conspicuous when it is offered to the notice day after day; and perhaps I have, without any distinct notice, seen thousands like my late companions; for, when the scene can be varied at pleasure, a slight disgust turns us aside before a deep impression can be made upon the mind.

There was a select set, supposed to be distinguished by superiority of intellects, who always passed the evening together. To be admitted to their conversation was the highest honour of the place; many youths inspired to distinction, by pretending to occasional invitations; and the ladies were often wishing to be men, that they might partake the pleasures of learned society.

I know not whether by merit or destiny, I was, soon after my arrival, admitted to this envied party, which I frequented till I had learned the art by which each endeavoured to support his character.

Tom Steady was a vehement assertor of uncontroverted truth; and, by keeping himself out of the reach of contradiction, had acquired all the confidence which the

consciousness of irresistible abilities could have given. I
was once mentioning a man of eminence, and, after having
recounted his virtues, endeavoured to represent him fully,
by mentioning his faults. "Sir," said Mr. Steady, "that he
has faults I can easily believe, for who is without them?
No man, sir, is now alive, among the innumerable multitudes that swarm upon the earth, however wise or however
good, who has not, in some degree, his failings and his
faults. If there be any man faultless, bring him forth into
public view, show him openly, and let him be known; but
I will venture to affirm, and, till the contrary be plainly
shown, shall always maintain, that no such man is to be
found. Tell not me, sir, of impeccability and perfection;
such talk is for those that are strangers in the world. I
have seen several nations, and conversed with all ranks of
people; I have known the great and the mean, the learned
and the ignorant, the old and the young, the clerical and
the lay; but I have never found a man without a fault; and
I suppose shall die in the opinion, that to be human is to
be frail."

To all this nothing could be opposed. I listened with a
hanging head. Mr. Steady looked round on the hearers
with triumph, and saw every eye congratulating his victory.
He departed, and spent the next morning in following
those who retired from the company, and telling them,
with injunctions of secrecy, how poor Spritely began to take
liberties with men wiser than himself; but that he suppressed him by a decisive argument, which put him totally
to silence.

Dick Snug is a man of sly remark and pithy sententious-
ness: he never immerges himself in the stream of conversation, but lies to catch his companions in the eddy: he is
often very successful in breaking narratives and confounding

eloquence. A gentleman giving the history of one of his acquaintance, made mention of a lady that had many lovers: "Then," said Dick, "she was either handsome or rich." This observation being well received, Dick watched the progress of the tale; and hearing of a man lost in a shipwreck, remarked, " that no man was ever drowned upon dry land."

Will Startle is a man of exquisite sensibility, whose delicacy of frame and quickness of discernment subject him to impressions from the slightest causes; and who therefore passes his life between rapture and horrour, in quiverings of delight, or convulsions of disgust. His emotions are too violent for many words; his thoughts are always discovered by exclamations. *Vile, odious, horrid, detestable,* and *sweet, charming, delightful, astonishing,* compose almost his whole vocabulary, which he utters with various contortions and gesticulations not easily related or described.

Jack Solid is a man of much reading, who utters nothing but quotations: but having been, I suppose, too confident of his memory, he has for some time neglected his books, and his stock grows every day more scanty. Mr. Solid has found an opportunity every night to repeat, from Hudibras,

> " Doubtless the pleasure is as great
> Of being cheated, as to cheat ; "

and from Waller,

> " Poets lose half the praise they would have got,
> Were it but known that they discreetly blot. "

Dick Misty is a man of deep research and forcible penetration. Others are content with superficial appearances; but Dick holds, that there is no effect without a cause, and values himself upon his power of explaining the

difficult and displaying the abstruse.   Upon a dispute
among us, which of two young strangers was more beautiful, "You," says Mr. Misty, turning to me, "like Amaranthia better than Chloris.   I do not wonder at the
preference, for the cause is evident: there is in man a
perception of harmony, and a sensibility of perfection,
which touches the finer fibres of the mental texture; and,
before Reason can descend from her throne to pass her
sentence upon the things compared, drives us towards the
object proportioned to our faculties, by an impulse gentle
yet irresistible; for the harmonick system of the Universe,
and the reciprocal magnetism of similar natures, are always
operating towards conformity and union; nor can the
powers of the soul cease from agitation, till they find
something on which they can repose."   To this nothing
was opposed; and Amaranthia was acknowledged to excel
Chloris.

  Of the rest you may expect an account from,
     Sir, yours,
       Robin Spritely.

Saturday, November 24, 1759.

BIOGRAPHY is, of the various kinds of narrative
  writing, that which is most eagerly read, and most
easily applied to the purposes of life.*

 In romances, when the wide field of possibility lies open
to invention, the incidents may easily be made more
numerous, the vicissitudes more sudden, and the events

    * Note XXXIII., Appendix.

more wonderful: but from the time of life when fancy begins to be over-ruled by reason and corrected by experience, the most artful tale raises little curiosity when it is known to be false; though it may, perhaps, be sometimes read as a model of a neat or elegant style, nor for the sake of knowing what it contains, but how it is written; or those that are weary of themselves may have recourse to it as a pleasing dream, of which, when they awake, they voluntarily dismiss the images from their minds.

The examples and events of history press, indeed, upon the mind with the weight of truth; but when they are reposited in the memory, they are oftener employed for show than use, and rather diversify conversation than regulate life. Few are engaged in such scenes as give them opportunities of growing wiser by the downfall of statesmen or the defeat of generals. The stratagems of war, and the intrigues of courts, are read by far the greater part of mankind with the same indifference as the adventures of fabled heroes, or the revolutions of a fairy region. Between falsehood and useless truth there is little difference. As gold which he cannot spend will make no man rich, so knowledge which he cannot apply will make no man wise.

The mischievous consequences of vice and folly, of irregular desires and predominant passions, are best discovered by those relations which are levelled with the general surface of life, which tell not how any man became great, but how he was made happy; not how he lost the favour of his prince, but how he became discontented with himself.

Those relations are therefore commonly of most value in which the writer tells his own story. He that recounts the life of another, commonly dwells most upon conspicuous events, lessens the familiarity of his tale to increase its dignity, shews his favourite at a distance, decorated and magnified like the ancient actors in their tragick dress, and endeavours to hide the man that he may produce a hero.

But if it be true, which was said by a French prince, *that no man was a hero to the servants of his chamber,* it is equally true, that every man is yet less a hero to himself. He that is most elevated above the crowd by the importance of his employments, or the reputation of his genius, feels himself affected by fame or business but as they influence his domestick life. The high and low, as they have the same faculties and the same senses, have no less similitude in their pains and pleasures. The sensations are the same in all, though produced by very different occasions. The prince feels the same pain when an invader seizes a province, as the farmer when a thief drives away his cow. Men thus equal in themselves will appear equal in honest and impartial biography; and those whom fortune or nature places at the greatest distance may afford instruction to each other.

The writer of his own life has at least the first qualification of an historian, the knowledge of the truth; and though it may be plausibly objected that his temptations to disguise it are equal to his opportunities of knowing it, yet I cannot but think that impartiality may be expected with equal confidence from him that relates the passages of his own life, as from him that delivers the transactions of another.*

Certainty of knowledge not only excludes mistake, but fortifies veracity. What we collect by conjecture, and by conjecture only can one man judge of another's motives or sentiments, is easily modified by fancy or by desire; as objects imperfectly discerned take forms from the hope or fear of the beholder. But that which is fully known cannot

* Note XXXIV., Appendix.

be falsified but with reluctance of understanding, and *Moral*
alarm of conscience: of understanding, the lover of truth;
of conscience, the sentinel of virtue.

He that writes the life of another is either his friend or *bio*
his enemy, and wishes either to exalt his praise or aggravate
his infamy: many temptations to falsehood will occur in
the disguise of passions, too specious to fear much resistance. Love of virtue will animate panegyrick, and hatred
of wickedness embitter censure. The zeal of gratitude, the
ardour of patriotism, fondness for an opinion, or fidelity to
a party, may easily overpower the vigilance of a mind
habitually well disposed, and prevail over unassisted and
unfriended veracity.

But he that speaks of himself has no motive to falsehood
or partiality except self-love, by which all have so often
been betrayed that all are on the watch against its artifices.
He that writes an apology for a single action, to confute an
accusation, to recommend himself to favour, is indeed
always to be suspected of favouring his own cause; but he *esp*
that sits down camly and voluntarily to review his life for *for*
the admonition of posterity, or to amuse himself, and leaves *poste*
this account unpublished, may be commonly presumed to
tell truth, since falsehood cannot appease his own mind,
and fame will not be heard beneath the tomb.

Saturday, December 1, 1759.

ONE of the pecularities which distinguish the present age
is the multiplication of books. Every day brings
new advertisements of literary undertakings, and we are

flattered with repeated promises of growing wise on easier terms than our progenitors.

How much either happiness or knowledge is advanced by this multitude of authors, is not very easy to decide.

He that teaches us any thing which we knew not before, is undoubtedly to be reverenced as a master.

He that conveys knowledge by more pleasing ways, may very properly be loved as a benefactor ; and he that supplies life with innocent amusement, will be certainly caressed as a pleasing companion.

But few of those who fill the world with books, have any pretensions to the hope either of pleasing or instructing. They have often no other task than to lay two books before them, out of which they compile a third, without any new materials of their own, and with very little application of judgment to those which former authors have supplied.*

That all compilations are useless, I do not assert. Particles of science are often very widely scattered. Writers of extensive comprehension have incidental remarks upon topicks very remote from the principal subject, which are often more valuable than formal treatises, and which yet are not known because they are not promised in the title. He that collects those under proper heads is very laudably employed; for though he exerts no great abilities in the work, he facilitates the progress of others, and, by making that easy of attainment which is already written, may give some mind, more vigorous or more adventurous than his own, leisure for new thoughts and original designs.

But the collections poured lately from the press have seldom made at any great expence of time or inquiry, and

* Note XXXV., Appendix.

therefore only serve to distract choice without supplying any real want.

It is observed that *a corrupt society has many laws ;* I know not whether it is not equally true, that *an ignorant age has many books.* When the treasures of ancient knowledge lie unexamined, and original authors are neglected and forgotten, compilers and plagiaries are encouraged, who give us again what we had before, and grow great by setting before us what our own sloth had hidden from our view.

Yet are not even these writers to be indiscriminately censured and rejected. Truth, like beauty, varies its fashions, and is best recommended by different dresses to different minds ; and he that recalls the attention of mankind to any part of learning which time has left behind it, may be truly said to advance the literature of his own age. As the manners of nations vary, new topicks of persuasion become necessary, and new combinations of imagery are produced ; and he that can accommodate himself to the reigning taste, may always have readers who perhaps would not have looked upon better performances.

To exact of every man who writes that he should say something new, would be to reduce authors to a small number ; to oblige the most fertile genius to say only what is new, would be to contract his volumes to a few pages. Yet, surely, there ought to be some bounds to repetition ; libraries ought no more to be heaped for ever with the same thoughts differently expressed, than with the same books differently decorated.

The good or evil which these secondary writers produce is seldom of any long duration. As they owe their existence to change of fashion, they commonly disappear when a new fashion becomes prevalent. The authors that in any nation last from age to age are very few, because there are very few that have any other claim to notice than that they catch hold on present curiosity, and gratify some accidental desire, or produce some temporary conveniency.

But however the writers of the day may despair of future fame, they ought at least to forbear any present mischief. Though they cannot arrive at eminent heights of excellence, they might keep themselves harmless. They might take care to inform themselves before they attempt to inform others, and exert the little influence which they have for honest purposes.

But such is the present state of our literature, that the ancient sage, who thought *a great book a great evil*, would now think the multitude of books a multitude of evils. He would consider a bulky writer who engrossed a year, and a swarm of pamphleteers who stole each an hour, as equal wasters of human life, and would make no other difference between them, than between a beast of prey and a flight of locusts.

Saturday, December 22, 1759.

WHEN the philosophers of the last age were first congregated into the Royal Society, great expectations were raised of the sudden progress of useful arts; the time was supposed to be near, when engines should turn by a perpetual motion, and health be secured by the universal medicine; when learning should be facilitated by a real character, and commerce extended by ships which could reach their ports in defiance of the tempest.

But improvement is naturally slow. The Society met and parted without any visible diminution of the miseries of life. The gout and stone were still painful, the ground that was not ploughed brought no harvest, and neither oranges nor grapes would grow upon the hawthorn. At last, those who were disappointed began to be angry: those likewise who hated innovation were glad to gain an opportunity of ridiculing men who had depreciated, perhaps with too much arrogance, the knowledge of antiquity. And it appears from some of their earliest apologies, that the philosophers. felt with great sensibility the unwelcome importunities of those who were daily asking, "What have ye done?"

The truth is, that little had been done compared with what fame had been suffered to promise; and the question could only be answered by general apologies, and by new hopes, which, when they were frustrated, gave a new occasion to the same vexatious inquiry.

This fatal question has disturbed the quiet of many other minds. He that in the latter part of his life too strictly inquires what he has done, can very seldom receive from his own heart such an account as will give him satisfaction.

We do not indeed so often disappoint others as ourselves. We not only think more highly than others of our own abilities, but allow ourselves to form hopes which we never communicate, and please our thoughts with employments which none ever will allot us, and with elevations to which we are never expected to rise; and when our days and years have passed away in common business or common amusements, and we find at last that we have suffered our purposes to sleep till the time of action is past, we are reproached only by our own reflections; neither our friends nor our enemies wonder that we live and die like the rest of mankind ; that we live without notice, and die without memorial ; they know not what task we had proposed, and therefore cannot discern whether it is finished.

He that compares what he has done with what he has left undone, will feel the effect which must always follow the comparison of imagination with reality ; he will look with contempt on his own unimportance, and wonder to what purpose he came into the world ; he will repine that he shall leave behind him no evidence of his having been, that he has added nothing to the system of life, but has glided from youth to age among the crowd, without any effort for distinction.

Man is seldom willing to let fall the opinion of his own dignity, or to believe that he does little only because every individual is a very little being. He is better content to want diligence than power, and sooner confesses the depravity of his will than the imbecility of his nature.

From this mistaken notion of human greatness it proceeds, that many who pretend to have made great advances in wisdom so loudly declare that they despise themselves. If I had ever found any of the self-contemners much irritated or pained by the consciousness of their meanness, I should have given them consolation by observing, that a little more than nothing is as much as can be expected from a being who, with respect to the multitudes about him, is himself little more than nothing. Every man is obliged by the Supreme Master of the universe to improve all the opportunities of good which are afforded him, and to keep in continual activity such abilities as are bestowed upon him. But he has no reason to repine, though his abilities are small and his opportunities few. He that has improved the virtue, or advanced the happiness, of one fellow-creature ; he that has ascertained a single moral proposition, or added one useful experiment to natural knowledge, may be contented with his own performance; and, with respect to mortals like himself, may demand, like Augustus, to be dismissed at his departure with applause.

Saturday, March 22, 1760.

OMAR, the son of Hussan, had passed seventy-five years in honour and prosperity. The favour of three successive califs had filled his house with gold and silver; and whenever he appeared, the benedictions of the people proclaimed his passage.

Terrestrial happiness is of short continuance. The brightness of the flame is wasting its fuel; the fragrant flower is passing away in its own odours. The vigour of Omar began to fail, the curls of beauty fell from his head, strength departed from his hands, and agility from his feet. He gave back to the calif the keys of trust and the seals of secrecy; and sought no other pleasure for the remains of life than the converse of the wise, and the gratitude of the good.

The powers of his mind were yet unimpaired. His chamber was filled with visitants, eager to catch the dictates of experience, and officious to pay the tribute of admiration. Caled, the son of the viceroy of Egypt, entered every day early, and retired late. He was beautiful and eloquent; Omar admired his wit, and loved his docility. "Tell me," said Caled, "thou to whose voice nations have listened, and whose wisdom is known to the extremities

of Asia, tell me how I may resemble Omar the prudent.
The arts by which you have gained power and preserved
it, are to you no longer necessary or useful; impart to
me the secret of your conduct, and teach me the plan
upon which your wisdom has built your fortune."

"Young man," said Omar, "it is of little use to form
plans of life. When I took my first survey of the world,
in my twentieth year, having considered the various
conditions of mankind, in the hour of solitude I said
thus to myself, leaning against a cedar which spread its
branches over my head : Seventy years are allowed to
a man : I have yet fifty remaining : ten years I will allot
to the attainment of knowledge, and ten I will pass in
foreign countries ; I shall be learned, and therefore shall
be honoured ; every city will shout at my arrival, and
every student will solicit my friendship. Twenty years
thus passed will store my mind with images which I
shall be busy through the rest of my life in combining
and comparing. I shall revel in inexhaustible accumulations of intellectual riches ; I shall find new pleasures
for every moment, and shall never more be weary of
myself. I will, however, not deviate too far from the
beaten track of life, but will try what can be found in
female delicacy. I will marry a wife beautiful as the
Houries, and wise as Zobeide ; with her I will live twenty
years within the suburbs of Bagdat, in every pleasure
that wealth can purchase, and fancy can invent. I will
then retire to a rural dwelling, pass my last days in
obscurity and contemplation, and lie silently down on
the bed of death. Through my life it shall be my settled
resolution, that I will never depend upon the smile of
princes ; that I will never stand exposed to the artificers
of courts ; I will never pant for publick honours, nor

disturb my quiet with affairs of state. Such was my scheme of life, which I impressed indelibly upon my memory.

"The first part of my ensuing time was to be spent in search of knowledge; and I know not how I was diverted from my design. I had no visible impediments without, nor any ungovernable passions within. I regarded knowledge as the highest honour and the most engaging pleasure; yet day stole upon day, and month glided after month, till I found that seven years of the first ten had vanished, and left nothing behind them. I now postponed my purpose of travelling; for why should I go abroad while so much remained to be learned at home? I immured myself for four years, and studied the laws of the empire. The fame of my skill reached the judges; I was found able to speak upon doubtful questions, and was commanded to stand at the footstool of the calif. I was heard with attention, I was consulted with confidence, and the love of praise fastened on my heart.

"I still wished to see distant countries, listened with rapture to the relations of travellers, and resolved some time to ask my dismission, that I might feast my soul with novelty; but my presence was always necessary, and the stream of business hurried me along. Sometimes I was afraid lest I should be charged with ingratitude; but I still proposed to travel, and therefore would not confine myself by marriage.

"In my fiftieth year I began to suspect that the time of travelling was past, and thought it best to lay hold on the felicity yet in my power, and indulge myself in domestick pleasures. But at fifty no man easily finds a woman beautiful as the Houries, and wise as Zobeide. I inquired and rejected, consulted and deliberated, till the sixty-second

22

year made me ashamed of gazing upon girls. I had now nothing left but retirement, and for retirement I never found a time, till disease forced me from public employment.

"Such was my scheme, and such has been its consequence. With an insatiable thirst for knowledge I trifled away the years of improvement; with a restless desire of seeing different countries, I have always resided in the same city; with the highest expectation of connubial felicity, I have lived unmarried; and with unalterable resolutions of contemplative retirement, I am going to die within the walls of Bagdat."

APPENDIX.

———◆◆◆———

THE RAMBLER.

I. (Page 10.)—"I mentioned Mallett's 'Elvira,' which had been acted the preceding winter at Drury Lane, and that the Hon. Andrew Erskine, Mr. Dempster, and myself, had joined in writing a pamphlet, entitled 'Critical Stricture,' against it. That the mildness of Dempster's disposition had, however, relented; and he had candidly said, 'We have hardly a right to abuse this tragedy; for bad as it is, how vain should either of us be to write one not near so good.' *Johnson.* 'Why no, sir; this is not just reasoning. You *may* abuse a tragedy, though you cannot write one. You may scold a carpenter who has made you a bad table, though you cannot make a table. It is not your trade to make tables."—Birkbeck Hill's *Boswell's Life of Johnson*, vol. i., 408.

II. (Page 23.)—Matthew Prior (1641-1721), of whose poetry Dr. Johnson speaks rather slightingly, had good reason to extol the Duke of Dorset. As a youth, Prior was employed by his uncle, who kept a fashionable tavern at Charing Cross. The lad, who had been educated at Westminster School under Dr. Busby, was, for his years, an accomplished classical scholar. One day Lord Dorset and some other gentlemen fell into a dispute in the tavern over a passage in the Odes of Horace, when one of the company exclaimed, "I find we are not like to agree in our criticisms; but if I am not mistaken, there is a young fellow in the house who is able to set us all right." Prior was accordingly summoned, and immediately solved the difficulty. Lord Dorset was so much impressed with the youth's ability and learning, that he sent him in 1682 to St. John's College, Cambridge, where he graduated in 1686, and was soon afterwards elected a Fellow.

III. (Page 30.)—Exactly the opposite was the case with Dr. Johnson himself, the affluence, vigour, and wit of whose talk was phenomenal.

IV. (Page 31.)—Johnson to Boswell : " All the complaints which are made of the world are unjust.   I never knew a man of merit neglected ; it was generally by his own fault that he failed of success. . . .   There is no reason why any person should exert himself for a man who has written a good book ; he has not written it for any individual."—Hill's *Boswell,* vol. iv., 172.

V. (Page 75.)—"When I was running about this town a very poor fellow, I was a great arguer for the advantages of poverty; but I was, at the same time, very sorry to be poor.   Sir, all the arguments which are brought to represent poverty as no evil, show it to be evidently a great evil.   You never find people labouring to convince you that you may live very happily upon a plentiful fortune.   So you hear people talking how miserable a king must be ; and yet they all wish to be in his place."— Dr. Johnson to Mr. Dempster, thirteen years later, 1763.—Hill's *Boswell,* vol. i., 441.

VI. (Page 80.)—"Dr. Johnson went home with me (1772) to my lodgings in Conduit Street and drank tea, previous to our going to the Pantheon, which neither of us had seen before.   He said, ' Goldsmith's *Life of Parnell* is poor ; not that it is poorly written, but that he had poor materials ; for nobody can write the life of a man but those who have ate and drunk and lived in social intercourse with him.' "— Hill's *Boswell's Life,* vol. ii. 166.

VII. (Page 83.)—Francis de Malherbe, French poet, 1555-1628.

VIII. (Page 95.)—" To let friendship die away by negligence and silence, is certainly not wise.   It is voluntarily to throw away one of the greatest comforts of this weary pilgrimage, of which when it is, as it must be taken finally away, he that travels on alone, will wonder how his esteem could be so little.   Do not forget me ; you see that I do not forget you.   It is pleasing in the silence of solitude to think, that there is one at least, however distant, of whose benevolence there is little doubt, and whom there is yet hope of seeing again."—Dr. Johnson (Ætat 79) writing to Captain Langton from Bolt Court, March 20, 1782.—Hill's *Boswell,* vol. iv., 145.

"He said to Sir Joshua Reynolds, 'If a man does not make new acquaintance as he advances through life, he will soon find himself left alone. A man, Sir, should keep his friendship *in constant repair.*'"—Hill's *Boswell*, vol. i., 300.

IX. (Page 106.)—"*Johnson:* 'It is wonderful, sir, how rare a quality good-humour is in life. We meet with very few good-humoured men.' I mentioned four of our friends, none of whom he would allow to be good-humoured. One was *acid*, another was *muddy*, and to the others he had objections, which have escaped me. Then, shaking his head, and stretching himself at ease in the coach, and smiling with much complacency, he turned to me, and said, 'I look upon *myself* as a good-humoured fellow.'"—Hill's *Boswell*, vol. ii., 362.

X. (Page 119.)—Alphonsus V., King of Arragon, surnamed the Magnanimous, 1384-1458. A great patron of learning, and the most accomplished sovereign of his time.

XI. (Page 138.)—" Yet think what ills the scholar's life assail,
Pride, envy, want, the garret and the jail."
Johnson's *Imitations of Juvenal*, Tenth Satire.

XII. (Page 143.)—Dr. Johnson's sly definition of Grub Street is worth recalling in this connection :—"Grub Street, the name of a street in London, much inhabited by writers of small histories, *dictionaries*, and temporary poems, whence any mean production is called Grub Street."

XIII. (Page 150.)—"Sir, you know courage is reckoned the greatest of all virtues, because, unless a man has that virtue, he has no security for preserving any other."—Hill's *Boswell*, vol. ii., 339.

XIV. (Page 180.)—The allusion is, of course, to two of the labours of Hercules. Erymanthus, a mountain of Arcadia, where the hero captured alive an enormous boar, and in the forest around Nemea he choked the lion which ravaged the country around Mycenæ.

XV. (Page 181.)—When asked how he felt upon the ill success of his tragedy (*Irene*), he replied—" Like the monument;" meaning that he continued firm and unmoved as that column. And let it be remembered, as an admonition to the *genus irritabile* of dramatick writers, that this great man, instead of peevishly complaining of the bad trade of the town, submitted to the decision without a murmur. He had, indeed, upon all occasions, a great deference for the general opinion : " A man (said he) who writes a book, thinks himself wiser and wittier than the rest of mankind ; he supposes that he can instruct or amuse them, and the public, to whom he appeals, must, after all, be the judge of his pretensions."—Hill's *Boswell's Life*, i., 199.

XVI. (Page 196.)—I mentioned that I was afraid I put into my journal too many little incidents. *Johnson :* " There is nothing, sir, too little for so little a creature as man. It is by studying little things that we attain the great art of having as little misery and as much happiness as possible."—Hill's *Boswell*, vol. i., 433.

XVII. (Page 198.)—Johnson's own lack of punctuality was notorious ; like other moralists, there were not wanting occasions when the wisdom of his lips uttered bitter things against the folly of his life.

XVIII. (Page 211.)—In the closing sentence of the next and final *Rambler* Dr. Johnson expresses the hope that he may be yet numbered with those authors who have given "ardour to virtue and confidence to truth." That his hope has been fully realised is now a matter of com- mon comment. The great moralist's wife died on the day on which the last number of the *Rambler* was published, and her removal from his side threw a gloom over his life, which time lessened but never effaced.

THE ADVENTURER.

XIX. (Page 220.)—" He inculcated upon all his friends the import- ance of perpetual vigilance against the slightest degrees of falsehood ; the effect of which, as Sir Joshua Reynolds observed to me, has been that all who were of his *school* are distinguished for a love of truth and accuracy, which they would not have possessed in the same degree if they had not been acquainted with Johnson."—Hill's *Boswell*, vol. iii., 229.

XX. (Page 230.)—Hermann Boerhaave (b. 1668, d. 1738) held the chairs of medicine and botany at the University of Leyden. A man of stainless character, whose fame rests chiefly on his *Institutiones Medicae*, published in 1708, and translated into every language in Europe.

XXI. (Page 242.)—He made the common remark on the unhappiness which men who have led a busy life experience, when they retire in expectation of enjoying themselves at ease, and that they generally languish for want of their habitual occupation and wish to return to it. He mentioned as strong an instance of this as can well be imagined. "An eminent tallow-chandler in London, who had acquired a considerable fortune, gave up the trade in favour of his foreman, and went to live at a country-house near town. He soon grew weary, and paid frequent visits to his old shop, where he desired they might let him know their *melting-days*, and he would come and assist them; which he accordingly did. Here, sir, was a man, to whom the most disgusting circumstance in the business to which he had been used was a relief from idleness."—Hill's *Boswell*, vol. ii., 337.

XXII. (Page 262.)—It was his custom to observe certain days with a pious abstraction—viz., New Year's day, the day of his wife's death, Good Friday, Easter-day, and his own birthday. He this year (1764) says—"I have now spent fifty-five years in resolving, having from the earliest time almost that I can remember, being forming schemes of a better life. I have done nothing. The need of doing, therefore, is pressing, since the time of doing is short. O God, grant me to resolve aright, and to keep my resolutions, for Jesus Christ's sake. Amen."— *Prayers and Meditations*, Boswell's *Life of Johnson*, vol. i., 483.

XXIII. (Page 265.)—"People in general do not willingly read, if they can have anything else to amuse them. There must be an external impulse; emulation or vanity, or avarice. The progress which the understanding makes through a book has more pain than pleasure in it. Language is scanty and inadequate to express the nice gradations and mixtures of our feelings. No man reads a book of science from pure inclination."—Hill's *Boswell*, vol iv., 218.

XXIV. (Page 272.)—"An account of the labours and productions of authors was for a long time among the deficiencies of English literature; but as the caprice of man is always starting from too little to too much, we have now among other disturbers of human quiet, a numerous body of *reviewers* and *remarkers*."—Johnson's *Preliminary Discourse* to the *London Chronicle*.

THE IDLER.

XXV. (Page 282.)—"Johnson's own superlative power of wit set
him above risk of such uneasiness. Garrick remarked to me of him,
'Rabelais and all the wits are nothing compared with him. You may
be diverted by them ; but Johnson gives you a forcible hug, and shakes
laughter out of you, whether you will or no.'"—*Boswell's Life*, ii., 231.

XXVI. (Page 292.)—Twenty years after Johnson wrote this phillipic
we find, from the following conversation, that his prejudice was still as
deeply rooted :—"The celebrated Mrs. Rudd being mentioned.
Johnson : 'Fifteen years ago I should have gone to see her.'
Spottiswoode : 'Because she was fifteen years younger?' 'No, Sir ; but
now they have a trick of putting everything into the newspapers.'"—
Boswell, iii., 330.

XXVII. (Page 294.)—The greatest living authority on the life and
times of Johnson—his nineteenth century Boswell, in fact—Dr. Birkbeck
Hill, thinks that in Mr. Sober we have a portrait of the Doctor, drawn
by his own hand.   There is unquestionably much in the sketch to
warrant such a conclusion.

XXVIII. (Page 294.)—Dr. Johnson's repugnance to early-rising is
well known. He struggled manfully, but unsuccessfully, against what
was in reality a constitutional infirmity.   When at the height of his
fame, the "Sultan of English Literature" was a man who was known
to be never ready to go to bed, and once there, never ready to get out.

XXIX. (Page 297.)—Dr. Johnson unconsciously describes himself
in a phrase which occurs in this essay—"the ponderous dictator of
sentences, whose notions are delivered in the lump, and are, like uncoined bullion, of more weight than use."   The racy vigour and brilliant
incisiveness of his reported talk, heightens the contrast which exists
between it, and the "terriffick diction" which marks his published
works. Johnson often played the part of "candid friend" to Oliver
Goldsmith, and sometimes the light-hearted poet ventured to pay him
back in his own coin, as the following incident shows :—"Goldsmith
was often very fortunate in his witty contests, even when he entered
the lists with Johnson himself. Sir Joshua Reynolds was in company

with them one day, when Goldsmith said, that he thought that he could write a good fable, mentioned the simplicity which that kind of composition requires, and observed that in most fables the animals introduced seldom talk in character. 'For instance,' said he, 'the fable of the little fishes, who saw birds fly over their heads, and envying them, petitioned Jupiter to be changed into birds. The skill,' he continued, 'consists in making them talk like little fishes.' While he indulged himself in this fanciful review, he observed Johnson shaking his sides, and laughing. Upon which he smartly proceeded, 'Why, Dr. Johnson, this is not so easy as you seem to think; for if you were to make little fishes talk, they would talk like whales.'"—*Boswell*, ii., 231.

XXX. (Page 300.)—A pathetic interest attaches to this number of the *Idler*. It was written two or three days after the death, at Lichfield, of Dr. Johnson's mother, at the advanced age of ninety; an event which, according to Boswell, "deeply affected him," since his "reverential affection for her was not abated by years, as indeed he retained all his tender feelings even to the latest period of his life."

XXXI. (Page 305.)—Writing to Dr. Burney, in the last year of his life (1784), Dr. Johnson says :—"I struggle hard for life. I take physic, and take air; my friend's chariot is always ready. We have been this morning twenty-four miles, and could run forty-eight more. *But who can run the race with death?*"

XXXII (Page 310.)—DR. JOHNSON TO MRS. THRALE.

"LONDON, *May* 1, 1780.

"DEAREST MADAM,

". . . Never let criticism operate on your face or your mind; it is very rarely that an author is hurt by his criticks. The blaze of reputation cannot be blown out, but it often dies in the socket ; a very few names may be considered as perpetual lamps that shine unconsumed."

XXXIII. (Page 326.)—[1772.] " Dr. Johnson went home with me to my lodgings in Conduit Street and drank tea, previous to our going to the Pantheon, which neither of us had seen before. He said, 'Goldsmith's *Life of Parnell* is poor; not that it is poorly written, but that he had poor materials; for nobody can write the life of a man but those who have eat and drunk and lived in social intercourse with him.' He censured Ruffhead s *Life of Pope*; and said 'he knew nothing of Pope and nothing of poetry.' "—*Boswell*, ii., 166.

XXXIV. (Page 328.)—" If a life be delayed till interest and envy are at an end, then we may hope for impartiality, but must expect little intelligence ; for the incidents which give excellence to biography are of a volatile and evanescent kind, such as soon escape the memory, and are rarely transmitted by tradition."—*The Rambler*, No. 60.

XXXV. (Page 330.)—" Sir, it is the great excellence of a writer to put into his book as much as his book will hold."—*Boswell's Life*, ii., 237.

THE WALTER SCOTT PRESS, NEWCASTLE-ON-TYNE.

BOOKS OF FAIRY TALES.

Crown 8vo, Cloth Elegant, Price 3/6 per Vol.

ENGLISH FAIRY AND OTHER FOLK TALES.

Selected and Edited, with an Introduction,

By EDWIN SIDNEY HARTLAND.

With Twelve Full-Page Illustrations by CHARLES E. BROCK.

SCOTTISH FAIRY AND FOLK TALES.

Selected and Edited, with an Introduction,

By SIR GEORGE DOUGLAS, BART.

With Twelve Full-Page Illustrations by JAMES TORRANCE

IRISH FAIRY AND FOLK TALES.

Selected and Edited, with an Introduction,

By W. B. YEATS.

With Twelve Full-Page Illustrations by JAMES TORRANCE.

London: WALTER SCOTT, LIMITED, Paternoster Square.

Crown 8vo, Cloth Elegant, in Box, Price 2s. 6d.

THE

CULT OF BEAUTY:

A MANUAL OF PERSONAL HYGIENE.

By C. J. S. THOMPSON.

[EXTRACT FROM PREFACE.]

Too much care cannot be taken of the exterior of the human body, on which the general health so largely depends. The most recent discoveries in science go to prove that cleanliness, with proper attention to bodily exercise, is the greatest enemy to disease and decay. Quackery has never been more rampant than it is to-day, and advertised secret preparations for beautifying the person meet us at every turn. It is with the object of showing how Beauty may be preserved and aided on purely hygienic principles, that this work has been written, the greatest secret of Beauty being Health.

CONTENTS—

" 'Quackery,' says Mr. Thompson, 'was never more rampant than it is to-day' with regard to 'aids in beautifying the person.' His little book is based on purely hygienic principles, and comprises recipes for toilet purposes which he warrants are 'practical and harmless.' These are virtues in any book of health and beauty, and Mr. Thompson's advice and guidance are, we find, not wanting in soundness and common-sense."
—*Saturday Review.*

London : WALTER SCOTT, LIMITED, Paternoster Square.

THE SCOTT LIBRARY.

Maroon Cloth, Gilt. Price 1s. net per Volume.

VOLUMES ALREADY ISSUED—

THE WALTER SCOTT PUBLISHING COMPANY, LIMITED,
LONDON AND FELLING-ON-TYNE.

THE SCOTT LIBRARY—continued.

THE WALTER SCOTT PUBLISHING COMPANY, LIMITED,
LONDON AND FELLING-ON-TYNE.

THE WALTER SCOTT PUBLISHING COMPANY, LIMITED,
LONDON AND FELLING-ON-TYNE.

THE WALTER SCOTT PUBLISHING COMPANY, LIMITED,
LONDON AND FELLING-ON-TYNE.

THE SCOTT LIBRARY—continued.

THE WALTER SCOTT PUBLISHING COMPANY, LIMITED,
LONDON AND FELLING-ON-TYNE

THE SCOTT LIBRARY—continued.

83 CARLYLE'S ESSAYS ON GERMAN LITERATURE. With an Introduction by Ernest Rhys.

84 PLAYS AND DRAMATIC ESSAYS OF CHARLES LAMB. Edited, with an Introduction, by Rudolf Dircks.

85 THE PROSE OF WORDSWORTH. SELECTED AND Edited, with an Introduction, by Professor William Knight.

86 ESSAYS, DIALOGUES, AND THOUGHTS OF COUNT Giacomo Leopardi. Translated, with an Introduction and Notes, by Major-General Patrick Maxwell.

87 THE INSPECTOR-GENERAL. A RUSSIAN COMEDY. By Nikolai V. Gogol. Translated from the original, with an Introduction and Notes, by Arthur A. Sykes.

88 ESSAYS AND APOTHEGMS OF FRANCIS, LORD BACON. Edited, with an Introduction, by John Buchan.

89 PROSE OF MILTON. SELECTED AND EDITED, WITH an Introduction, by Richard Garnett, LL.D.

90 THE REPUBLIC OF PLATO. TRANSLATED BY Thomas Taylor, with an Introduction by Theodore Wratislaw.

✕ 91 PASSAGES FROM FROISSART. WITH AN INTRO-duction by Frank T. Marzials.

✕ 92 THE PROSE AND TABLE TALK OF COLERIDGE. Edited by Will H. Dircks.

93 HEINE IN ART AND LETTERS. TRANSLATED BY Elizabeth A. Sharp.

94 SELECTED ESSAYS OF DE QUINCEY. WITH AN Introduction by Sir George Douglas, Bart.

95 VASARI'S LIVES OF ITALIAN PAINTERS. SELECTED and Prefaced by Havelock Ellis.

? ✕ 96 LAOCOON, AND OTHER PROSE WRITINGS OF LESSING. A new Translation by W. B. Rönnfeldt.

97 PELLEAS AND MELISANDA, AND THE SIGHTLESS. Two Plays by Maurice Maeterlinck. Translated from the French by Laurence Alma Tadema.

98 THE COMPLETE ANGLER OF WALTON AND COTTON. Edited, with an Introduction, by Charles Hill Dick.

THE WALTER SCOTT PUBLISHING COMPANY, LIMITED,
LONDON AND FELLING-ON-TYNE.

THE SCOTT LIBRARY—continued.

THE WALTER SCOTT PUBLISHING COMPANY, LIMITED,
LONDON AND FELLING-ON-TYNE.

MANUALS OF EMPLOYMENT FOR EDUCATED WOMEN.

The object of this series of manuals will be to give to girls, more particularly to those belonging to the educated classes, who from inclination or necessity are looking forward to earning their own living, some assistance with reference to the choice of a profession, and to the best method of preparing for it when chosen.

Foolscap 8vo, Stiff Paper Cover, Price 1s.; or in Limp Cloth, 1s. 6d.

I.—SECONDARY TEACHING.

This manual contains particulars of the qualifications necessary for a secondary teacher, with a list of the colleges and universities where training may be had, the cost of training, and the prospect of employment when trained.

II.—ELEMENTARY TEACHING.

This manual sums up clearly the chief facts which need to be known respecting the work to be done in elementary schools, and the conditions under which women may take a share in such work.

III.—SICK NURSING.

This manual contains useful information with regard to every branch of Nursing — Hospital, District, Private, and Mental Nursing, and Nursing in the Army and Navy and in Poor Law Institutions, with particulars of the best method of training, the usual salaries given, and the prospect of employment, with some account of the general advantages and drawbacks of the work.

IV.—MEDICINE.

This manual gives particulars of all the medical qualifications recognised by the General Medical Council which are open to women, and of the methods by which they can be obtained, with full details of the different universities and colleges at which women can pursue their medical studies.

THE WALTER SCOTT PUBLISHING COMPANY, LIMITED,
LONDON AND FELLING-ON-TYNE.

Crown 8vo, Cloth, 3s. 6d. each; some vols., 6s.

The
Contemporary Science Series.

EDITED BY HAVELOCK ELLIS.

Illustrated Vols. between 300 and 400 pp. each.

EVOLUTION OF SEX. By Professors GEDDES and THOMSON. 6s.

ELECTRICITY IN MODERN LIFE. By G. W. DE TUNZELMANN.

THE ORIGIN OF THE ARYANS. By Dr. TAYLOR.

PHYSIOGNOMY AND EXPRESSION. By P. MANTEGAZZA.

EVOLUTION AND DISEASE. By J. B. SUTTON.

THE VILLAGE COMMUNITY. By G. L. GOMME.

THE CRIMINAL. By HAVELOCK ELLIS. New Edition. 6s.

SANITY AND INSANITY. By Dr. C. MERCIER.

HYPNOTISM. By Dr. ALBERT MOLL (Berlin).

MANUAL TRAINING. By Dr. WOODWARD (St. Louis).

SCIENCE OF FAIRY TALES. By E. S. HARTLAND.

PRIMITIVE FOLK. By ELIE RECLUS.

EVOLUTION OF MARRIAGE. By CH. LETOURNEAU.

BACTERIA AND THEIR PRODUCTS. By Dr. WOODHEAD.

EDUCATION AND HEREDITY. By J. M. GUYAU.

THE MAN OF GENIUS. By Prof. LOMBROSO.

PROPERTY: ITS ORIGIN. By CH. LETOURNEAU.

VOLCANOES PAST AND PRESENT. By Prof. HULL.

PUBLIC HEALTH PROBLEMS. By Dr. J. F. SYKES.

MODERN METEOROLOGY. By FRANK WALDO, Ph.D.

THE GERM-PLASM. By Professor WEISMANN. 6s.

THE INDUSTRIES OF ANIMALS. By F. HOUSSAY.

MAN AND WOMAN. By HAVELOCK ELLIS. 6s.

THE WALTER SCOTT PUBLISHING COMPANY, LIMITED,
LONDON AND FELLING-ON-TYNE.

THE WALTER SCOTT PUBLISHING COMPANY, LIMITED,
LONDON AND FELLING-ON-TYNE.

THE WALTER SCOTT PUBLISHING COMPANY, LIMITED,
LONDON AND FELLING-ON-TYNE.

The Music Story Series.

A SERIES OF LITERARY-MUSICAL MONOGRAPHS.

Edited by FREDERICK J. CROWEST,

Author of " The Great Tone Poets."

Illustrated with Photogravure and Collotype Portraits, Half-tone and Line Pictures, Facsimiles, etc.

Square Crown 8vo, Cloth, 3s. 6d. net.

VOLUMES NOW READY.

THE STORY OF ORATORIO. By ANNIE W. PATTERSON, B.A., Mus. Doc.

THE STORY OF NOTATION. By C. F. ABDY WILLIAMS, M.A., Mus. Bac.

THE STORY OF THE ORGAN. By C. F. ABDY WILLIAMS, M.A., Author of " Bach " and " Handel " ("Master Musicians' Series").

THE STORY OF CHAMBER MUSIC. By N. KILBURN, Mus. Bac. (Cantab.), Conductor of the Middlesbrough, Sunderland, and Bishop Auckland Musical Societies.

THE STORY OF THE VIOLIN. By PAUL STOEVING, Professor of the Violin, Guildhall School of Music, London.

THE STORY OF THE HARP. By WILLIAM H. GRATTAN FLOOD, Author of " History of Irish Music."

NEXT VOLUME.

THE STORY OF ORGAN MUSIC. By C. F. ABDY WILLIAMS, M.A., Mus. Bac.

IN PREPARATION.

THE STORY OF THE PIANOFORTE. By ALGERNON S. ROSE, Author of " Talks with Bandsmen."

THE STORY OF HARMONY. By EUSTACE J. BREAKSPEARE, Author of " Mozart," " Musical Æsthetics," etc.

THE STORY OF THE ORCHESTRA. By STEWART MACPHERSON, Fellow and Professor, Royal Academy of Music.

THE STORY OF BIBLE MUSIC. By ELEONORE D'ESTERRE-KEELING, Author of " The Musicians' Birthday Book."

THE STORY OF CHURCH MUSIC. By THE EDITOR.

ETC., ETC., ETC.

THE WALTER SCOTT PUBLISHING COMPANY, LIMITED, LONDON AND FELLING-ON-TYNE.

LaVergne, TN USA
07 September 2009
157140LV00003B/211/A